Roland Allen
A Theology of Mission

Roland Allen
A Theology of Mission

Towards a Missiology of Spirit and Order

Steven Richard Rutt

The Lutterworth Press

The Lutterworth Press
P.O. Box 60
Cambridge
CB1 2NT
United Kingdom

www.lutterworth.com
publishing@lutterworth.com

ISBN: 978 0 7188 9476 4

British Library Cataloguing in Publication Data
A record is available from the British Library

First Published by The Lutterworth Press, 2018

Contents

A Legacy and Dedication

for
Our Children
Shannon, Sherri, Steven and Seth
and

Our Children's Spouses and Our Eleven Grandchildren
Shannon & Ron Wills (Ella, Wyatt, Juliet and Luke)
Sherri and Bram Wouters (Bram, Colbie and Kale)
Steven and Joanne Rutt (Annie, Ginger and Holly)
Seth and Katilyn Rutt (Bryson Richard Rutt)

My wife, Sue, and I affirm this covenantal blessing upon our family:
For He established a testimony in Jacob,
And appointed a law in Israel,
Which He commanded our fathers,
That they should make them known to their children;
That the generation to come might know them,
The children who would be born,
That they may arise and declare them to their children,
That they may set their hope in God,
And not forget the works of God
But keep His commandments.
(Psalm 78:5-7, NKJV)

Acknowledgements

My first book, *Roland Allen: A Missionary Life*, specified that there are many to whom I am indebted for their encouragement, support, assistance and guidance during my research for and writing of this thesis which has now developed into the publication of two volumes on Roland Allen's missionary life and theology of mission. As this second volume began to take shape I wanted to thank my doctoral supervisor and friend Professor Christopher Partridge (University of Lancaster, England) for his continued wise counsel and helpful advice as I was refining this volume's content and style. Also, I am genuinely appreciative that Hubert J.B. Allen has continued to contribute reflections of his grandfather's life with me as disclosed within the Foreword. Special thanks is given to the Rt Rev Michael Nazir-Ali PhD, (former Bishop of Rochester, England) who, due to his familiarity with the missiology of Roland Allen, generously agreed to write the Forewords for these two volumes.

I am particularly indebted to Lucy McCann – the Senior Archivist of Weston Library (Bodleian Libraries, Oxford) – as she and the staff at Rhodes House, Oxford, always helped me locate specific archival documents of missionaries and mission societies (USPG), and, in particular, for their willingness to always provide access to the Roland Allen archives. I want to especially thank Dr David Emmanuel Singh (Research Tutor, Oxford Centre for Mission Studies; Editor, SAGE Publications) for his endorsement. Special thanks to my valued friends who serve on the board of Covenant Renewal Ministries – Jeff Gordon, Bill O'Brien, and, former board member Grant Sardachuk – because of their patronage and encouragement along the way. In addition, I want to acknowledge Dr Rod Tussing because of his objective analysis of my original thesis statement, as well as his encouragement of my research. I am also grateful to Fr Jacob 'Koos' van Leeuwen for his ongoing encouragement and prayers for my research to be published.

My 'missionary' parents – Richard and Kathleen Rutt – nurtured me and my sister, Faith, in the Christian faith and significantly shaped my belief that 'every Christian is a missionary'. I owe so much to my parents because of their evangelical faith, love for the Bible and their tireless devotion to evangelism. This biblically-based child-rearing shaped my faith and prepared me for global mission. This passion for mission is rooted in and stems from many years of missionary service that our family – my wife, Sue, and our four wonderful children, Shannon, Sherri, Steven and Seth – experienced as we served Christ in various countries. I am continually thankful that our children continue in the Christian faith, married Christian spouses and have given us eleven delightful grandchildren. Therefore, I lovingly dedicate this book to my children and grandchildren.

Foreword

by Hubert J.B. Allen

It is remarkable that fresh books examining my grandfather and his ideas are still being considered worthy of publication seventy years after his death. Dr Rutt's magisterial study is an important and wide-ranging contribution, so I am happy to have been invited to express some introductory thoughts. For more than that, however, I must simply refer to the brief biography which I composed over twenty years' ago, largely to edify his descendants.[1]

I need, however, to emphasize that I myself and the only other three persons known to me who can remember him in his lifetime, were, in those War-time days, mere schoolchildren. My contemporary accurately described Roland as *'a fine-looking man who was both kind and also rather stern and austere'*.[2] I only recall one example of the impatience some people attributed to him, at a time when he flung a book on the floor, expostulating: *'Calls himself a scholar – and his book doesn't even have an Index!'*

But in those declining years in Nairobi, his health was not good, so his wife Beatrice became formidably protective. Consequently, just as one of us three grandchildren had begun some truly fascinating conversation with him – not, of course, at our age discussing his controversial adult ideas about missionary methods, the established Church, or the Apostolic succession, but rather such topics as poetry, or cathedral architecture, or maps, or public speaking – then only too often Grannie would intervene and tell us to *'run along now, and stop tiring your grandfather'*. Nobody ever argued with Grannie, so all of

---

1. Roland Allen, *Pioneer, Priest & Prophet*, Eerdmans/Forward Movement, 1995.

2. This third living witness is Valerie, the daughter of Mr Hermann Fliess, a German Jew, who early in the war acted as spokesman for all his fellow Germans in Kenya's internment camp at Kabete. Roland and Beatrice removed her and her brother from a feckless landlady, and took care of her until the end of the war.

us – including our equally disappointed 'Granfer' – would dutifully disperse: he, probably, to work on classical Swahili poetry at his desk, we children to read on the verandah or to play in the *banda* – the circle of eucalyptus poles supporting a thatched roof, which served as a simple gazebo, protecting us from the tropical rain or sun. My two sisters remember Granfer using that *banda* to teach them how to project their voices, so that a whisper could be heard right across it, notwithstanding the lack of walls.

In 1945, after spending almost the whole of World War II in East Africa, we three children set out for England with our parents by train, bus and river steamer down the Nile to Cairo. On the final morning, Granfer, knowing that it was extremely unlikely that we should ever all be together again, celebrated full Holy Communion for the whole family, assuring my doubtful mother: '*Of* course, *Nell shall receive both the Bread and the Wine!*' – although she was only seven years' old, and none of us three were yet confirmed.

In spite of my emphasizing this background, Dr Rutt is not alone in attributing to me a very much more profound knowledge and understanding of my grandfather's life, ideas and literary legacy than I, in fact, possess. It is true that in my own declining years I sought to provide – especially for his direct descendants – an outline of his eventful life-story, together with an ignorant layman's understanding of some reasons for his continuing notoriety. But I have spent very much less time than many scholars studying his published works – and indeed some of his books I have never read at all. On the other hand, I have been privileged to live close to Oxford University's Bodleian Library, where I have been able to read much of his private correspondence and a few of his unpublished (or incomplete) writings, which the librarians have carefully preserved.

Furthermore, our children and grandchildren are able to share the family's pride in such memorabilia as the little brass gong, which Granfer made use of instead of a church bell to summon people to prayer in Peking (Beijing) during the summer of 1900, when the Boxer movement was besieging the greatly hated foreign Legations. From that same episode, we also possess a small brass tray, on which he was carrying refreshments to a patient in the makeshift hospital, when a sniper's bullet knocked a chip off its rim, instead of hitting his heart. His medals, unmounted on their ribbons and never worn, we found in an old tobacco tin long after his death. He had great admiration for courage, so he respected any award for brave deeds; but he had no patience with medals '*simply for* being *there*', like his China Medal or his

1914 War Medal.[1] Such medals, he considered, if awarded at all, should have been awarded to *everyone* – to all people in any way adversely affected by the war (even – or perhaps especially – to non-combatants and conscientious objectors).

Most of what I learned about my grandfather's character, and idiosyncracies, was derived at second hand, from my father and other older friends and relatives; and in this book and its anticipated companion volume Dr Rutt alludes to nearly all the incidents and episodes, by which I sought in my monograph to illustrate such aspects of my 'Granfer'. So I think it only remains for me to express admiration and gratitude for such a very learned and painstaking tribute to the Rev. Roland Allen.

Hubert J.B. Allen

---

1. This was awarded for his wartime chaplaincy in the hospital ship 'Rohilla', from which he succeeded in swimming ashore when she was wrecked off the coast of Yorkshire on her way to Belgium in October 1914.

Foreword

by Bishop Michael Nazir-Ali

Roland Allen has Still Much to Teach us

Most people have diverse experiences in life and are formed by different influences. The media likes to group us and stereotype us as 'conservative' or 'radical', 'evangelical' or 'catholic', etc. In fact, we are often the result of myriad influences during the course of our lives. Roland Allen was no different. His mother's Evangelical faith was formative for him and remained with him for the rest of his life. His interest in evangelism and mission stemmed from it, as did his reverence for biblical authority. At Oxford, he encountered some of the finest minds of the burgeoning Anglo-Catholic movement. His concern for a proper ecclesiology and his emphasis on the sacramental life arose from such exposure.

It is, of course, well known that Allen's interpretive approach to Church, mission and faith was based on his reading of St Paul's missionary methods as set out in the Acts of the Apostles and in Paul's Letters to churches and individuals. Thus, he is not only Pauline but Lucan in the way he reads history as a history of mission. From the *Didachē*, he acquired a view of how the primitive church would organise itself, taught new converts and administered the sacraments, as well as his ideas about local and 'trans-local' ministries. His beliefs about the local church, the role of the laity, the relation between the Priesthood of all Believers and the Ministerial Priesthood all derive from what might be called 'primitive catholicity'. Although Allen is well aware of the dangers of 'African', 'Asian' or 'American' Christianity, he does not face issues arising from claims to radical autonomy. He is content with the Quadrilateral of Bible, Creeds, Sacraments and Ministry as the marks of catholicity but does not ask how such catholicity is to be maintained as a legitimate diversity in unity. What is the place of a proper teaching authority in the Church? How are decisions that affect everyone, to be made together and what are the proper instruments to do this? Perhaps such questions had to wait for a later age to be asked, if not answered.

Allen believed passionately in church-planting strategies which did not perpetuate mission structures. Following the educationalists of his day, he held that a good church-planter should first assess the social and spiritual situation, then, in the light of this, to share the good news of the Gospel with the people, to disciple converts, to train the leadership of the new church and then to move on. He rejects the possibility of church and mission continuing indefinitely to exist side by side but fulfilling different roles, rather, the church is to be the vehicle of its own missionary mandate. In his belief that such a church should be self-supporting, self-governing and self-propagating, he is thinking of every aspect of a church's life, not merely economic independence, but structures of governance, training of clergy and other leaders, organising for mission etc. Once again, however, as a man of his times, he does not discuss, in detail, the partnership and interdependence which these churches would also need.

The social and cultural context should alert the missionaries to the necessity of what today we would call inculturation or contextualisation. The Chinese love for order and propriety or the spiritual longings of East African Sufism should be reflected in the kind of Christian faith that emerges among a people. Equally, Christianity is also a world view and this would assist the people to develop a world view and a proper anthropology which aids all round development of all that is God-given in their culture. Allen was, like William Reed Huntington, wary of religious systems, whether administrative, hierarchical or even liturgical from becoming dominant over the fundamental principles of mission and church. He believed that a local church should possess everything it needs for its common life. His passion about the necessity of sacramental life in a church led him to the somewhat odd conclusion that, in the absence of a priest, lay leaders should be allowed to preside at celebrations of sacraments. It may have been that rigid ideas in his day about what constituted 'proper training' for ordained ministry, which led him to this startling conclusion. There is, however, no necessary conflict between the requirement that a duly ordained person should preside at celebrations of the sacraments and the belief that a local church should have all the ordinary ministry it needs for its common life. What is necessary is a process of discerning gifts and callings in the local church so that the wider Church can recognize them and so that, those whom Allen labels, 'trans-local' ministers, can then ordain, authorize and commission such people for appropriate ministries in their local church and beyond. Anything can happen in an emergency and this is never 'nothing' but it cannot be made a basis of church order. In the process of inculturation, a proper balance has to be maintained between what is

Apostolic and, therefore, required of every local church so that it may truly be in fellowship with the Church down the ages and across the world, and what is *cultural* in the way it orders its worship, discipleship and decision-making.

Allen did see the local church as having a mission beyond its own community. He was affected by the practice in China of a newly planted church in a village setting out to evangelize the next village, a practice which still continues. Such a view of mission could, of course, be extended across regional, cultural, linguistic and national boundaries, though there would need to be careful co-ordination and co-operation amongst the churches to avoid duplication, optimize resources, develop centres of training and so on.

Allen knew that the *Pax Britannica* had provided an opportunity for mission in many parts of the world but he knew also from personal experience, during the Boxer Rebellion, the ugly fruit colonialism can produce on every side. Indeed, much of Christian mission has been about withstanding the temporal rulers, colonial or communist, nationalist or fundamentalist, whether in his day or in ours.

The fact that books have continued to be written about Roland Allen since his death and that they are still being written alerts us to his significance for mission-minded thinking for today's Church – and tomorrow's. Steven Richard Rutt has put us all in his debt by bringing Allen's thought and practice, once again, to our attention.

Bishop Michael Nazir-Ali
Advent 2016

Introduction

An Analysis of the Development of Roland Allen's Missiology

After extensive archival research and analysis of Roland Allen's engagement with the Pauline apostolic principles, which are recorded in the Lucan 'missionary' account in the Acts of the Apostles and the epistles of St Paul, this second volume attempts to observe and unpack Allen's personal analysis of Western colonial missionary methods (1903-47) in light of Pauline practice. After Allen's initial missionary experiences in China (1895-1903) and subsequent missionary journeys to India, Canada and Africa (1910-47), it makes sense that he developed as an acute missionary methods analyst. During his missionary survey work, he observed that the practices of benevolent paternalism within 'mission stations' was a major problem and came to the conclusion that the mission societies of his day tended to impede indigenous Church growth and maturity. Therefore, he spent the rest of his life addressing the missionary situation through his itinerant teaching ministry and writings. It is within this historical context of colonial missionary efforts (good and bad) that an overview for the discipline of missiology is provided by demonstrating Allen's significant contribution as a missionary methods analyst: first, through examination of the church-planting principles, which he claimed resided in Pauline practice; and second, through his analysis of Western colonial missionary methods contrasted with, what he believed were, apostolic methods. In many ways, *Roland Allen: A Theology of Mission* examines and seeks to advance his understanding of a Pauline hermeneutic for missionary principles and practices.

This volume, therefore, consists of ten chapters and aims to disclose the central planks of the apostolic principles that shaped his missionary ecclesiology of 'Spirit and Order'. In Chapter 1, 'The Problem: Allen's Assessment of Western Missions', the problem is located as seen through Allen's diagnosis of Western missionary paternalism and institutional devolution. This identification will be contrasted with what he believed was a biblical missionary methodology, which originated from his hermeneutic of Pauline practice. Roland Allen, on one hand,

1

believed that the *Pax Britannica* made it possible for missionaries to freely advance Gospel ministry within the colonies, similar to the way that the *Pax Romana* provided a *milieu* for the Gospel to advance during the early Church era. As a missionary, he was an enthusiastic advocate of Christian mission through evangelism and church-planting. On the other hand, he was the first to acknowledge that there existed a problem of 'mission station' hegemony. His diagnosis of this problem of institutional devolution (termed here 'Peter Pan' paternalism) was forthrightly confronted by him through his writings because he saw how various missionary societies' structural systems kept indigenous leadership dependent upon the foreign missionaries and did not allow them to 'grow up'. Allen observed how the indigenous 'natives' understood the mission stations as foreign businesses – held in trust by Europeans – where the missionaries financially organized and permanently managed these properties. For Allen, the 'mission station' system lacked apostolic precedent and created a dependency on foreigners. This chapter unpacks Allen's analysis of the problem and discloses his solution for church-planting strategies.

Allen's solution to the problem is addressed within Chapter 2 entitled 'Allen's Missiological Remedy: What Would Paul Do?' Allen conformed to and argued for the quintessence of St Paul's missionary methods and practices in order to address the problem. His writings were shaped more and more by Pauline practice and it was this understanding that motivated Allen to proactively argue for implementing a 'Gospel method' for Church growth. He believed that as a trans-local church planter, Paul's example of investing his time and energy in mentoring and appointing indigenous leadership was indicative of why he was so successful with church-planting in Galatia, Macedonia, Achaia and Asia. This significantly influenced Allen's thought, especially because of how Paul proactively applied these principles to promote self-extending churches that were not dependent on him to be their resident leader. His understanding of what Paul did cannot be understood from an autocratic practice – operating in isolation – Allen argued, but from a selfless practice of his apostolic ministry which sought the wellbeing of the indigenous Church and the Church's ability to be self-governing.

Allen's argument for the planting of the indigenous Church is supported by and stemmed from the central planks of the apostolic principles disclosed within Chapter 3 – 'Unpacking Roland Allen's Missionary Theology'. He wasted no time in defining his 'missionary theology' than by contrasting the difference between the Church and the 'mission station' system. It is interesting to discover that Allen's thinking, which tended towards solving some of these problems, was actually shaped by various educational principles which were promoted by some contemporaneous educators such as Maria Montessori, Johann Friedrich Herbart and Johann Heinrich Pestalozzi. This chapter aims to show, in particular, how Maria Montessori's educational methods provided some impetus for Allen's emphasis on 'timeless principles' that are designed to work in any area of life. The basis for the argument at hand tugs at the development of a pedagogy that was based upon Montessori's principles, which enable the educational process to adapt to any given situation. Allen believed that these educational principles could easily work within the missionary *milieu*. Rather than only criticizing certain missionary practices, he drew attention (within his writings from 1913-19) to these scholastics of his day and showed that the way they challenged various educational institutions could also, by analogy, be proposed to the current missionary setting so that the missionaries could possibly learn from them. Further clarity is revealed in Chapter 4 – 'Allen's Theology of 'Spirit and Order' in order to set the parameters for his missionary ecclesiology, the apostolic principles that encompass his missionary theology need to be unpacked. This chapter discloses his belief in the transcendence of the Spirit's work in the life of the Church and argued for a return to, what he believed was, a proper apostolic emphasis – *Spirit* and *Order*. His integrated pneumatology and ecclesiology formed the basis for his church-planting missionary theology, which he was convinced encompassed true historic apostolicity and catholicity. The focus of Chapter 5 – 'Roland Allen's Charismatic Missiology' consists of my analysis of two of his published works: *Missionary Principles – and Practice* (1913) and *Pentecost and the World: the Revelation of the Holy Spirit in the Acts of the Apostles* (1917); also, his sermons, teaching notes, articles and correspondence, especially his teaching notes, which he entitled 'The Doctrine of the Holy Spirit'. These writings disclose his understanding of the Holy Spirit's transcendence and imminence with the advancement of the Church's global expansion and provides an *apologia* for the significance of the Spirit's descent at Pentecost and the ongoing empowerment of the Church. In particular, his teaching notes incorporate a symphonic blend of 'pneumatology, ecclesiology and missiology' which shaped his overall missionary ecclesiology.

The emphasis turns to a specific case study in Chapter 6 – 'The Influence of Roland Allen's Missiology in India'. This consists of an analysis of the ecclesiastical conversation between Allen and two Indian bishops – both critical and complimentary – disclosing the relevance of his thought for leadership issues then (and now). In general, Allen frequently corresponded with bishops throughout the global Anglican Communion, as my research has already disclosed. Attempts to carefully analyze the significant contribution he made to missionary ecclesiology as he engaged with various bishops who embraced his teachings, and conversely, with other bishops who refused to adapt to changing structures within the Church of England, are highlighted in this volume. The following case study of two such bishops in India – Vedanayagam Samuel Azariah (1874-1945) of the diocese of Dornakal and George Clay Hubback (1882-1955) of the diocese of Assam – will provide greater clarity on the way that Allen tended to engage with duly appointed episcopal leadership, in particular, during his itinerant missionary journeys within India (1927-28). By examining these two bishops' responses of his ideas, we will be able to see how, on one hand, Allen's missiology was able to facilitate Church renewal and transformation significantly without costly infrastructural apparatuses within the diocese of Dornakal, while, on the other, this missiological renewal was inhibited by leadership inflexibility and a lack of missional foresight within the diocese of Assam.

This case study is now augmented in Chapter 7 by the infrastructure of Allen's missionary ecclesiology and is entitled *Spontaneous Church Growth: Catholicity, Sacramentalism & Volunteerism*. Firstly, Allen believed that the Church is the true mission society. He believed that the Church expresses her true catholicity from the essence of *e pluribus unum* – out of many, one. He believed that the Church (universal) is *one* and that local churches (particular) are spiritually united to the *one*, holy, catholic and apostolic Church by the Holy Trinity. For Allen, the *missio Dei* means that because our Triune God is 'One' and 'Missional', it ought to be understood that the Church (the 'one' body of Christ) is also 'missional' – a mission society – that is sent and empowered by the Trinity. He understood Church growth in organic terms, in which the essence of God's life in the Church 'naturally' (supernaturally!) flows to the world, thereby releasing the spontaneous expansion of the Church. Secondly, he believed that the substance of the Church's health and growth was determined by her belief in the Bible, creedal confessions, ministry gifts, and sacramental life. Thirdly, he believed that 'every Christian is a missionary' and that the expansion of the Church is enhanced by volunteer service. This chapter explores his belief that Church growth is spontaneous when she is spiritually nourished by the sacraments and that the pneumatological dynamic works in harmony to nurture an emerging Church in which 'the missionary Spirit' empowers *all members* for missionary action. This chapter carefully unpacks various articles and books that Allen wrote from 1920-30, in order to highlight his thoughts on: volunteerism within Islam and Christianity, Church indigenization, devolution, voluntary clergy practice and spontaneous Church growth.

Chapter 8 is entitled 'Roland Allen's Apostolic Principles: An Analysis of his 'The Ministry of Expansion: the Priesthood of the Laity'.[1] This chapter highlights the historical context of the missionary situation in certain parts of the British colonies, where there existed a shortage of ordained clergymen. This presented a problem because the Church of England required that the sacraments could only be administered by duly ordained clergy. He dealt with this apparent tension between a strict form of clericalism, which denied sacramental celebration as a means of grace whenever professional clerics were absent, in contrast to a sacramental practice that refused to withhold grace to those who gathered together as a community of faith. His response, simply, was to argue that Christ was 'spiritually present' to consecrate the elements of bread and wine whenever clergy were not present to preside over the Holy Communion. This chapter reveals his belief that to withhold the sacrament was a violation of apostolic principle, especially because Anglican doctrine emphasizes the necessity to administer the Eucharist for the believer's spiritual health. His sacramental emphasis moved away from a theoretical treatise on the subject by personally identifying himself with the Anglican 'scattered sheep' in various countries who were living where no ordained priests existed. From one angle, as a High Church Anglican, he did believe in the appropriate administration of the Holy Communion by ordained priests and bishops (that was divine order), but from another, his view for the Church's expansion to pioneer regions organically emerging within new territories – even if properly ordained clergy were not locally present – still necessitated the continuance of the sacramental meal whenever Christians met together. I carefully explain how Allen understood this as 'Spirit-directed apostolic order' within pioneer regions in which Christianity was beginning to spread throughout Africa.

Furthermore, Roland Allen continued to unpack his sacramental theology at the mature age of 75 by disclosing with great clarity the ways in which the sacramental practice impacts the Church's growth, which is the topic of Chapter 9 – 'The Church as 'The Family Rite'.[2] The thesis

---

1. Formerly an unpublished work by Roland Allen – 'The Ministry of Expansion: the Priesthood of the Laity' (1930), USPG X622, Box 3, Number 27, Oxford, Bodleian Library. Recently published edition: *The Ministry of Expansion by Roland Allen: The Priesthood of the Laity*, ed. J.D. Payne (William Carey Library, 2017).

2. Roland Allen, 'The Family Rite' (1943), USPG X622, Box 7, Oxford, Bodleian

of this work is an *apologia* for 'The Family Rite' as the core foundation
for the local church and he believed that it is to be understood that the
head of the household was to lead his family in worship. 'The Family
Rite', as Allen argued, sheds light on his understanding of the father's
priestly role within the family structure, as patterned and practised by
families during the Feast of Passover (Exodus 12). According to this
form of reasoning, he believed that the Passover provided a basis for
a New Covenant model of church-planting within homes. He argued
that this was the normal pattern during the early stages of the Church's
expansion. But, he argued, a 'Temple Rite' replaced the 'Family Rite' once
the Church began to become more organized and professionalized. This
chapter aims to explain his thinking and does include ongoing discussions
with his son, John (Iohn), on this matter during the early to mid-1940s.
That said, during Roland Allen's later years of life in Africa, he argued
for and consistently practised a 'Family Rite' sacramental approach on
a daily basis with his wife in their home and believed this to be a model
for the Church's expansion. In many ways, this 'Family Rite' emphasis
within Allen's theology of mission is an advocacy for the planting of
house churches.

   Roland Allen: A Theology of Mission concludes with Chapter 10 –
'Epilogue: Volume One and Volume Two' and proposes to summarize
what Allen believed was a prototypical apostolic ministry of the Apostle
Paul for the indigenous Church's expansion. The changing circumstances
within colonial hegemony compelled Allen to argue for a missionary
ecclesiology of indigenous nature that was *in, of* and *by* the Church. The
conclusion itemizes Allen's contribution to missiological studies within
a framework of a historical theology. Critical observations concerning
his missionary ecclesiology in light of postcolonial theory are addressed,
as well as a critique of some anti-Western biased assumptions within
postcolonial studies. A proposal to apply Allen's missionary ecclesiology
to contemporary missiology is encouraged due to the current missionary
situation within World Christianity.

   Library. This was later published in David M. Paton's *Reform of the Ministry:*
   a Study of the Work of Roland Allen (London: The Lutterworth Press, 1968).

1. The Problem
Allen's Assessment of Western Missions

Roland Allen sets out to examine the ecclesiastical problems surrounding paternal mission stations and its negative effect on the indigenous Church. Not only did he evaluate the problems of growing resentment towards foreign missionaries, but in response, he proposed principled solutions to these problems. This overview for the discipline of missiology demonstrates his significant contribution as a methods analyst: first, through examination of the church-planting principles that he claimed resided in Pauline practice; and second, through his analysis of Western colonial missionary methods contrasted with what he believed were apostolic methods. This chapter attempts to examine his understanding of a Pauline hermeneutic for missionary practice.

The primary interpretative model which shaped his missiology was rooted in Pauline principles and his missionary practice. What were the basic presuppositions that formed his ecclesiological ethos to focus on Paul rather than any other apostle or missionary? Firstly, after his father's untimely death in Belize – without his family[1] – young Roland (less than five years of age)[2] was the product of a conventional Anglican rearing in England, where '[h]is upbringing was then solely put into the hands of his mother, who was a very strict person with a strong evangelical persuasion'.[3] This backdrop of conventional Anglican rearing discloses his propensity towards an evangelical view of the Scriptures and a deep regard for Pauline epistolary, as evidenced throughout his lifetime. Secondly, his classical education at Oxford influenced the way he reasoned through and engaged with philosophical

---

1. Hubert Allen, *Roland Allen: Pioneer, Priest, and Prophet* (Grand Rapids: Eerdmans and Cincinnati: Forward Movement Publications, 1995), 10.
2. See David Sanderson, 'Roland Allen and his Vision of the Spontaneous Expansion of the Church', Lambeth Diploma thesis, 1989.
3. Ake Talltorp, 'Sacraments for Growth in Mission: Eucharistic Faith and Practice in the Theology of Roland Allen', *Transformation*, 29(3) (July 2012): 214-24 (214).

questions and theological doctrine.[1] Thirdly, his spiritual formation
was enhanced by some leading fathers of the Oxford Movement, who
personally influenced his thinking on sacramental theology, patristic
ministry and apostolic order.[2] Fourthly, his missionary experience in
China was pivotal in adding competence to his missionary theology, all
of which moulded the way he thought and approached a contemporary
application of Pauline missiology. This ecclesiological ethos played a
significant role in how his missionary ecclesiology developed and the
kind of questions concerning certain problematic missionary methods
that he had started to raise, which were entrenched in the missionary
situation he encountered. He specifically began to argue for a missiology
which promoted 'independence' – shaped from Pauline influence – for
indigenous converts and implicitly contended for all its members to take
responsibility for its own development and maturity, which, he believed,
was antithetical to a 'Peter Pan' (i.e., perpetual childhood) philosophy of
'mission station' paternalism.

Mission Stations and Allen's Critique of 'Peter Pan' Paternalism

After he returned from missionary work in China (1903) he was invited
to present a paper at the John Rylands Library before the Federation of
Junior Clergy Missionary Associations (JCMA) at their 19th Conference
of Delegates from 71 distinctive associations (included in attendance
were various bishops, canons and archdeacons from northern England).[3]
His thesis clearly stated that 'our Mission system'[4] expects indigenous
converts to be 'like automatons', even though 'the native church' has
'never grasped the fundamental principles on which it is based'.[5] This

1. Nias, *Flame from an Oxford Cloister: The Life and Writings of Philip Napier Waggett S.S.J.E. Scientist, Religious, Theologian, Missionary Philosopher, Diplomat, Author, Orator, Poet* (London: The Faith Press, 1961), 20-24, 47-56.

2. Charles Gore (ed.), *Lux Mundi: A Series of Studies in the Religion of the Incarnation* (London: John Murray, 1889. Repr., 1890); see Ragnar Ekstrom, *The Theology of Charles Gore* (Lund, 1994); Bardwell L. Smith, 'Liberal Catholicism: An Anglican Perspective', *Anglican Theological Review*, 3/1972, vol. 54, 175-193; H.N. Bate, 'Frank Edward Brightman 1856-1932', Proceedings of the British Academy, volume 19, (London: Humphrey Milford, Oxford University Press), 1-8.

3. Roland Allen, 'The Work of the Missionary in Preparing the Way for Independent Native Churches,' USPG X622, Box 2, File J: 4, 12, Oxford, Bodleian Library.

4. Ibid.

5. Ibid., 11.

comment was based upon a report that the delegates were familiar with, which, on one hand, promoted the idea of independence for the indigenous churches, but on the other hand, suggested that independence was 'far distant'.[6] He attributes this failure of missions to stem from how they imposed systems of 'laws and customs' instead of apostolic principles.[7] He suggested an evaluation for 'the true state of affairs' of past and present mission work accomplished by missionaries, in light of the 'accepted doctrine' and 'official policy of our great Missionary Societies' which was beginning to place more emphasis on planting 'independent native churches'.[8] He encouraged the delegates to study these 'theories' and the 'new methods tested' and then to set out to determine what was the 'germ of independence' for these newer churches.[9]

Firstly, although he agreed with this shift towards planting indigenous churches, he disagreed with the general missionary methodology which still expected their converts to adapt by using 'semi-Europeanized' rituals, prayer books, church buildings and styles of worship based on the ways of 'Rome, or of Sarum, or of Keswick'.[10] Charles Kraft agrees and argues that 'establishment' branches of Christianity which are afraid 'to alter the forms' of worship in order to reach the current culture and have contented 'itself with indoctrinating new generations and new cultures into forms of Christianity that are no longer culturally appropriate', tend to 'superstitiously' preserve what they believe to be 'the 'sacred forms of worship' that have been maintained for a long time.[11] Allen argued for an indigenous 'how to' methodology that focused on 'how to win Native Converts . . . how to organize village churches . . . how to educate Coreans [sic] to understand and use intelligently any Prayer Book at all . . . [and] how to adapt a native hut for worship'.[12] Lamin Sanneh correctly interprets Allen's argument here when he suggests that he was challenging 'the Western cultural captivity of the gospel', which was, in effect, 'strangling the gospel'.[13] He called this a misrepresentation of Christianity, 'slavery to a Foreign system' which was 'not their own' and,

---

6. Ibid., 13.

7. Ibid., 12.

8. Ibid., 7.

9. Ibid., 7.

10. Ibid., 4, 8.

11. Charles Kraft, *Christianity in Culture: A Study in Dynamic Biblical Theologizing in Cross-Cultural Perspective* (Maryknoll: Orbis Books, 1980), 382-83.

12. Allen, 'The Work of the Missionary', Box 2, File J: 4, 8.

13. Lamin Sanneh, *Disciples of All Nations: Pillars of World Christianity* (Oxford and New York: Oxford University Press, 2008), 224-225.

consequently, the imposition of a 'foreigner's Church'.[1] As far as Allen was concerned, this was a betrayal of Pauline missiology, which opposed slavery to a 'foreign system', as clearly demonstrated when he defended the 'freedom' of the Galatian churches to reject the 'Judaizing' system which they attempted to impose upon the churches.[2]

Secondly, he believed the only way for the missionaries to reverse what Robert Young has referred to as the 'long-lasting political hegemony'[3] towards 'independence' would be to apply the following 'three principles' as part of the training process:

> (1) to teach the native converts to recognize their responsibility as members of the Church; (2) to avoid the introduction of any foreign element unless it is absolutely essential; (3) to be always retiring from the people to prepare the way for final retirement.[4]

These three apostolic principles began to shape his thinking as he was attempting to train catechists in China. He recognized that the Anglican conventional methodology for leadership training actually limited any possibility to expand beyond his context. He quickly realized that unless the local converts took responsibility immediately to disciple, train and lead their own faith communities, then any idea of expansion would be slow. He reflects upon what he did in China:

> I called the people together, told them it was high time that they were doing something for the spread of the Gospel, and asked them what they meant to do. I observe that people in England sometimes view such conduct with surprise. If they treated their people at home in the same way, I believe they would feel less surprise that it succeeded in China.[5]

Allen argued that his successful experiences in China shaped his missionary thinking to undergo reform by embracing a different methodology. This reform was shaped more through praxis than theory. He began to 'flesh out' his missiology by analyzing every aspect of missionary societies' practices. This led him to develop as a methods analyst concerning the 'whys' and 'wherefores' of missionary methods.

---

1. Allen, 'The Work of the Missionary', Box 2, File J: 4, 12.
2. Cf. the Epistle to the Galatians.
3. Robert Young, *Postcolonialism: An Historical Introduction* (Oxford: Blackwell Publishers, 2001), 334.
4. Allen, 'The Work of the Missionary', Box 2, File J: 4, 9.
5. Ibid., 4, 11.

Thirdly, he warned against missionaries forcing foreign 'laws and customs' rather than allowing the converts to adopt familiar local customs with 'principles which they valued'[6] as part of the contextualization process for local church development. He emphasized the need for missionaries to be more self-critical concerning their tendency to 'force' conformity to a foreign system that would likely be abandoned once either independence came through a devolved process, or, if the indigenous churches' frustrations with paternalism would eventually 'lead to rebellion'.[7]

Fourthly, he applied the principles of self-government and self-support to the Chinese catechists so that they would make 'what they have learnt their own'.[8] He told the delegates how his 'reformed' methodology in China worked in bringing 'independence' to the local churches but that it was contingent on the locals taking ownership of their worship services and daily responsibilities within the faith communities. He said that the missionaries who expected quick results by imposing a 'cast-iron system', what Kwame Bediako calls 'missionary ethnocentrism',[9] generally failed. In contrast, he told the delegates that the principle he applied was to build slowly and that 'we had better at first give them only so much as they can easily assimilate'.[10]

Finally, Allen comments on the extent to which the 'three principles' had been adopted: the first principle (i.e., converts recognizing their responsibility) was 'practised in different shapes very widely'; the second principle (i.e., restraint from imposing foreign elements unless it's necessary) was 'less widely' practised; and the third (i.e., missionaries retiring from their converts) was 'scarcely recognized at all'.[11]

Hence, he concluded that the 'problem of independent native churches is the great problem of the day' and that the Western Church's missionaries needed to come to terms with: (1) understanding 'the native mind'; (2) feeling 'sympathy for the natives in their early

---

6. Ibid., 4, 12.

7. Ibid., 4, 12.

8. Ibid., 4, 13.

9. Kwame Bediako, 'Biblical Christologies in the Context of African Traditional Religions', in Vinay Samuel and Chris Sugden (eds), *Sharing Jesus in the Two Thirds World: Evangelical Christologies from the contexts of poverty, powerlessness and religious pluralism*, The Papers of the First Conference of Evangelical Theologians from the Two Thirds World, Bangkok, Thailand, 22-25 March, 1982, (Grand Rapids: Eerdmans, 1983), 87.

10. Allen, 'The Work of the Missionary', Box 2, File J: 4, 13.

11. Ibid., 4, 15.

efforts'; (3) watching 'slow growth with patience and hope'; (4) realizing 'that Western Christianity is not the whole of Christianity'; and (5) watching how 'the Holy Spirit transforms strange forms of life into Christian forms of life unlike our own' by uniting multi-ethnic Christians as a 'complement of our own needs'.[1] As such, his thesis unpacked an emerging theology for Church unity seven years prior to the Edinburgh Conference of 1910. His developing ecclesiology presupposed an application of principles which reinforced 'independent native churches' to emerge slowly and which were 'indigenously led'.[2] Allen's insistence that all members take responsibility for their own development and maturity is an argument against a 'Peter Pan' philosophy of mission station paternalism.

The Influence of 'Mission Stations' Upon the Establishment of Indigenous Churches[3]

The generally agreed upon practice and 'object' of foreign missions in 1912 was for the planting and 'establishment of indigenous Churches'.[4] However, for some time foreign missions practised an 'inherited' system – mission stations – which operated under a different philosophy of mission and was still being maintained in an increasing fashion 'year by year'.[5] On one hand, not only was the practice widespread, accounting for the growth of Christianity in 'India and Africa and China', but, observed Allen, the number of Christians was 'rising more rapidly than any other is due, without doubt, to the establishment of these Missions'.[6] On the other hand, he believed these 'mission stations' created a foreign subculture of which 'the first impression by which all later impressions are interpreted' actually misrepresented gospel ministry for the local converts. They tended to interpret the ways that missionaries claimed that their church buildings, rituals, houses and relationships with their 'paid helpers' were a necessity for the sake of establishing a civilized Christianity.[7] The first impressions that missionaries gave to those they sought to convert frequently tended

---

1. Ibid., 4, 14–15.
2. Sanneh, *Disciples of All Nations*, 278.
3. Roland Allen, 'Mission Stations: The Influence of "Mission Stations" Upon the Establishment of Indigenous Churches', *English Church Review*, vol. III, no. 35 (November 1912): 499–508.
4. Ibid., 500.
5. Ibid.
6. Ibid.
7. Ibid., 501.

to shape their subsequent relationships with communities. His point was that, frequently, their first impressions were ultimately detrimental to the application of apostolic principles for the establishment of indigenous churches, in that the converts tended to view the missionaries as businessmen.[8] He describes this in three ways:

(1) The establishment of a Mission is primarily a financial operation;

(2) Secondly, the missionary who opens a new centre and establishes a Mission is commonly a European, and the land and property is held in trust by Europeans, therefore emphasis is laid upon the fact that the business on which he is engaged is a foreign business;

(3) In the mission station the permanence of the foreign element is emphasized.[9]

He saw within this system 'a certain incongruity'[10] which misrepresented the Christian faith. He came to the conclusion that mission stations ultimately 'controlled and directed every action',[11] and embraced a threefold course of action of paternalism. Firstly, it imposed an authoritarian framework of ministry, which was designed to support, strengthen, guide and educate the converts until they were self-governing.[12] Secondly, it set out later to produce a co-operative approach 'side by side with the growing Native Church life'.[13] Thirdly, missionaries were supposedly prepared to operate with an intentional plan of retirement from the indigenous setting by giving the converts the mechanism to manage everything themselves.[14] Allen regarded how this plan of action was flawed from the beginning due to its pervasive hegemonic infrastructure. However, this practice was not new. Andrew Porter writes that, in 1890, Harry Johnston, 'Britain's first administrator in Nyasaland and himself an unbeliever . . . none the less [sic] praised the missions'[15] because

their immediate object is not profit, they can afford to reside at places till they become profitable. They strengthen our hold over

---

8. Ibid., 502.

9. Ibid.

10. Ibid., 503.

11. Ibid.

12. Ibid.

13. Ibid.

14. Ibid.

15. Andrew Porter, *Religion versus empire? British Protestant missionaries and overseas expansion, 1700-1914* (Manchester/New York: Manchester University Press, 2004), 269.

the country, they spread the use of the English language, they induct the natives into the best kind of civilization and in fact each mission station is an essay in colonization.[1]

This illustrates the hegemonic attitude characteristic among advocates of what has been called 'the scramble for Africa'. Missionaries were caught in the midst of what Allen called 'the imperialistic spirit'[2] of the times and had to deal with the tension between leadership through service and leadership by control. Jehu Hanciles has argued how colonial hegemonic thinking was prevalent even later, noting that Stephen Neill, in his influential studies of mission,[3] consistently failed 'to take this into consideration', and in the process presented 'solutions that implicitly romanticize the role and involvement of the foreign missionary'.[4]

In actuality, the surrounding community benefited from these foreign resources, especially the converts who received various privileges due to their association with the mission, in contrast to those who lived outside its system. Instead of empowering the converts to cultivate a level of independence, Allen noticed that their infrastructure created negative results where independence 'was sapped' morally, spiritually and intellectually.[5] Similarly, Young points out that Mahatma Gandhi's 'different epistemology' sought to propose a 'third way' whereby 'a whole social system' was created 'with its own economics, moral and spiritual culture'[6] to encourage independence. That said, as he notes, as far as Gandhi was concerned, the ideal

> is that capital and labour should supplement and help each other. They should be a great family living in unity and harmony, capital not only looking to the material welfare of the labourers but their moral welfare also – capitalists being trustees for the welfare of the labouring classes under them.[7]

---

1. Ibid.
2. Roland Allen, 'Jerusalem: A Critical Review of "The World Mission of Christianity"' (London: World Dominion Press, 1928), 27.
3. See, Stephen Neill, *The Unfinished Task* (London: The Lutterworth Press, 1957); Stephen Neill, *A History of Christian Missions* (London: Penguin Books, 1964. Repr., Harmondsworth: Penguin Books, 1986).
4. Jehu Hanciles, *Euthanasia of a Mission: African Church Autonomy in a Colonial Context* (London & Westport: Praeger, 2002), 254.
5. Allen, 'Mission Stations', English Church Review, 504.
6. Young, *Postcolonialism*, 322-23.
7. Sunil Kumar Sen, *Working Class Movements in India, 1885-1975* (Delhi: Oxford University Press, 1994), 96; M.K. Gandhi, *The Collected Works of Mahatma*

Young argues that this supports a practice of 'capitalist as trustee' and makes Gandhi's idea no different than that of 'colonial administrators'.[8] Allen seems to have been fully aware of this problem and sought ways to correct it in his own work.

The converts invariably continued 'to look on the Mission as "the cow" . . .' which was 'not really a healthy condition, either for the converts or for the missionary'.[9] These converts served within the mission station and received some financial compensation for their work, even though 'they were not highly paid' yet for them it was regular 'material benefits'.[10] However, the sustainability of the mission station was all hinged on foreign money and he argued that this system inevitably postponed any plan for missionaries to retire from controlling their organization.[11] His observations of this hegemony caused him to contend against a mentality of 'dependency', that being a 'welfare' mission system, and instead he argued for progress towards inculcating principles of dignity, responsibility and independence. His thinking progressed towards ways of empowering indigenous converts to break from dependency on foreign control by taking the initiative to manage their own independent churches.

Herein lies his *apologia* for 'a fundamental teaching of the Gospel, the principle of self-sacrifice'[12] as taught and lived within the framework of the indigenous Church, in contrast to the paternalistic system of foreign mission stations which taught and practised 'it is more blessed to receive than to give'.[13] For Allen, although the *principle* of self-sacrifice was generally taught by the 'individual missionaries', it was the *system* of the mission stations that actually undermined the *principle*.[14] He argued that the mission station is *not* the Church. Consequently, dependency on the missionary and the mission station directly contradicts what he delineates in *Missionary Methods*:

if the first converts are taught to depend on the missionary, if all work, evangelistic, educational, social is concentrated in his

Gandhi, 90 vols., Delhi: Publications Division, Ministry of Information and Broadcasting, Govt. of India, 1958-84, 28: 47, as cited in Young, *Postcolonialism*, 334.

8. Young, *Postcolonialism*, 323; cf. Frederick John D. Lugard, *The Dual Mandate in British Tropical Africa* (Edinburgh: Blackwood, 1922).

9. Allen, 'Mission Stations', *English Church Review*, 504.

10. Ibid., 503.

11. Ibid., 505.

12. Ibid.

13. Ibid.

14. Ibid.

hands . . . a tradition very rapidly grows up that nothing can be done without the authority and guidance of the missionary, the people wait for him to move, and, the longer they do so, the more incapable they become of any independent action.[1]

He believed that missionaries were to work themselves out of their temporary vocations. And yet, the system of the mission station acted as centrepiece for all its missionary organizational services of health, education and welfare. Eventually, missionaries realized that if the mission station began to decay the whole structure would collapse, especially if foreign financial support began to decline.[2]

Hanciles argues this very point in *Euthanasia of a Mission*, which examines Henry Venn's (1796-1873) indigenous 'three self' model and identifies 'the unhelpful dichotomy between church and mission inherent in Venn's thinking'.[3] He rightly contrasts Allen's 'three self' viewpoint from Venn's in this way: 'Allen's central thesis – that the primary difference between the Apostle Paul's missionary method and the modern approach was that he founded 'churches' instead of 'missions' – and gives his arguments a different conceptual framework from Venn.[4] To use a modern term, for Allen's missiology it can be said that he believed the Church to be *missional*. In his thinking, Church and mission cannot be dichotomized for the two are interwoven and that the Church inherently produced mission *not* that mission stations or mission societies produced the Church.

This distinction led him to critique another system which the missionaries had created as a solution to the 'fatal mistake' they had made.[5] The missionaries eventually erected another organization 'side by side'[6] designed to assist the existing 'mission station' structure. This new organization intended to function separately from the mission and was called 'the native church'.[7] The indigenous converts were not only confused with the imposition of 'another system' but he said 'they preferred the easy irresponsibility of the old régime'.[8] He thought that this reaction against the newer 'native Church' model indicated the way

---

1. Allen, *Missionary Methods*, 81.
2. Allen, 'Mission Stations', *English Church Review*, 505.
3. Hanciles, *Euthanasia of a Mission*, 254.
4. Ibid.
5. Allen, 'Mission Stations', *English Church Review*, 505.
6. Ibid.
7. Ibid.
8. Ibid.

that 'children think, who dimly see that increasing responsibility involves larger effort, and are afraid of the demand which it makes upon them'.[9] His retort was that the missionary societies created a 'dual organization': (1) the mission station; and (2) the 'native Christian community with its organization'.[10] His solution to this problematic 'new situation' was, firstly, to fix the system by applying the missionary principle of planting local churches *first* – not later – before introducing schools, hospitals or any other institutions. This back-to-front 'dual organization' system contributed to reinforcing his 'ecclesiocentric' missiology, but it also made room for what Hanciles calls the 'semiautonomous status'[11] of emergent indigenous leadership. The problematic situation where indigenous 'paid agents' in the mission stations were 'paid in a different form from those which the native community could supply', he believed, hindered the 'natives' from taking the initiative to develop their own independent churches because 'of financial security in the service of the Mission, which they would not enjoy under native control'.[12] He regarded this system as detrimental to the principle of unity, which he believed was the basis for diocesan networking churches. Secondly, his next solution was for the foreign missionaries to give these stations 'to the native Christian community'.[13] Thirdly, after the missionaries retire and transfer the mission properties over to the indigenous communities, he argued that the independent churches should freely exercise their right to discontinue 'the larger and more expensive' missions 'because the native Church will not see any importance in maintaining them'. Moreover, since these missions 'have not grown up with the natural growth of the people on the spot, they have been imposed on them by the needs of foreigners, and when the foreigners are removed the needs are removed'.[14]

Consequently, Allen concludes that this mission station system needs to be seen 'as a thing of the past' due to its creation 'as the schools of a Christianity which is not of the country'.[15] Again, his concern was that this imposition of foreign methodologies needed to discontinue since it seemed to create various difficulties for the future development of the indigenous Church.

---

9. Ibid.
10. Ibid., 506.
11. Hanciles, *Euthanasia of a Mission*, 209.
12. Allen, 'Mission Stations', *English Church Review*, 506.
13. Ibid.
14. Ibid., 507–508.
15. Ibid., 508.

A Question of Priorities: Educational Emphasis as Primary

Roland Allen was an advocate of holistic education. That said, when examining his view of education in the missionary situation, he makes some clear distinctions. Firstly, he was *not* an advocate for mission societies building schools to 'evangelize' children of non-Christian families. He argued against this method because it had 'created a very confused idea among the people generally as to their real object'.[1] The initial intention of the mission societies to 'educate leaders for the Native Church' in their schools and to use these schools as institutions 'for the conversion of the non-Christian children committed to their care' he believed, was a deceptive methodology on the part of the missions since the non-Christian parents were under the assumption that their children were being 'fitted to hold posts of influence and emolument in the country'.[2] His defence for 'the advantages of Western education',[3] which the Chinese government requested remained intact; however, he was concerned with how the disingenuous mission practice cultivated a growing 'suspicious' perception of and resentment against Christianity'.[4]

Secondly, he was an advocate for indigenous Church teachers who were appointed to educate the children and young people coming from Christian families. His argument for understanding this distinction is disclosed in the following response to H.J. Wallace when he questioned Allen's article 'The Chinese Government and Mission Schools':[5]

> I am persuaded that the true mission education lies outside schools created for the 'education' of the young, and is an education of the whole local Church, by the local Church, in the local Church, an education which missionary educationists today rarely mention, and scarcely attempt to practise, but an education of the most profound and fundamental character.[6]

---

1. Roland Allen, 'Education in the Native Church', in *World Dominion* (London: World Dominion Press, 1926. Repr., 1928), 14.
2. Ibid.
3. Ibid.
4. Ibid., 15.
5. Roland Allen, letter to the editor of *World Dominion* (London: World Dominion Press, April 1931) 19-23; Roland Allen, 'Christian Education in China' in The Report of the China Educational Commission of 1921-1922, *Theology*, March 1923 (London: World Dominion Press, repr., 1930).
6. Allen, *World Dominion*, 22.

Allen's *apologia* for holistic education stemmed from his ecclesiocentric mission theology.[7] The educational system was based upon: (1) the principle of indigenous Christian teachers hired by the local villages to educate their own people; and (2) the principle of 'liberty' where the teachers function as 'free agents' to train children and youth with applicable curriculum, vocational training, life skills and character development.[8] He argued against mission stations attempting to educate from the foreign mission's base of operation and subsidized by foreigners. He did contend for the right of Christian 'native' teachers to freely educate out from the context of their locally managed churches. Thirdly, did Allen oppose Christian education? No. He clearly articulated his defence of Christian education.

> Now what is needed is a Christian education which will grow with the growth of the Church and wax steadily in proportion as the Church increases in numbers and strength. What is needed is a Christian education which is of the Church, by the Church, for the Church, a Christian education which depends in no sense upon the supply of men or money from a foreign country, but which lives in the life of the Church.[9]

For indigenous Christian education to be currently effective and integrally ongoing, he believed, it is incumbent for the local churches to develop policies that refuse foreign aid for the general maintenance of its local work. Hanciles, similarly, wrote how these problems were also evident in West Africa's Sierra Leone Mission whereupon 'the spirit of paternalism which engendered chronic dependence' needed to be addressed.[10] That said, Allen warned against not only foreign paternalism but also the hegemony extended through national government grants for schools – mission and indigenous – which was being encouraged and promoted among some Protestant denominations and mission societies who embraced the 'social gospel' methodology.

Allen's likes and dislikes for introducing Western learning for non-Western people groups must be examined carefully. He was *not* opposed to Western education being introduced into a non-Western culture *if* the

---

7. Cf. Kwame Bediako, 'Biblical Christologies in the Context of African Traditional Religions', Vinay Samuel & Chris Sugden (eds.), *Sharing Jesus In the Two Thirds World* (Grand Rapids: Eerdmans, 1983) 81.

8. Roland Allen, 'Educational Principles and Missionary Methods', *English Church Review* (January 1913): 23.

9. Allen, 'Education in the Native Church', 18.

10. Hanciles, *Euthanasia of a Mission*, 16.

country's government desired to implement aspects of its educational principles, as in the case of Chang Chih-tung.[1] He argued that Chih-tung's pragmatic desire for Western learning in China was incomplete if it was divorced from Christian faith and morals. Therefore, according to his understanding of what principles constituted Western education, he articulated:

(1) that an ecclesiocentric educational system says 'The Church is the School of Christ',[2] which educates her members in the principles of personal discipleship, biblical teaching, community relationships and mutual responsibility;

(2) that Pauline principles 'and his system of education [were] strictly by observation and experiment'[3] and which provided the West's educational milieu for educators such as 'Pestalozzi, and Froebel, and Herbart, and Montessori'[4] to contextualize these principles;

(3) that the Pauline *spiritual* 'method was a training in activities'[5] motivated by the charismatic dynamism, whereas Froebel's *natural* educational system 'was the principle of self-activity';[6] and

(4) the Western emphasis on 'scientific pedagogy' has as its foundation in Montessori's 'fundamental principle . . . the liberty of the pupil'[7] which echoes the Pauline principle of 'liberty'.[8] Leonard Elliott-Binns recalls how in the 1830s 'the minds of Englishmen turned again towards liberty; and the revival of a belief in the principle became a striking feature of the period'.[9] The principle of liberty is integral to Western education's ethos and he argued that its roots were embedded in Pauline theology and practice.

---

1. Roland Allen, 'The Progress of Education in China', *Cornhill* (November 1908): 665.

2. Allen, 'Educational Principles', *English Church Review,* 19.

3. Ibid., 21.

4. Ibid., 20.

5. Ibid., 21.

6. Ibid.

7. Ibid., 23.

8. Cf. II Corinthians 3:17; Galatians 5:1ff; Allen, 'Educational Principles', 22-23.

9. L.E. Elliott-Binns, *Religion in the Victorian Era,* 1936, 21.

Education Designed to Proselytize

The missionaries' educational plan to proselytize the children of non-Christians rather than 'to educate leaders for the Native Church'[10] was the primary cause of Allen's initial frustration. Not only did he think that missionary societies had been diverted from their main objective, but he was also concerned that they had lost their vision for an all-inclusive evangelism and instead sought 'to gain an influence over the more enlightened, progressive, and socially influential classes of the country in order to open doors for the propagation of their religion among these classes'.[11] He argued against this method, firstly because it was, he believed, a substitute of the Pauline principle to plant the indigenous Church within the environment of *all* classes of people groups. Secondly, this reminded him of a disturbing trend promoted at Edinburgh 1910. Stanley discloses this trend in his discussion of Timothy Richard's emphasis:

> Educational missionaries had not yet realized that what was needed in response was a corresponding revolutionary readjustment in their methods: a world civilization (Richard even used the term 'a world Empire') was being born, and it was the responsibility of Christian missions to infuse the emerging new order with principles of divine wisdom. Richard's call for a 'higher type of missionary' who could fulfill the role of a Confucian sage and advise the rulers of the land on what would make for the good of the nation was a distinctive and rather eccentric variant of the Commission's theme of the role of education in the Christianisation of national life.[12]

Thirdly, Allen defined and contrasted the difference between 'proselytize' and 'convert'. He argued that 'to proselytize' was an endeavour to persuade a person 'from one system of thought and practice to another' and 'to convert' emphasizes bringing a person 'into relation with Christ'.[13] In terms of missionary societies, he believed that their purpose for Christian education was designed specifically 'for

---

10. Allen, 'Education in the Native Church', 14.

11. Ibid., 14–15.

12. Brian Stanley, *The World Missionary Conference, Edinburgh 1910*, Studies in the History of Christian Missions (Grand Rapids/Cambridge: Eerdmans, 2009), 190; cf. Ecumenical Centre, Geneva, Commission III replies, vol. 4: 268-69; and also, *Report of Commission III*, 83-84.

13. Roland Allen, 'Christian Education in China: The Report of the China Educational Commission of 1921-1922' in *Theology* (March 1923): 129-134, Box 2, File J: 17, 134.

Christians' not non-Christians and that its primary aim was to cultivate an educational environment which centred on children being 'instructed in Christ'.[1] Consequently, he was opposed to missionary societies proselytizing in order to 'introduce Christianity as a system of moral and religious thought'.[2]

Fourthly, he argues that there was sufficient evidence to prove how the failure of the 'Mission institutions' to convert 'large numbers of non-Christians' made room to 'naturally educate some opponents of the religion which they represent'.[3] Institutional casualties are not an uncommon phenomenon. He referred to the 'anti-Christian societies' in China and how their publications quite often had contributing articles by 'students and ex-students of mission schools and colleges'.[4] What is 'needed' to solve this dilemma, he suggests, is that Christian education ought to 'grow with the growth of the Church' so as to develop gradually 'in proportion as the Church increases in numbers and strength'.[5] His ecclesiocentric approach to Christian education presupposes a comprehensive philosophy of indigenous ministry, 'which is of the Church, by the Church, for the Church'.[6] That said, Allen's missionary ecclesiology inculcated the *apologia* – 'The Church is a school of the most valuable order' – for it assumes that her members are learning the 'virtues of self-control' as a disciplined approach for holistic life and for the purpose of promoting the 'practice' and 'the meaning of Christian government'.[7] He believed that this *apologia* was 'the true foundation of all social and political progress'.[8]

Finally, the missionary calling to educate from a Christian world view, Allen believed, ought to stem from distinctly 'Christian' schools with indigenous faculty and administration that function 'independently' from government schools and choose not to depend upon government subsidies[9] or foreign benevolence. His understanding was that school enrollment ought to consist of children from Christian homes who know what to expect in the curriculum, classroom management and religious emphasis which underpins the educational process.

---

1. Ibid.
2. Ibid.
3. Roland Allen, 'Education in the Native Church', *World Dominion* (London: World Dominion Press, 1926. Repr., 1928), 15.
4. Ibid., 16.
5. Ibid., 18.
6. Ibid.
7. Ibid., 21.
8. Ibid.
9. Ibid., 12.

The Hegemonic Dilemma:
Indigenous Leaders Perceived as 'Inferior'

A cogent reaction to his exposure of 'the imperialistic spirit' is disclosed in a letter to the editor of *The Living Church* by John Nichols (Shanghai, China).[10] Nichols corrects Allen's definition of 'imperialism' saying instead that it 'is the desire and effort to extend national interests in external fields'.[11] Nichols states that the 'missionary body in China is, flatly, not imperialistic' and that missionaries have attempted to make Christianity 'native and free' but 'to turn things over to Chinese control is far in advance of the inherent rights of the situation' and he argues that even the Chinese recognized [that] they were not ready to assume this level of responsibility'.[12] He assumed that Allen's method was 'to ordain at random' those who have not been trained and tested.[13] Nichols argued for the 'duty' of missionaries to make sure that 'the true faith is taught and a regulated ministry set up'.[14] On one hand, Allen would theologically concur that the indigenous converts need 'the true faith'. On the other hand, his ecclesiology anticipated 'a ministry' of men who were 'above reproach' (I Timothy 3:2)[15] and who were not regulated by foreign missionaries, but were duly ordained indigenous ministers. He envisioned 'fully equipped' churches served by locally trained ministers who were *not* inferior to the missionaries who had mentored them. Nichols also assumed that he was *naïve* to suggest that Anglican missionary bishops could actually consecrate 'native unpaid bishops'.[16] Allen disagreed, because his visionary forecast for this practice was based on Pauline precedent and English Christianity. He argued that this was the historic practice of Anglicanism: 'In our

---

10. John W. Nichols, letter to the editor, 'The Imperialism of Missions in China', *The Living Church* (13 April 1929): 833.

11. Ibid.

12. Ibid.

13. Ibid.

14. Ibid.

15. Patrick Daniel, my teaching assistant at Arizona Christian University argues 'that Paul was echoing Greco-Roman culture sentiment when it came to the issue of being "above reproach" in I Timothy 3:2, for the purpose of evangelism' (Patrick Daniel, 'The Overseer as a Witness for the Gospel,' a paper submitted to Dr Andrew Pitts at Phoenix Seminary for BL595 – Judeo/Greco-Roman Backgrounds to the New Testament, 2015).

16. Ibid.

own history, St Augustine was consecrated bishop, not of England, but of Canterbury (AD 597) . . . and at that time all the bishops derived from Augustine were natives.'[1]

An argument can be made for 'native' leadership to emerge through the means of a 'foreign' representative's prompting, as in the case of Augustine of Canterbury. Although Rome's papacy sent Augustine as a missionary bishop to England, it was only a matter of time before the ecclesiastical leaders who emerged were of English origin not transplanted foreigners. The English Church's self-governing process was actually initiated by foreign leadership, and yet, was able to quickly propagate indigenous bishops and priests without foreign restraints.[2] That said, the hegemonic dilemma does exist where indigenous leaders are assumed to be inferior.

Today, this is a concern within postcolonial discourse, especially by what Young said concerning 'empowering the poor, the dispossessed, and the disadvantaged, for tolerance of difference and diversity, for the establishment of minorities' rights, women's rights, and cultural rights within a broad framework of democratic egalitarianism. . . . '[3] Although Allen was not a direct influence, it is clear that his work is prescient – it had much in common with the ideas of thinkers such as Young. Allen's concerns about these items were addressed by him a century ago and are articulated in *Missionary Methods* (1912):

> We have allowed racial and religious pride to direct our attitude towards those whom we have been wont to call 'poor heathen'. We have approached them as superior beings, moved by charity to impart of our wealth to destitute and perishing souls. . . . We have managed their funds, ordered their services, built their churches, provided their teachers. . . . We have done everything for them, but very little with them. We have done everything for them except give place to them. We have treated them as 'dear children' but not as 'brethren'.[4]

Allen articulated a clarion call for missionaries to *renounce* the attitude of superiority and recognize the commonality that exists with their converts as is exemplified within the principles of Christian unity.

1. Paton, *The Ministry of the Spirit*, 179.
2. This is not to dismiss Celtic Christianity's influence within the Britannic Isles.
3. Young, *Postcolonialism*, 113.
4. Allen, *Missionary Methods*, 142-143.

Foreign hegemonic mannerisms quite often had difficulty recognizing local potential to lead without their assistance and when paternalistic attitudes could only envision indigenous immaturity, that being, again, a sort of 'Peter Pan' philosophy, by which the 'natives' never seemed to measure up to the foreign missionaries' standards, then this 'imperialistic spirit' reinforces the racial divide where 'the stamp of being the white man's religion, a foreign religion'[5] misrepresents the catholicity of the Church.

Another problem that missionaries encountered was the issue of 'class' distinction, not only as a result of the differences between Western and non-Western Christians, but also the 'denominational' class distinction between 'liberal' and 'conservative' missionaries. On the one side, the 'liberal hope,' Stanley says, was 'that the great religions of the world would, under sympathetic missionary tutelage, locate the fulfilment of their highest ideals in the teachings of Jesus Christ.'[6] For example, J.N. Farquhar's *The Crown of Hinduism* (1913) presented Jesus Christ as the fulfilment of the highest ethical aspirations of Hinduism[7] and promoted 'the dogma-less Christ of social gospel liberalism, a teacher of ethical idealism and social justice who could command the devotion of all men'.[8] On the other side, 'conservative evangelicals', such as Hudson Taylor, 'adopted Chinese dress' and was not interested in promoting 'the values of Western civilization' or 'social regeneration' but chose instead to contextualize the Gospel by emphasizing conversion as a personal faith in knowing Christ.[9] Allen identified himself amongst the side of conservative evangelicals.

Stanley describes 'a thesis defending the possibility of Christian missionary activity without empire' and 'was in part confessional, readily admitting the high-handed arrogance and easy dismissiveness with which many missionaries had approached religions and cultures other

5. Henrik Kraemer, *The Christian Message in a Non-Christian World* (Grand Rapids: Kregel Publications [1938], 1969), 337.

6. Brian Stanley, *The Bible and the Flag: Protestant Missions and British Imperialism in the Nineteenth and Twentieth Centuries* (Leicester: Apollos [IVP], 1990), 166.

7. See Eric Sharpe, *Not to Destroy But to Fulfil: the Contribution of J.N. Farquhar to Protestant Missionary Thought in India before 1914* (Uppsala: Svenska Institutet för Missionsforskningvenska); *Faith Meets Faith: Some Christian Attitudes to Hinduism in the Nineteenth and Twentieth Centuries* (London: SCM, 1977).

8. Stanley, 164; see J.N. Farquhar, *The Crown of Hinduism* (London, 1913).

9. Stanley, 165.

than their own'.[1] Allen's apostolic principles, however, influenced the way he engaged cross-culturally with the ancient faiths and religious systems which developed from them. This is especially evidenced later in life, when he engaged with Muslims in Nairobi by translating 'Muslim epics from Swahili into English'.[2]

1. Andrew Porter, *Religion versus empire? British Protestant missionaries and overseas expansion, 1700-1914* (Manchester/New York: Manchester University Press, [2004], 2005) 6; cf. Stanley, *The Bible and the Flag*, 1990.
2. Hubert Allen, 'Would Roland Allen still have anything to say to us today?' 184.

2. Roland Allen's Missiological Remedy
What Would Paul Do?

Allen experienced a paradigm shift in his missionary thinking after serving in China the five years prior to the Boxer Uprising (1900). Returning to England for a two-year furlough, he reflected on questions that emerged during his missionary experiences as he 'became more and more uneasy' about the vast 'six provinces' to be evangelized.[1] He questioned how the Anglican Church could possibly be planted in those immense provinces with the limited evangelistic work currently being done by his colleagues.[2] He also queried the methodology he was using to train Chinese catechists for ordination because it took so long and replied, 'I shall not see a great advance in my lifetime', which caused him 'great doubt and perplexity'.[3] For solace during his furlough, he turned to the apostle Paul to understand his missionary methods:

> From that day forward I began to see light, and gradually as I studied the method of the Apostle I entered into a large liberty, difficulties were smoothed away, doubts removed, and I began to understand what the establishment of the Church might be. I do not mean that I attained without a struggle. At first I was horrified and dismayed. I thought that I must be quite mad, because I could not imagine how other men wiser than I had not seen what I saw. I wrote down what I saw in St Paul's work. I simply wrote: 'The Apostle did this; we do that.' Then men like Bishop Gore and Father Waggett read it, and they said that it was illuminating. That dismayed me all the more because I could not understand how wise men could see what I saw and not change their whole manner of action.[4]

---

1. Roland Allen, 'Indigenous Churches: The Way of St Paul' (a paper read at the CMS Conference of Missionaries, High Leigh, 1927), *Church Missionary Review* (June 1927), USPG X622, Box 2: 23, 147, Oxford, Bodleian Library.
2. Ibid.
3. Ibid.
4. Ibid., 148.

These spiritual mentors while at Oxford appreciated much of what
Allen had come to understand, but this did not satisfy his quest for a
paradigmatic shift towards Pauline missiology. Was he on the right track?
He thought so. His missiological journey led him to conclude that 'St
Paul was right and we were wrong'.[1] However, some 'modern missionary
statesmen' disagreed with his conclusions in *Missionary Methods* (1912),[2]
claiming that the changing times and circumstances had made Paul's
methods inconsequential.[3] He replied: 'To that I answer that principles do
not change.'[4] His belief in the abiding validity of Pauline principles is what
Thomas Oden would call 'paleo-orthodoxy', that being 'classic consensual
teaching'.[5] Allen preached that biblical inspiration was the 'Spirit's influence
of inspired men's words'[6] and affirmed the immutability of Scripture
where 'inspiration cannot be touched by criticism'.[7] His rootedness in a
conservative theology of biblical revelation argued for its relevance in any
age. 'Nothing can touch this power,' he says, because 'it is a fact'.[8] Revelation
as 'fact' implies that there is 'truth', as Lesslie Newbigin argues, 'because
there was a concern for truth and a belief that it could be known'.[9] Although
he argued against applying a 'how to' methodology learned from or
directed by foreign leadership, he nevertheless challenged all missionaries
to contextualize the faith that stems from the pneumatological influence
within their own lives. Allen, therefore, believed that 'Pauline Christianity'

---

1. Ibid.
2. Ibid.
3. Ibid.
4. Ibid.
5. Thomas Oden, *The Rebirth of Orthodoxy*, San Francisco: HarperCollins
    Publishers, 2003, 34. Oden's belief is that '[s]ince 1979 I have used the term
    paleo-orthodoxy for the orthodoxy that holds steadfast to classic consensual
    teaching, in order to make it clear that the ancient consensus of faith is starkly
    distinguishable from neo-orthodoxy. The "paleo" stratum of orthodoxy is its
    oldest layer. For Christians this means that which is apostolic and patristic.'
    Oden, *Rebirth of Orthodoxy*, 34. Although Oden is not directly engaging with
    Allen here, his *paleo-orthodoxy* would coincide with Allen's Anglo-Catholic
    emphasis on the apostolic faith and patristic theology.
6. Roland Allen, Sermon for Lent (Psalm 139:6), Beaconsfield 1922, USPG
    X622, Box 5, sermon 371, Oxford, Bodleian Library.
7. Ibid.
8. Ibid.
9. Lesslie Newbigin, 'Religious Pluralism and the Uniqueness of Jesus Christ'
    an article from the *International Bulletin of Missionary Research*, Repr. in *The
    Best in Theology*, vol. Four, J.I. Packer, gen. ed. (Carol Stream: Christianity
    Today, 1990) 270.

propagated this kind of truth (as Newbigin argued) and that Paul's 'method was a method of Gospel, not a method of law'.[10] Allen's emphasis on the 'Gospel method' is similarly expressed later by Peter Jensen in 'that priority must be given to the Gospel as the interpretative grid for all experience'.[11] And it is this type of understanding that motivated Allen to proactively argue for implementing a Gospel method for Church growth. Therefore, what would Paul do? Allen believed that as a trans-local church planter, Paul would invest his time and energy mentoring and appointing indigenous leadership and then proactively apply these apostolic principles to promote self-extending churches. His understanding of what Paul would do cannot be understood from an autocratic practice – operating in isolation – but from a selfless practice of his apostolic ministry, which sought the wellbeing of the indigenous Church.

Allen's Hermeneutic
Pauline theology and ecclesiology in perspective

To decipher Allen's definition of 'indigenous', clarity is essential. Firstly, in 'The Use of the Term "Indigenous" ' (1927), he defines it as 'born in a country; native . . . born or produced naturally in a land . . . belonging naturally to the soil. . . . '[12] In the technical usage of this word, he did *not* believe that the 'local church' could 'spring out of the soil naturally, but was introduced supernaturally at a late date' and that it was 'impossible to use the term indigenous' in this sense.[13] On one hand, he argued that 'Christianity and the Church' were 'imported' into countries and 'are essentially not local, but universal'.[14] Recently this point was made by J.D. Payne: 'In the proper sense, a church can never be indigenous; the church was never natural to an area. The church was and is foreign. The church was an intruder.'[15] On the other hand, and in a 'secondary sense', the usage of the word 'native' can be understood to refer to 'growing on the soil, reproducing itself, propagating

---

10. Allen, *Missionary Methods*, 148.

11. Peter Jensen, *The Revelation of God: Contours of Christian Theology* (Downers Grove: InterVarsity Press, 2002) 141.

12. Roland Allen, 'The Use of the Term "Indigenous"', *International Review of Missions*, vol. 16 (1927) 262-270; cited James Murray, *New English Dictionary* (Oxford, 1928).

13. Roland Allen, 'The Use of the Term "Indigenous"', *International Review of Missions*, 262.

14. Ibid.

15. J.D. Payne, *Roland Allen: Pioneer of Spontaneous Expansion* (USA: self-published, 2012) 42.

itself on the soil – it is quite possible to speak of Christianity or of the
Church as indigenous, in this country or in that'.[1] He argues that if 'we say
that Christianity is indigenous to England . . . the word is not illegitimately
used'; if it is understood in its 'spiritual signification', such as that 'in the
mind of God before the foundation of the world',[2] it was predetermined
to be realized. Allen's sense of divine decrees makes the point concerning
the 'spiritual' dynamic which cultivates the possibility of indigenization.
Pneumatology shaped the way he defined 'indigenous' in that:

(1) the Church is propagated not only because missionaries are
     sent, but because 'that procreative power being the Holy Ghost
     in the Church [fosters] self-supporting, self-governing and
     self-extending' faith communities 'at home';[3] and
(2) that the Church's character is 'true' because it is 'spontaneous,
     uncontrolled or unforced from without'.[4] That said, in his
     missionary theology, he concluded that 'before England was an
     inhabited country, the Church of Christ existed in England and
     that Christ came into England when He came into the world'.[5]
     Therefore, his 'spiritual' use of indigenous, in this sense,
     'means that, in time, and to our apprehension, the Church has
     so established itself as to be in a sense at home in England, so
     that it can grow and increase'.[6] This provides the backdrop for
     his usage of 'indigenous'.

His earlier interpretation of Pauline ministry was seen through the
lens of Ramsay's examination of Paul's missionary travels and Harnack's
ecclesiological hermeneutic. After extensive archival analysis of Allen's
outlined comments on Paul's letters, epistolary sermons and periodic
translations from the Greek text, the evidence discloses that his research,
reflection and engagement with Pauline missiology is well thought through.
Consider Dean Gilliland's *Pauline Theology & Mission Practice* (1983),
which argues that 'Pauline kerygma was concrete, experience-oriented,
personally applied and contextually relevant'.[7] He argues that much of
today's 'system for theologizing' is scholastic and abstract, whereupon it

---

1. Allen, 'The Use of the Term "Indigenous"', 262-63.
2. Ibid., 263.
3. Ibid.
4. Ibid.
5. Ibid.
6. Ibid.
7. Dean S. Gilliland, *Pauline Theology & Mission Practice* (Eugene: Wipf and
   Stock Publishers, 1983), 11.

has the tendency to force Pauline theology into a framework of 'classic theology', which, he concludes, is 'not Pauline theology'.[8] Rather than categorizing Paul's writings as 'dogmatic theology', which Gilliland says 'is oriented [*sic*] to the past', he argues that there 'are four characteristics about Paul's theology that underlie everything else that can be said about it: it is dynamic, it is evangelical, it is pastoral and it is holistic'.[9] Firstly, by 'dynamic' theology he means 'one that relates specifically to the needs of people in a particular place and situation' and that it 'is addressed to the present as well as the future'.[10] Gilliland's interpretation of Allen's Pauline theology assumes his focus on the 'dynamic' characteristic, thus, what Gilliland calls 'dynamic theology', or, 'contextual (dynamic) theology',[11] and especially when he 'shows his concepts to be very close to the concept of dynamic equivalence'[12] in line with Charles Kraft's ecclesiologically framed idea of 'dynamic equivalence churches'.[13] These types of churches – also called contextualized churches[14] – tend to focus on the 'dynamic' characteristic, and, according to J.D. Payne, as indigenous churches, spring 'from the soil and manifests many of the cultural traits and expression of the people themselves, rather than being a church that consists, primarily, of an outside culture imported onto the new believers'.[15] Would Allen have thought that 'dynamic theology' was Pauline? Using Gilliland's definition, the answer would be positive. Allen clearly made this point as he wrote that Paul did not 'allow the universal application of precedents' from other regions, such as; imposing the 'decrees of the Jerusalem Council [which] were addressed to the churches of Syria and Cilicia' as if they also applied for the regions of 'Macedonia and Achaia'.[16] For Allen, fully equipped

---

8. Ibid.

9. Ibid., 12.

10. Ibid., 12-13.

11. Ibid., 12.

12. Ibid., 44.

13. Charles H. Kraft, 'Dynamic Equivalence Churches: An Ethnotheological Approach to Indigeneity', *Missiology*, vol. 1, no. 1 (January 1973): 39-57, as cited in Gilliland, *Pauline Theology & Mission Practice*, 43; see also, Charles Kraft, *Christianity in Culture: A Study in Dynamic Biblical Theologizing in Cross-Cultural Perspective* (Maryknoll: Orbis Books, 1980), 321, where Kraft cites Allen's *The Spontaneous Expansion of the Church* (1956).

14. J.D. Payne, *Discovering Church Planting: An Introduction to the Whats, Whys, and Hows of Global Church Planting* (Colorado Springs: Paternoster, 2009), 4, 18.

15. Ibid., 20.

16. Allen, *Missionary Methods*, 133.

indigenous churches were capable of self-government since, he said, if 'it is a true doctrine that "every man must bear his own burden", it is equally true that every age must produce its own definitions and every church its own precedents'.[1]

Paul's theology, secondly, was also 'evangelical'.[2] By 'evangelical' theology he means 'that what God has accomplished in Christ is the word of the Gospel, that the central message of the cross is the very content of the Gospel . . . and that all that Paul did, taught, and preached is judged by the Gospel. . . .'[3] He agrees and calls this theology or 'doctrine' the kind that transcends the 'intellectual theory' and is 'the complement of experience' in which the 'doctrine renews its youth from age to age' and yet it is not 'divorced from experience' since 'it is expressed with power'.[4] Gilliland's two remaining characteristics of Paul's theology were, thirdly, the 'pastoral' theology which nurtures the 'soul and the spirit' that being is 'the cure of souls before any other issue in his ministry'[5] and, fourthly, the 'holistic' theology which caused Paul to be 'concerned with people in their total life, and with the effect that the Gospel could have on the whole of life'.[6] Gilliland's holistic emphasis agrees with Allen's church-planting *apologia* because it assumes that by 'throwing upon the shoulders of the native Christians all responsibility that they can carry, and more than they can carry' emerges a practice that 'is a sound one'.[7] Therefore, these independent churches quickly experience a holistic theology for 'the whole of life'[8] as the laity are empowered and encouraged to do gospel ministry.

As he engaged with Pauline theology, he did not separate it from mission, for he believed that theology leads to mission and mission is an extension of theology. Twenty-one handwritten pages exist of his outlined commentary on the Acts of the Apostles.[9] This includes his own 'Chronology of Acts'[10] in which he maps out a historical account of apostolic actions and compares the different assumed dates for these events

1. Ibid.
2. Gilliland, *Pauline Theology & Mission Practice*, 12.
3. Ibid., 13.
4. Allen, *Spontaneous Expansion*, 50-51; also, Allen, *Missionary Methods*, 72-74.
5. Gilliland, *Pauline Theology & Mission Practice*, 14.
6. Ibid., 15.
7. Allen, *Missionary Methods*, 156.
8. Gilliland, *Pauline Theology & Mission Practice*, 14.
9. Roland Allen archives, Outlined commentary on Acts 1:1-20:28, Box 3, 29 (21 pages). The 'Chronology of Acts' includes events up to Acts 24:27, USPG, Oxford, Bodleian Library.
10. Ibid.

by referring to Harnack, Turner, Ramsay and Lightfoot.[11] He highlights Paul's conversion experience, commenting how he immediately confessed Christ as the Son of God in the synagogues of Damascus.[12] Paul's immediate fearless evangelistic confession before the Syrian Jews, Allen argues, emerged from his transforming salvific epiphany and charismatic experience.[13] This is central to his missiology because he connects the missionary impetus with pneumatological experience. Schnabel agrees and argues that, for this reason, 'Allen's work deserves to be read in the twenty-first century'.[14]

The main object of his description of Paul's missionary journeys focused on the essentials of his theological discourse and missionary practice. His outline of these missionary journeys sheds light on how his thinking was shaped by Paul's apostolic preaching on: John the Baptist's prophetic call to repentance and faith in the promised Messiah; forgiveness; the Messiah's kingdom; cross-cultural ministry to the Greeks; charismatic signs and wonders; church-planting methods; apostolic leadership mentoring, imparting and training; sacramental practice; teaching and preaching repentance to God and faith in Jesus Christ both publicly and privately to Jews and Greeks.[15] An example of Paul's practice, which shaped his thought, was the apostolic mentoring process of future leaders within the Church where he noticed that Paul 'did not send young teachers, he took them away'.[16] Paul's practice, he argued, was different from the conventional Anglican – 'and other denominations' – way of training ordinands through theological colleges in order to supply ministers for the churches.[17] This method of sending foreign teachers for long-term placement within local churches was antithetical to Pauline practice, he argued, and was also a foreign imposition on the younger churches.[18] Paul's pedagogical method for training teachers, as

---

11. The dating of Paul's conversion differs among scholars, e.g. Harnack (AD 30); Turner (AD 35-36); Ramsay (AD 33); and Lightfoot (AD 34); USPG X622, Box 3, 29: 9, Oxford, Bodleian Library.

12. Acts 9:19-22.

13. Allen archives, Commentary on Acts 1:1-20:28, USPG X622, Box 3, 29: 9, Oxford, Bodleian Library.

14. Schnabel, *Paul the Missionary*, Preface, 11-13.

15. Allen archives, Commentary on Acts 1:1-20:28, USPG X622, Box 3, 29, 11-20, Oxford, Bodleian Library.

16. Ibid., Box 3, 29, 14.

17. Allen, *Missionary Methods*, 106.

18. Ibid., 156.

disclosed with the mentoring of Timothy,[1] influenced Allen to implement a methodology of ministerial apprenticeship – practical and theoretical – as internship training quintessentially based upon the principle that Christ used with training his twelve disciples.

For Allen, the ecclesiology of Paul asserted that there is only *one* Church – *e pluribus unum* ('out of many, one').[2] He clearly articulated that the Church is a 'body', which has certain sacramental 'rites' and a 'priesthood' whereby the 'universal is in the particular as truly as the particular is in the universal Church'.[3] He formulated an ecclesiocentric belief as he engaged with Pauline epistolary.[4] Firstly, although Allen questioned whether Paul's first epistle to the Church in Thessalonica was 'the earliest [Christian] writing',[5] he did believe it was the 'earliest intimation of the mission preaching' of Paul.[6] He also understood it was written while Paul was in Corinth for eighteen months 'at the end' of his second missionary journey and that it 'must be within 20 years' of Christ's resurrection.[7] His unpublished comments begin with Paul's salutation where he discloses the unity that exists – 'equally'[8] – in the Trinity and is demonstrated through the Church by three 'cardinal virtues . . . faith . . . love . . . hope',[9] which, for Allen, theologically provided the basis for unity among members in the Church. He continues to assert that Paul's Gospel was communicated to the Thessalonian Church within the timeframe of about '5 months' – Ramsay's calculation[10] – in which there was evidence that they had 'turned' from idols and had begun to 'serve' Christ substantiated by a living 'faith, love and hope'.[11] He argues that 'if we treat this simply, it is quite possible to see' that Paul's Gospel to the Thessalonian Church could 'all be very quickly

---

1. Allen archives, Commentary on Acts 1:1–20:28, Box 3, 29, 14.
2. Cf. Introduction.
3. Roland Allen, 'The Priesthood of the Church' in *Church Quarterly Review* (January 1933) 239.
4. The following dating arrangement of Pauline epistolary is based on John A.T. Robinson's *Redating the New Testament* (Philadelphia: Westminster Press, 1976). Robinson dates 1 Thessalonians (AD 50) and 2 Thessalonians (AD 50–51).
5. Roland Allen archives, Outlined commentary on I Thessalonians, USPG X622, Box 3, Oxford, Bodleian Library.
6. Ibid.
7. Ibid.
8. Ibid.
9. Ibid.
10. Allen, *Missionary Methods* (1962) 68.
11. Roland Allen archives, Outlined commentary on I Thessalonians, USPG X622, Box 3, Oxford, Bodleian Library.

taught'.[12] This is significant in understanding Allen's apostolic principle for the practice of 'short term' church planting and remains a major principle within his missionary ecclesiology.

Secondly, his analysis concerning the kind of ecclesiology the Thessalonians demonstrated is found in Paul's description of their persevering faith and authentic Christian 'example' that was known 'all over the world',[13] including the 'churches in Judaea'.[14] He shows how Paul did *not* flaunt his apostolic authority, but rather was 'declining' of any special privileges even though he nurtured them in 'gospel' ministry as a 'nurse' and 'father'.[15] His focus on this apostolic reticence in Paul's ministry shaped his missionary ecclesiology by establishing a non-hegemonic example for missionary methods. He views Paul's concern for the Church as pre-eminent. Towards the end of the first epistle, he adds a *nota bene* when describing the 'health' of the Church: it 'depends largely upon *mutual* support' in that 'not everything [is] left to officials'.[16] This reveals his understanding of the Church as a united body. He understands this 'mutual support' within a 'united' body as an extension of Paul's earlier thematic emphasis on Trinitarian unity and the Church's living *apologia* of its 'faith, love and hope'.[17]

Thirdly, a brief examination of the first epistle to the Church in Corinth[18] sheds light on what Allen refers to as 'almost' a Catholic epistle due to Paul's audience – 'with all who in every place' – are united to express faith in Christ.[19] His repeated emphasis on both the catholicity and localness of the Church is purposeful in the way he does ecclesiology and for him is non-negotiable. His careful exegesis on Pauline epistolary – especially the Corinthian letters, Galatians, Ephesians[20] and Philippians – are heightened in four ways:

---

12. Ibid.

13. Cf. I Thessalonians 1:8 (ἐν παντὶ τόπῳ); also, Romans 1:8 (ἐν ὅλῳ τῷ κόσμῳ).

14. Allen archives, Commentary on I Thessalonians, USPG X622, Box 3, Oxford, Bodleian Library.

15. Ibid.

16. Ibid., I Thessalonians 5:14 (his emphasis).

17. Ibid.

18. Robinson's epistle date is AD 55.

19. Roland Allen archives, Outlined commentary on I Corinthians, USPG X622, Box 3, Oxford, Bodleian Library; I Corinthians 1:2.

20. In light of current Pauline scholarship N.T. Wright regards Ephesians to be written by Paul rather 'than by an imitator', N.T. Wright, *What St Paul Really Said* (Grand Rapids: Eerdmans and Cincinnati: Forward Movement Publications, 1997), 8.

(1) his translation and exposition of the Greek text intensified and enriched his theological commentary;

(2) his ecclesiological comments included how local church discipline ought to be administered by the whole body;

(3) he developed a theology of the cross that shaped and sharpened his ecclesiology by articulating the pneumatological dynamic at work through 'the mystery of redemption' for the Church's life and mission; and

(4) he extended this redemptive understanding by establishing an apologia that the Christian faith is not based upon intellectual arguments but upon the gospel dynamic proclamation of the cross, as it is experientially realized within the Church's faith and practice.[1] With regard to church discipline, he comments on the situation of incest that Paul confronted in his letter:[2]

As regards the individual inside the [Church] [Christ] is Lord, outside is a [spiritual] power of Evil Satan. We hand over the offender to the Devil [which] result[s] [in] death to the body; but in hope of salvation of the Spirit. There is [great] dispute about this, but I [question] whether Africans [would] see any difficulty. They expect the solemn curse [to] cut off [from] all the social life of the community to produce physical results. And I see no reason why the death [should] be suppressed to precede the repentance. . . . An offence of this kind is not a private matter. It affects the Body & the Body must be purged. Indifference to it is spiritually demoralizing, & lowers the moral tone of the whole Body. . . . Purge the Body of leaven, & become what you really are a body free [from] the leaven of sin.[3]

Allen agreed with the Pauline practice to remind the Corinthian Christians of their mutual responsibility as a body to confront immorality directly. This stemmed from his commitment to properly understand and apply the text, rely upon historic ecclesiastical practice and enhance cross-cultural contextualization. Because of his missionary experience, he stated that within the African context, the indigenous

---

1. Allen archives, Outlined commentary on I Corinthians, USPG X622, Box 3, Oxford, Bodleian Library; I Corinthians 1-5; cf. Gerhard O. Forde, *On Being a Theologian of the Cross: Reflections on Luther's Heidelberg Disputation, 1518* (Grand Rapids: Eerdmans, 1997).

2. I Corinthians 5.

3. Allen archives, Outlined commentary on I Corinthians, USPG X622, Box 3, Oxford, Bodleian Library; I Corinthians 5:6.

church would not hesitate to administer discipline to any of its members who committed incest. Current African theological scholarship discloses this to be the case. For example, Dachollom Datiri's discussion of incest makes the point that 'Paul's strong response to immorality teaches a very practical lesson – church discipline must sometimes be administered for the benefit of the church, as well as for the correction of the person concerned'.[4] After he identifies the need for excommunication from the community of faith of those who practise incest, he says that, 'while discipline must never be done in a spirit of hostility, a congregation that ignores immorality will end up with a sick and corrupted church'.[5] He thus agrees with Allen's principles of missionary ecclesiology, which stress how the local body ought to maintain a 'corporate conscience', not only to keep the peace, but also to maintain local spiritual health within the community, lest 'tolerating even one case of immorality will corrupt the whole church'.[6] Similarly, there have been concerns that elements within the Anglican Communion were being compromised by the questioning of a 'lifelong monogamous union of a man and a woman' as a biblical 'unchangeable standard'. The point is that African Christians forced this issue to be addressed at the 1998 Lambeth Conference.[7] The former primate of Nigeria, Peter Akinola, said that the 1998 decision to uphold the traditional understanding was 'supported by an overwhelming majority of the bishops of the Communion'.[8] Indeed, GAFCON's theological resource group consisting of forty theologians from fourteen countries produced a commentary entitled *Being Faithful: The Shape of Historic Anglicanism Today*, which stated: 'Most African Anglicans have affirmed monogamy; the prevalence of polygamy among some professing Christians, and also the keeping of concubines, are scandals requiring attention by the Church.'[9] Again, this confirms Allen's conclusions:

---

4. Dachollom Datiri, 'I Corinthians' in *Africa Bible Commentary: A One-Volume Commentary Written by 70 African Scholars*, Tokunboh Adeyemo, (gen. ed.), (Nairobi: WordAlive Publishers, 2006), 1408-1409.

5. Ibid., 1409.

6. Ibid., 1408.

7. Nicholas Okoh, Vinay Samuel and Chris Sugden, (gen. eds.) *Being Faithful: The Shape of Historic Anglicanism Today*, a Commentary on the Jerusalem Declaration (London: The Latimer Trust, 2009), 55.

8. Peter Akinola in Sarah Finch, (ed.), *The Way, the Truth and the Life: Theological Resources for a Pilgrimage to a Global Anglican Future*, Theological Resource Team of GAFCON (Vancouver: Regent College Publishing and London: The Latimer Trust, 2008), 4-5.

9. Okoh, Samuel and Sugden, *Being Faithful*, 55.

(1) the Jerusalem Declaration reaffirmed the Lambeth Quadrilateral (1888) which essentially reiterated Allen's 'signs of the kingdom' for the Church – Bible, Creed, Sacraments, Ministry;

(2) it was representative of indigenous leadership from various countries;

(3) it was united upon traditional apostolic principles; and

(4) it did *not* function as a manifestation of central hegemonic power from any particular 'see', but rather articulated the views of 'marginalized' non-Western leaders and Western advocates regarding the traditional Anglican values on human sexuality.[1]

In brief, the previous examples of African Christianity affirm what Allen naturally assumed would emerge from the 'spontaneous expansion' of the African Church. He believed that when foreign missionaries stepped aside from the management of indigenous church affairs, 'Christianity's local promise'[2] – using Sanneh's understanding of Allen's missiology – to responsibly govern, support and extend their churches would organically emerge.

Pauline Church Planting in the Four Provinces

Since Allen's thesis has clearly determined the paternalistic nature of the 'mission station' system as not representative of Pauline practice, it is necessary to look more closely at how he unpacked Paul's church planting methodology. Missiologists for the past century have discussed his classic argument in *Missionary Methods* for taking Pauline missiology seriously:

> In little more than ten years St Paul established the Church in four provinces of the Empire – Galatia, Macedonia, Achaia and Asia. Before AD 47, there were no churches in these provinces; in AD 57 St Paul could speak as if his work there was done, and could plan extensive tours into the far west without anxiety lest the churches which he had founded might perish in his absence for want of his guidance and support.[3]

This statement is his church-planting credo. F.F. Bruce said Allen's 'summary' demonstrated that 'his confidence was justified: they did not perish, but grew and prospered'.[4] Firstly, he communicated that he

---

1. Finch, *The Way, the Truth and the Life*, 4.

2. Sanneh, *Disciples of All Nations*, 231.

3. Allen, *Missionary Methods*, 3.

4. F.F. Bruce, *Paul: Apostle of the Heart Set Free* (Grand Rapids: Eerdmans, 1995 [1977]), 18.

'established the Church in four provinces'. When Allen speaks of 'Church'
he generally uses the upper case 'C' to emphasize the one, holy, catholic and
apostolic Church as this is distinguished from a single local 'church' for
which he consistently used the lower case 'c'. This distinction is articulated
throughout his writings both published and unpublished. Secondly, as he
addressed the 'provinces' in which Paul planted churches he refused to call
them, for example, the 'Church of Galatia' or the 'Church of Macedonia'
in a similar way that the 'Church of England' is referred to. In fact,
Allen believed it was more appropriate to say that in the sixth century
'Augustine was consecrated bishop, not of England, but of Canterbury'.[5]
This highlights the way he understood districts or spheres of ecclesiastical
ministry. When speaking of the province of Galatia, his unpublished notes
on Paul's epistle to the Galatians discloses this distinction: 'to the churches
of [Galatia] (not the Church) but to all the churches in the district'.[6] The
churches of Galatia, he believed, were local Christian societies that were
networked together and where each congregation supplied its own local
leadership and sacramental rites. He assumed that Paul's ecclesiology
blended the good qualities of episcopal shepherding, presbyterial
governance and congregational democracy to form churches that were
networked together by the pastoral bishop, directed locally by the elders
and facilitated by all members mutually responding to local needs.

Pauline church planting principles pivot around his methodology: (1)
of inculcating 'the Gospel'[7] to new converts and making sure they have
learned its core teachings of first importance spiritually, intellectually and
socially; and (2) by communicating this Gospel message and ministry 'in
such a way that they can propagate it' as an extension of the local church
to other regions.[8] Firstly, Paul's trans-local principle practice of ordaining
leadership – both permanent and charismatic[9] – before he departed from
the new faith community provided space for the local churches, not
only managing their affairs, but also to sharpen their leadership skills
through trial and error. On one hand, Paul's principle approach did *not*
legitimize 'apostolic hegemony', as he told the Corinthian Christians.
Rather, Paul 'repudiates the idea that he had "lordship over their faith"'.[10]
Paul respected the spiritual development of the newer churches by not

5. Paton, *The Ministry of the Spirit*, 179.
6. Roland Allen archives, Outlined commentary on Galatians, Box 3, USPG
   X622, Box 3, Oxford, Bodleian Library.
7. Allen, *Missionary Methods*, 13.
8. Ibid.; cf. I Corinthians 15:1-6.
9. Ibid., 111.
10. Ibid., 112; cf. Allen's citation of II Corinthians 1:24.

controlling or interfering with their progress. On the other hand, as a duly called and recognized apostle, Paul 'sparingly'[1] used his authority to correct ecclesiastical problems but he did confront issues through his instructional epistles[2] and by his presence on return visits during which his custom consistently demonstrated servant leadership. Allen says of Paul that 'he scarcely ever lays down the law, preferring doubt and strife to an enforced obedience to a rule'.[3] He believed that Paul's principle of apostolic impartation and the initial deposit of 'Gospel' faith sufficiently enabled a new church to possess all it needed to function successfully. That said, he also believed:

> Now with regard to these assertions of the apostolic authority, it is necessary to observe that they all occur in the epistles to one church, and that they were called forth for the most part by the outrageous conduct of unreasonable and disorderly men. They certainly do not represent St Paul's general attitude to his churches. They do not even represent the attitude of St Paul to the Corinthians as a body.[4]

Secondly, Paul's principles for the Church's spontaneous expansion incorporated, he believed, a proactive idea that the 'Church must beget church'[5] in a way that the interwoven 'three self' approach provided the foundation where 'we might see such an expansion of Christianity throughout the world as now we little dream of'.[6] Since the time Allen articulated his vision, the sizable growth of World Christianity – particularly in the majority world – has experienced its expansion within indigenous churches, as he predicted. For example, Jenkins' *The Next Christendom: The Coming of Global Christianity* cites Adrian Hastings' analysis of Christianity's growth in Africa: 'Black Africa today is totally inconceivable apart from the presence of Christianity.'[7] In terms of his understanding of how Paul's

---

1. Ibid.
2. Hans Urs von Balthasar, *Paul Struggles with His Congregation: The Pastoral Message of the Letters to the Corinthians* (San Francisco: Ignatius Press, Translated by Brigitte L. Bojarska, 1992 [1st edition in German *Paulus ringt mit seiner Gemeinde* 1988]), 20, 53-63.
3. Allen, *Missionary Methods*, 112.
4. Ibid.
5. Allen, *Spontaneous Expansion*, 40.
6. Ibid., 40-41.
7. Adrian Hastings, *A History of African Christianity, 1950-1975* (Cambridge: Cambridge University Press, 1979); see Adrian Hastings in 'Christianity in Africa', in Ursula King (ed.), *Turning Points in Religious Studies* (Edinburgh: T

indigenous principle of expansion could work within Africa, it is safe to say
that his principle has proven to be a current expression of indigenization
'mission accomplished' in terms of its ever-expanding numerical growth
and independence from foreign supervision.[8] His vision for Christianity's
expansion, as he engaged with Pauline principle and practice, originates from
his presuppositional framework that 'every Christian is a missionary' and is
motivated by a 'missionary spirit',[9] so that 'the Church is', that being in her
nature, 'a missionary society'.[10] How, then, did Allen interpret the Pauline
principle on where it should begin? He believed that church-planting ought
to begin small and needs to develop slowly.

Pauline Practice to Plant Small Indigenous Churches

F.F. Bruce engaged with Allen's comments on Pauline church-planting
methods in 'strategic centres' where his gospel ministry 'would be
disseminated' and concluded that 'Thessalonica served as a base for the
further evangelization of Macedonia, Corinth for Achaia and Ephesus
for proconsular Asia'.[11] Paul's mission in Macedonia implied a method
of frequent travelling throughout the province, but *not* a desire to
establish a centralized long-term base of ministry, where a mega-
church could develop around his ministry gifts. This also substantiates
his unwillingness to practise apostolic hegemony. In another of Bruce's
works, *New Testament History*, 1969, he identifies Thessalonica as 'the
principal city of Macedonia'[12] which, although he chooses to only remain
in a cultured city for five months before ministering within the rural
areas, actually highlights his missionary passion to do apostolic work
anywhere and the flexibility to serve cross-culturally. In the Editions
Haitalis, *Paul the Apostle of the Gentiles: Journeys in Greece*, 2003, the
Greek authors place Paul's first visit to be 'in 49 AD'[13] and states that after
Paul finished 'his visits to the cities of Macedonia and had travelled to

& T Clark, 1990) 208, as cited from Philip Jenkins, *The Next Christendom: The
Coming of Global Christianity* (New York: Oxford University Press, 2002) 56.

8. Allen, *Spontaneous Expansion*, 18, 64–67, 75, 90, 95, 102, 111, 140, 144–46.

9. Francis Anekwe Oborji, *Concepts of Mission: The Evolution of Contemporary
Missiology* (Maryknoll: Orbis Books, 2006), 9; also, Allen, *Spontaneous
Expansion*, 114–116.

10. Allen, *Spontaneous Expansion*, 97, 117–118.

11. F.F. Bruce, *Paul*, 18ff.

12. F.F. Bruce, *New Testament History* (Garden City: Doubleday-Galilee, 1980
[1969]), 307.

13. Editions Haitalis, *Paul the Apostle of the Gentiles: Journeys in Greece* (Athens:
Lithografiki S.A., 2003), 78.

southern Greece as far as Athens, he sent Timothy to Thessaloniki to obtain information about the progress of the church there', and then, after that 'commission' he 'met up with Paul in Corinth' whereupon Paul then wrote both of his letters, 'the earliest texts in the New Testament to the Christians in 'Thessaloniki'.[1]

The concept of Church growth,[2] according to Allen, was not based upon a mega-church concept,[3] but rather upon the establishment of 'the little congregation' model.[4]

> The missionary can observe the rule that no organization should be introduced which the people cannot understand and maintain. He need not begin by establishing buildings, he need not begin by importing foreign books and foreign ornaments of worship. The people can begin as they can with what they have. As they feel the need of organization and external conveniences they will begin to seek about for some way of providing them.[5]

This does not mean that he was opposed to large congregations as long as they were missional in practice. He believed that wherever a group of Christians formed as a body and centred its existence on their engagement with the Bible, a basic 'tradition or elementary' creed understood by all, the administration of the sacraments and its own ordained ministry, then this community could rightfully be called a 'local' church.[6] In this sense, the local church does not need its own 'church' building to be considered a 'real' church.

---

1. Ibid., 80-81; cf. Ramsay, *St Paul the Traveller*, 275, 286, 395; also, John A.T. Robinson, *Redating the New Testament* (Philadelphia: Westminster Press, 1976).

2. Donald A. McGavran, (ed.), *Church Growth and Christian Mission* (New York: Harper & Row, 1965), 9-23, 69-86, 228-245; also Donald A. McGavran, *Understanding Church Growth* (Grand Rapids: Eerdmans, 1970); C. Peter Wagner, *Frontiers in Missionary Strategy* (Chicago: Moody Press, 1971), 44, 47; C. Peter Wagner, *Church Planting for a Greater Harvest: A Comprehensive Guide* (Ventura: Regal Books, 1990).

3. C. Peter Wagner, *Strategies for Church Growth: Tools for Effective mission and Evangelism* (Ventura: Regal Books, 1989), 55; Wagner, *Church Planting for a Greater Harvest* (1990).

4. Allen, *Missionary Methods*, 161.

5. Ibid.

6. Ibid., 107, 132; cf. Lesslie Newbigin, *The Gospel in a Pluralist Society* (London: SPCK, 2000 [1989]), 146-47.

3. Unpacking Roland Allen's Missionary Theology

'The Montessori Method'[1] and 'Missionary Methods' (1913)

Roland Allen wasted no time in defining his *missionary theology* than by contrasting the difference between the Church and the Mission Station system. The first two sentences reveal his concern when he wrote that 'the Church is the School of Christ. The foreign Mission is the elementary School'.[2] The basis for the argument at hand tugs at the development of a pedagogy which is based upon 'fundamental principles'[3] which enable the educational process to adapt to any given situation. He goes on to say, 'We have clung to the old-fashioned formula: "Repeat what you are told, whether you understand or whether you don't." '[4] He saw this as a major defect in how foreign missionaries sought to educate their converts. Rather than only criticizing missionary practices he drew attention to scholastics of his day that challenged the educational institutions and by analogy proposed how missionaries could possibly learn from them. The scholastics whom he believed understood pedagogic principles were Montessori,[5] Herbart and Pestalozzi.[6]

In 1913, Allen referred to Maria Montessori as a 'new apostle of education'.[7] In the early part of the twentieth century, her remarkable

---

1. See Gerald Lee Gutek (ed.) *The Montessori Method: The Origins of an Educational Innovation: Including an Abridged and Annotated Edition of Maria Montessori's Method* (Lanham: Rowman & Littlefield, 2004).

2. Allen, 'Educational Principles and Missionary Methods', *English Church Review*, 19.

3. Ibid., 20.

4. Ibid.

5. Roland Allen, 'The Montessori Method and Missionary Methods', *The International Review of Missions*, Volume 2 (1913), J.H. Oldham, (ed.) (Edinburgh: Henry Frowde/Oxford University Press): 329-341.

6. Allen, 'Educational Principles and Missionary Methods', *English Church Review*, 20-24.

7. Allen, 'The Montessori Method and Missionary Methods', 330.

accomplishments occurred among the 'feeble minded' and 'poorest'
children with learning disabilities from the asylums in Rome and San
Lorenzo.[1] Allen was impressed with her innovative system that he called
'the great principle [and] spirit which informed her search for true
methods of education'.[2] By referring to her 'apostolic' spirit for education
– by way of analogy – he called for consideration of 'whether evangelistic
missionaries may not be able to learn some lesson from the work of this
new apostle of education'.[3] He proposes to his missiological audience
how 'closely akin' Montessori's work was to 'our work' in evangelism: (1)
'from the nature of the work itself'; and (2) 'from the similarity of the
conditions produced by the employment of false methods'.[4]

Firstly, Allen highlights how the nature of evangelistic work
creates a context for the engagement of education among both
'hearers and converts'.[5] He purposefully suggests the need for some
level of 'educational theory' in which 'sound educational methods are
therefore of the first importance' for those who desire training as
'catechists, evangelists, and pastors'.[6] What his criticism produced was
a re-evaluation of the methodology used for 'evangelistic education'
which he believed was 'yet to be discovered'.[7] Secondly, by analogy he
juxtaposed Montessori's portrayal of various 'consequences of false
educational methods' with certain educational 'missionary methods'
which had detrimental effects in the missionary situation.[8] He agrees
with her concern in the way that the educational process produced a
form of 'slavery' by introducing and imposing the 'modern school desk
as proof' of a system that forces the child to conform to an unnatural
'position considered to be hygienically comfortable', but actually
'made it possible for them to become humpbacked!'[9] By analogy,
he takes this 'description' and makes application to the 'missionary
organization' that had the tendency for 'cramping our converts in a
form of church organization which was wholly unnatural to them' and
ultimately resulted in 'a spiritual curvature of the spine'.[10] His point

1. Ibid., 331.
2. Ibid., 331.
3. Ibid., 330.
4. Ibid., 331.
5. Ibid.
6. Ibid.
7. Ibid.
8. Ibid., 332.
9. Ibid.
10. Ibid.

addressed the unintended consequences wherein the converts 'ceased to be able to support their own religious life' since they had the 'props with which we supported them' through the means of paternalistic practice.[11] He identified the 'props' as the well-intentioned 'men's societies, temperance societies, mothers' unions, children's leagues' which he believed did not address or cure the 'spiritual disease' of certain false educational methods which young converts, who, through 'docility and gentleness', willingly submitted to until the time they possibly might 'revolt'.[12] Thirdly, Montessori proposed her 'threefold' methodology – study, observation and experiment.[13] He engages with her method of study by explaining why she translated the works of two physicians – Jean Marc Gaspard Itard and Edouard Seguin – from French into Italian, in order to familiarize herself with 'the spirit of the author' [Itard] and to develop in 'her study a prepared mind looking for definite light for a definite purpose'.[14] He contrasts her studious efforts in pursuit for understanding the educational methods of observation and experimentation with the understanding of Paul's 'principles of missionary education' and his 'practice of missions' as a 'far greater master of the missionary method than Seguin or Itard'.[15]

The significance of Montessori's methodology of study, observation and experiment,[16] influenced Allen's thinking and became a framework for his educational emphasis in missions,[17] as disclosed in his other writings.[18] His practice of using an empirical methodology 'based on observation' has Montessori's fingerprints all over it.[19] He commented that missionaries would be more effective if they would 'begin to observe our people with new eyes', that being, to 'observe' how the

---

11. Ibid., 332-33.

12. Ibid., 334.

13. Ibid.

14. Ibid., 334-35.

15. Ibid., 335.

16. Maria Montessori, *The Advanced Montessori Method: Scientific Pedagogy as Applied to the Education of Children from Seven to Eleven Years*, vol. 1 – Spontaneous Activity in Education [translated from Italian by Florence Simmonds and Lily Hutchinson], (London: William Heinemann, 1919 [1918]) 67-141.

17. Ibid., 334-36.

18. Roland Allen, 'Educational Principles and Missionary Methods', 19-25; also, Roland Allen, *Educational Principles and Missionary Methods* (London: Robert Scott Roxburghe House, 1919).

19. Allen, 'The Montessori Method and Missionary Methods', 336.

converts solved local problems and exercised leadership without foreign interference.[1] Likewise, her teaching method for children – education by experiment – helped shape his ideas on how missionaries ought to consider other methods and forms for training their converts based upon her 'principle of liberty' which he believed coalesced both methods 'founded on observation and experiment'.[2] He attempted to clarify any misrepresentation of Montessori's classroom management style whereby children actively learn by doing (observation and experiment), as though the children were somehow free to do their own thing without supervision. His response is that her 'scheme' of liberty was 'closely connected with discipline' and that this discipline 'must come through liberty'.[3] Furthermore, she believed that 'real discipline comes through work'.[4]

Allen's theological understanding of 'law and gospel' plays into this scheme by contrast: 'Law is the government of external discipline, gospel is the life of internal discipline.'[5] He then cites James' 'law of liberty'[6] as a backdrop for how Montessori's Christian faith[7] (Roman Catholic)[8] understood 'this law'.[9]

> When Moses gave the Decalogue which was to guide the Hebrews to salvation, he preceded it by the law: 'Thou shalt love the Lord thy God with all thine heart, and thy neighbour as thyself.' When the Pharisees came to Christ, asking Him to declare the Law, He answered: 'Do ye not know? Thou shalt love thy neighbour as thyself,' as if to say: the law is evident and unique, it is the law of life, and for this reason must always have existed, from the very beginning of the world.[10]

---

1. Ibid.
2. Ibid., 338.
3. Ibid., 339; cf. Montessori, *The Advanced Montessori Method*, vol. 1, 157.
4. Montessori, *The Advanced Montessori Method*, vol. 1, 163-67.
5. Allen, 'The Montessori Method and Missionary Methods', 339.
6. Ibid.; James 2:12.
7. Maria Montessori, *The Absorbent Mind* (Madras: Kalakshetra Publications, 1969 [1949]), 288-94.
8. Maria Montessori, *The Discovery of the Child* (Madras: Kalakshetra Publications, 1966 [1948]), v, 38, 347-49; also, Montessori, *The Advanced Montessori Method*, vol. 1, 33.
9. Ibid. See E.P. Culverwell, *The Montessori Principles and Practice: A Book for Parents and Teachers* (London: G. Bell & Sons, 1918), 282-83.
10. Montessori, *The Advanced Montessori Method*, vol. 1, 330-31.

In short, he believed that Montessori felt that educators needed to move beyond the 'mechanism' or 'mechanical skill' and grasp the quintessential values of 'the spirit of reverent curiosity' and 'the spirit of reverent love' when training teachers how to teach their students.[11] He argues that her method was exactly what 'our missionaries' needed to overcome its propensity to conduct

> training in the practice of the church system [with] a spirit of mechanical obedience to rules [wherein] our native teachers have been for the most part mechanics rather than scientists. They have learned how to work the machine. They have not learned how to enjoy a scientific experiment.[12]

Today, in a late-modern culture, Stuart Murray agrees[13] and has proposed various experimental forms for building 'post-Christendom churches' in a non-mechanical way by applying a philosophy of 'principled flexibility'[14] in ministry that seeks to demonstrate Christian love to the unconverted. Here, Allen differentiates between 'reverent love' and 'condescending love' for the missionary, wherein the latter resulted in 'apathy and failure because it is not based on respect and reverence for those whom we teach'.[15] This understanding that Montessori had 'for the personality of her pupils',[16] even though they suffered with various levels of mental and developmental disabilities, made an impact on Allen's ministry among the disenfranchised, as evidenced by his grandson's perception that '[m]y grandfather was endlessly patient with anyone who lacked education' or who was in any way mentally disabled.[17] His pastoral approach of training the uneducated and slow-learners was significantly influenced by Montessori's ideological system and shaped the way he performed cross-cultural ministry, especially among the underdeveloped non-Westerners.[18]

---

11. Ibid., 340.

12. Ibid.

13. Stuart Murray, *Church After Christendom* (Milton Keynes, UK: Paternoster Press, 2008), 99-101.

14. Ibid., 66.

15. Allen, 'The Montessori Method and Missionary Methods,' 340-41.

16. Ibid., 341.

17. Hubert Allen, 'The Parables of Christ are Timeless: An example of Roland Allen's originality introduced by his grandson,' in *Transformation: An International Journal of Holistic Mission Studies*, vol. 29, no. 3 (July 2012) 186.

18. Allen, 'The Montessori Method and Missionary Methods', 341.

His 'Educational Principles and Missionary Methods' (mentioned earlier) provided a framework for understanding his use of various dynamic principles located in the writings of Montessori, Pestalozzi, Froebel and Herbart.[1] His compelling passion to convey this principle that 'liberty is activity'[2] was furthermore developed in his *Educational Principles and Missionary Methods* (1919).

'Educational Principles and Missionary Methods The Application of Educational Principles to Missionary Evangelism' (1919)[3]

As was his custom, he submitted *Educational Principles and Missionary Methods* for a bishop to examine before its publication. Charles Gore, then bishop of Oxford and formerly principal of Pusey House, where, '[o]ne of the young persons under his influence was Roland Allen',[4] wrote the introduction to this work. Gore, unassumingly, wrote that he was neither 'an expert on education' nor 'missionary methods', yet he encouraged missionaries to look past what he thought was an 'excessive reaction' within the contemporary 'modern school of educationalists' and to find ways to set aside criticisms of Allen's conclusions by lending 'sympathetic attention' to the 'truth which the author's view contains'.[5] His reticent comments did not diminish his willingness to consider that the institutional side of Anglican mission needed to 'be sufficiently converted to recognize that a very deep and difficult change is required of us' both in 'our educational methods' but also through 'the method for propagating the truth'.[6] What in particular was Gore reacting to and challenged by? He believed that the book was rather 'one-sided' and that it promoted the 'modern school' system as opposed to the overall significance of the standard form of education and 'the dogmatic element in education'.[7] It appears that Gore had difficulty with some aspects of the modern approach that challenged the conventional method whereby 'the teacher must be the one active force . . . the pupil must be passive',

---

1. Allen, 'Educational Principles and Missionary Methods', 19-25.
2. Ibid., 23.
3. Roland Allen, *Educational Principles and Missionary Methods: The Application of Educational Principles to Missionary Evangelism*, Introduction by Charles Gore (London: Robert Scott Roxburghe House, 1919).
4. Talltorp, *Sacrament and Growth*, 10.
5. Allen, *Educational Principles and Missionary Methods*, vi.
6. Ibid.
7. Ibid.

whereas Adams, Froebel, James, Montessori and Pestalozzi,[8] emphasized the significance of education in which the students learn quickly how to apply the 'principles' of 'sympathetic observation' (Pestalozzi and Froebel),[9] applied knowledge as an outgrowth of learning by doing (Adams),[10] 'sense perception' (Pestalozzi),[11] teachers' imitable character (James)[12] and the educational negativity that emerges from 'the fallacy of confusing goodness with stillness' of children within a classroom setting (Montessori).[13] Allen's thesis attempts to challenge the currently practised missionary form of education that tended towards a rote methodology of learning by proposing an applied method of learning by doing. Gore did not specify what 'modern' methods was an 'excessive reaction' to conventional education, but he did invite missionaries to 'welcome this book' as a source to evaluate their methods.[14]

Within the preface, he proposes to extend the thesis of *Missionary Methods* (1912) by shifting from his earlier focus 'between the methods and results of our missionary work' to another way of understanding the missionary situation from 'the point of view of the modern educationalist'.[15] Again, he builds his thesis upon the 'most important principles', which he believed could be understood as 'general principles' generally accepted among 'modern educationalists' worldwide.[16] He was captivated by his conclusions that 'the application of modern educational principles leads us to the same conclusion which the study of St Paul's methods suggested'.[17] Throughout the book he parallels the 'general principles' located within the writings of 'modern educationalists' and argues that those timeless principles stemmed from

8. J. Adams, *The Evolution of Education* and *The Herbartian Psychology Applied to Education* (London: Ishister and Company, 1897); Friedrich W.A. Froebel, *Chief Writings on Education*, translated by Fletcher and Welton; Froebel, *The Student's Froebel*; Johann Friedrich Herbart, *The Science of Education*, translated by H.M. and E. Felkin (1892); William James, *Talks to Teachers* (1899); Maria Montessori, *The Montessori Method* (New York: Frederick A. Stokes Company, 1912).

9. Allen, *Educational Principles and Missionary Methods*, 25.

10. Ibid., 63-64.

11. Ibid., 73

12. Ibid., 78-79.

13. Ibid., 90.

14. Allen, *Educational Principles and Missionary Methods*, vi.

15. Ibid., vii.

16. Ibid.

17. Ibid.

biblical precedent.[1] He chose not to overload this book 'with quotations from educational authorities', but instead 'added a short list of the books' that demonstrated, in particular, the influence of John Adams.[2]

The principle approach to education and its commonality with Allen's proposed missionary methods pervade this work. Chapter 1 begins with his presupposition that '[m]issionary work is educational work', in terms of directing and guiding their converts towards some level of maturity.[3] He raises the question by saying how can maturity be accomplished if the only form of missionary education is that which resides in the 'mission schools and colleges' and is not available to all the converts?[4]

> In this case, since the work is educational, the theory also must be educational, and the principles involved must be educational principles. Now when we enquire what this theory is, when we ask upon what principles this work is done, and how the principles are applied, we are met by the astonishing fact that there is no answer. So far as I know, there does not exist a single book which treats of the application of educational principles to this most important educational work. . . . We have never yet attempted to distinguish the principles upon which we ought to conduct the education of that vast mass of our converts whom the schools and colleges do not reach.[5]

Allen's apologetic for educational reform within missiology begins with a renewed interest in personal knowing. He begins Chapter 2 with the premise that the objective to facilitate the student's progress must begin at the point at which 'the pupil must take the first place'.[6] He is not advocating narcissism, but rather a focused approach to know and understand the student. Chapter 3 enlarges upon this 'knowledge of the pupil' in two ways: (1) by implementing a 'study of physiology and psychology' so that the educator is able to know the governing laws which heighten the understanding of the human's body and mind; and (2) by observing the student's individuality with all of his or her 'characteristics and foibles'.[7] Similarly, Michael Goheen correctly

---

1. Ibid., vii–x.
2. John Adams, *The Evolution of Education and The Herbartian Psychology Applied to Education* (London: Ishister and Company, 1897).
3. Allen, *Educational Principles and Missionary Methods*, 1.
4. Ibid., 5.
5. Ibid.
6. Ibid., 11.
7. Ibid., 24.

interprets how Newbigin addressed this contrast between 'scientific knowing with personal knowing' – while writing during his final year of theological training under the tutelage of H.H. Farmer – he explained that one can only get to know another person's 'will' or understand their 'purpose' if, while listening, the person willingly 'chooses to reveal himself'.[8] Allen places emphasis on this sense of personal knowing and 'sympathetic observation' on the part of the teacher to the pupil.[9] He argues that this translates into the missionary situation when, after studying the evangelized 'by patient and sympathetic observation, we can attain such knowledge as will enable us to educate, and not merely to train or to teach them'.[10] Just when it looks like Allen is 'beating up on' the missionaries for their failure to educate properly, he highlights their 'affectionate interest' and selfless sacrifice towards those they are reaching 'better than any other class of foreigners'.[11]

Allen begins his apologetic for educational principles by focusing on the purpose of education. Chapter 4 provides the foundation for his *apostolic principle* of being fully equipped from the beginning towards self-government, self-sufficiency and self-extension. Firstly, he argues against the 'mistake of over-direction' where parents, teachers and educators tend to do too much 'for the child which he could very well learn to do for himself'.[12] Of course, he is not implying that children do not need supervision and care, but rather he is advocating against a repression of the child's abilities to comprehend, adjust, make mistakes and learn

8.   Michael W. Goheen, *As the Father Has Sent Me, I Am Sending You: J.E. Lesslie Newbigin's Missionary Ecclesiology* (Zoetermeer, Netherlands: Uitgeverij Boekencentrum, 2000) 20; Lesslie Newbigin, 'Revelation,' Unpublished theology paper presented at Westminster College, Cambridge (1936); cf. Martin Buber, *I and Thou*, (Edinburgh: T and T Clark Publishers, 1937). Goheen says: 'Ronald Gregor Smith, translator of Buber, mentions in his introduction to the second edition of *I and Thou* that contemporary theology was shaped by Buber. Specifically he points to J.H. Oldham and H.H. Farmer who acknowledge their indebtedness to Buber's book. Oldham's influence on Newbigin was significant. H.H. Farmer was Newbigin's theology professor during the time he wrote this paper. Perhaps it was through these men that Newbigin embraced this important distinction,' Goheen (2000) 20, footnote 3; see H.H. Farmer, *Reconciliation and Religion: Some Aspects of the Uniqueness of Christianity as a Reconciling Faith*, Gifford Lectures University of Glasgow 1951, edited and introduced by C.H. Partridge, (Lewiston: The Edwin Mellen Press, 1998).

9.   Allen, *Educational Principles and Missionary Methods*, 25.

10. Ibid., 30.

11. Ibid., 31.

12. Ibid., 35.

from their mistakes – learning by doing – so that they do not develop a dependency mentality. Herein lies Allen's view of independence,[1] which carried over to his missionary ecclesiology which inculcated individual and mutual responsibility within the faith community.

Secondly, he argues that the 'true method of education is a method of transference', by which he means that the student has to 'learn to do for himself and by himself acts which at first he does only under direction', enhancing this delegation of 'control' from the teacher to the student.[2] How that plays out in his educational missiology is foundationally set forth 'from the bottom', at which he argues that '[t]he end must be implicit in the beginning' and then provides an example that, when looking to appoint archdeacons and bishops, ought *not* attempt to 'find exceptional individuals' but rather 'what is needed is a society prepared for the progress which the appointment of archdeacons and bishops implies'.[3] This missiological emphasis embraces the concept by which 'a people' learn 'to express their missionary zeal spontaneously'.[4] Newbigin agrees and cites Allen's *Missionary Methods* while arguing against types of missional tasks that only function in terms of paternalism, instead of belief in the charismatic dynamic within the Church:

> On the contrary, St Paul appeared to base his entire faith on the power of the Holy Spirit to create new forms of churchmanship very different from the forms that had existed in Judea in the old church of Jerusalem. And I believe that in this time that lies immediately ahead of us, in which as I say the missionary enterprise has to learn to swim against the stream of world events, we may be forced to take much more seriously the pattern of the New Testament in this matter, rather than the pattern of the previous one and a half or two centuries.[5]

Thirdly, just as Newbigin recognized the need to proactively develop newer types of ministries within the Church, even so in Chapter 5, Allen argues against the 'imposition of our church system' as a basis for

---

1. See Timothy Yates, *Christian Mission in the Twentieth Century*, (Cambridge: Cambridge University Press, 1999) 62-63.
2. Allen, *Educational Principles and Missionary Methods*, 37.
3. Ibid., 41.
4. Ibid.
5. Lesslie Newbigin, *A Word in Season: Perspectives on Christian World Missions* (Grand Rapids: Eerdmans, 1994) 22; also, Lesslie Newbigin, 'Bringing Our Missionary Methods under the Word of God', *Occasional Bulletin from the Missionary Research Library* 13 (1962) 1-9.

education.[6] He believed the 'external' system or 'education under law' misrepresented the 'Gospel' emphasis which the missionaries originally intended to proclaim and instead were distracted to enforce a system that was: 'passive, mechanical, grudging observance of laws, rules, forms imposed from without by authority, external, unreal, foreign'.[7] Just as the modern educators encouraged their students to learn through 'discovery', so he challenged the missionaries to empower the converts 'to discover, to know, and to use, the grace of the Holy Spirit', whereby they as the indigenous people of God could begin to vocationally discover their opportunities to participate in spontaneous Church expansion without hegemony.[8] This is precisely what Linda Woodhead articulates when describing the shift within the missionary situation that followed Edinburgh's 1910 World Missionary Conference:

> The short-lived optimism that reigned at the start of the twentieth century and was encapsulated in the mission slogan 'The evangelization of the world in this generation' quickly dissipated as the expected harvest of souls failed to materialize. Though the foundations had been laid, it was only once the colonial powers had departed that Christian growth really took off.[9]

David Bosch also delineated a similar position when describing this shift within the missionary situation after Edinburgh's 1910 World Missionary Conference and the subsequent decades:

> The world was being rebuilt feverishly and the Christian Church had a decisive role to play in this. The upsurge in missionary interest during this period was astounding. Both ecumenical and evangelical mission agencies got involved on an unprecedented scale, although the former's emphasis had shifted to cooperation with the younger churches rather than unilaterally undertaking missionary, educational and other projects.[10]

On one hand, in the midst of colonialism, missionaries had brought Christianity's truth claims to foreign cultures that provided the building blocks for establishing the Church through its mission station system. On the other hand, Allen's compelling arguments of independence for

6. Allen, *Educational Principles and Missionary Methods*, 46-49.

7. Ibid., 49-57.

8. Ibid.

9. Linda Woodhead, *An Introduction to Christianity* (Cambridge: Cambridge University Press, 2011 [2004]), 392.

10. Bosch, *Transforming Mission*, 338-39.

the indigenous Church created philosophical havoc among paternalistic leaders who were unwilling to release control, and as Sanneh correctly said this is 'why Roland Allen protested missionary endorsement of Western political interests as a betrayal of their vocation'.[1] Not until decolonization began to emerge did missiologists admit that his philosophy of missionary ecclesiology was not only the wave of the future, but that it had its rootedness in Pauline missiology.[2] His educational principles were designed to inculcate the indigenous younger churches to embrace the spiritual framework that could facilitate spontaneous growth once the missionaries retired from one region to serve elsewhere or due to missionary departure because of decolonization, especially in reference to Church growth in Africa.

Between Chapters 6 and 12, certain principles for missionary education are presented which incorporate biblical values along with various modern educators' ideas. These main beliefs and methods promote:

(1) 'the principle of development' which extends from discovery, knowledge and 'the grace of the Holy Spirit';[3]

(2) the principle of learning 'simple lessons of faith . . . simple acts of charity, simple expressions of felt needs' where the converts' proactive posture is: 'let us do it';[4]

(3) the conscious effort to reject a passive acceptance of 'perpetual infancy' by slowly – but systematically – applying self-governing principles that encourage younger churches 'how to direct their own course';[5]

(4) Christian education that emphasizes 'religious knowledge [that is] based on experience' and which enables children to actively test and practise the lessons taught by means of 'a true experimental method of teaching [that] keeps curiosity alive';[6]

(5) the 'fundamental principles' of Pestalozzi, Froebel and Montessori that can be applied to the missionary situation by means of 'an experimental method of teaching'[7] (e.g. the Socratic method) which engages the converts to learn biblical truth;

1. Sanneh, *Disciples of All Nations*, 248.
2. Donald A. McGavran, *The Bridges of God: a Study in the Strategy of Missions* (London: World Dominion Press, 1955); also, Sanneh, *Disciples of All Nations*, 232.
3. Allen, Educational Principles and Missionary Methods, 62.
4. Ibid., 96.
5. Ibid., 99.
6. Ibid., 102-103.
7. Ibid., 104-111.

(6) the 'principle of liberty' which provides enough flexibility for the implementation of educational content and 'to be encouraged' to contextualize it for different cultural settings;[8] and

(7) the principle of 'religious education'[9] where the 'spirit of the educator'[10] stimulates the converts to inquisitively progress to a more experimental level of learning and excelling.

Allen concludes this book with an 'illustration' from a letter sent from V.S. Azariah (a few months before his consecration as Bishop of Dornakal) who wrote concerning a spontaneous prayer from one of the congregations.[11] The man prayed:

> Oh Father who art in Heaven, You are our Father, we are Your children. Keep us all well. Heal my rheumatism and my child's boil. Keep us from all wild animals, the bear and the tiger. Forgive us our sins, our quarrels, angry words, all that we have done since morning. Make us good. Bring all the castes to kneel down to You and call You Father.[12]

Azariah's main objective was 'to assist his hearers to learn the meaning of prayer' and not necessarily that they learn 'the Greek "Amen" ' or 'the Telugu Lord's Prayer' word for word.[13] Both Azariah and Allen attempted to educate the converts with a form of discipleship which incorporated the principle of learning by doing, rather than the rote method. They believed that this practice of 'an experimental method of teaching'[14] was the best way to bring all members into understanding their identity within the priesthood of the Church (i.e., that which Protestantism calls the priesthood of all believers). Newbigin learned from both Allen's teaching and Azariah's apostolic ministry by 'experimentally' implementing the substance of their educational methods in India's situation to develop the 'fully native ministerial leadership'[15] as an extension of 'the laity scattered abroad in every department of life'.[16]

---

8. Ibid., 125.

9. Ibid., 137.

10. Ibid., 128.

11. Ibid., 134–137.

12. Ibid., 134.

13. Ibid.

14. Ibid., 104–111.

15. Newbigin, *The Open Secret*, 130.

16. Lesslie Newbigin, 'The New Delhi Report: The Third Assembly of the World Council of Churches', *New Delhi* (New York: Association Press, 1962)

Summary

The growing resentments towards the missionary presence in various countries caused Allen to assess the problems and propose ways to correct the escalating tension. He started by implementing – not radically 'new' ideas – but rather by restoring 'old' methods rediscovered in his hermeneutic of Pauline missionary practice. The apologetic for indigenous principles rooted in Pauline theology and practice, he believed, trumped the prevalent mission station system that had already created Christian 'ghettoes' among converts who learned how to be totally dependent on the missionaries and their foreign sources. On one hand, the clarion call for restoring Pauline missionary methodology was generally met with resistance by institutional missions just after the signs of sanguinity due to the 1910 Edinburgh Conference. On the other hand, in the years between both of the World Wars, the shifting towards decolonization, and the decrease in mission giving, many foreign missionaries and missiologists began to seriously consider what steps were needed to take place in preparation for mission devolution. Although there were those who embraced Allen's missiology – selectively – his overall influence did not materialize until approximately a decade after his death.

Allen believed that the mission station system was not the Church. The Church must be indigenous and 'independent' he argued, whereas, the mission stations perpetuated foreign hegemony. His missionary apologetic advocated 'independence' for the indigenous Church in three ways:

(1) by teaching the converts from the beginning to identify their responsibilities to manage their own churches;
(2) by limiting and decreasing any use of foreign elements; and
(3) for the missionaries to intentionally prepare for retirement from the churches they have planted.[1] These three apostolic principles shaped his thinking as he directly trained and indirectly influenced indigenous leaders to lead their own congregations. Jehu Hanciles disagreed with Henry Venn's 'unhelpful dichotomy between church and mission',[2] but instead agreed with Allen's 'three self' teaching and implementation.

88-89.

1. Roland Allen, 'The Work of the Missionary in Preparing the Way for Independent Native Churches', File J: 4, 9.
2. Hanciles, *Euthanasia of a Mission*, 254.

Further problems developed with mission societies when they went beyond maintaining mission stations and created native churches. On one hand, Allen was obviously favourable of indigenous churches being planted but he believed the mission societies should have prioritized the establishment of churches first, instead of building mission stations. On the other hand, he did not believe the societies had the right to plant churches without episcopal authorization and oversight. Herein places his missionary ecclesiology within the missionary situation.

The principles that constituted Western education which Allen believed to be essential were:

(1) that true education which stems from the Church wherein she educates her members in the principles of personal discipleship, biblical teaching, community relationships and mutual responsibility, is a healthy ecclesiocentric educational system;

(2) that Pauline principles and his system of education by – observation and experiment – provided the West's educational milieu for educators such as 'Pestalozzi, and Froebel, and Herbart, and Montessori'[3] to contextualize these principles;

(3) that both the Pauline *spiritual* training in activities which was motivated by the charismatic dynamism, and, Froebel's *natural* educational system towards self-activity, provided principle-based educational methods; and

(4) the Western emphasis on scientific pedagogy has as its foundation Montessori's 'fundamental principle . . . the liberty of the pupil' which echoes the Pauline principle of 'liberty'.[4] The principle of liberty is integral to Western education's ethos and he argued that its roots were embedded in Pauline theology and practice.

His ecclesiocentric approach to Christian education presupposed a comprehensive philosophy of indigenous ministry 'which is of the Church, by the Church, for the Church'.[5] His missionary ecclesiology inculcated the *apologia* – 'The Church is a school of the most valuable order' – for it assumes that her members are learning the 'virtues of self-control' as a disciplined approach for holistic life and for the purpose of promoting

---

3. Allen, 'Educational Principles and Missionary Methods', *English Church Review* (January 1913): 20.

4. Cf. II Corinthians 3:17; Galatians 5:1ff; Allen, 'Educational Principles and Missionary Methods', 22-23.

5. Roland Allen, 'Education in the Native Church' in *World Dominion* (London: World Dominion Press, 1928 [1926]), 18.

the 'practice' and 'the meaning of Christian government'.[1] He believed
that this *apologia* was foundational to social and political advancement.
When explaining what Paul did in the missionary situation of his day,
Allen believed that as a trans-local church-planter, Paul, invested his
time and energy mentoring and appointing indigenous leadership with
foundational principles in order to promote self-extending churches. His
understanding of what Paul did cannot be understood from an autocratic
practice – operating in isolation – but from the selfless practice of his
apostolic ministry that sought the wellbeing of the indigenous Church.

---

1. Ibid., 21.

4. Roland Allen's Theology of 'Spirit and Order'

Chapter 4 sets the parameters for Allen's missionary ecclesiology by unpacking the central apostolic principles which permeated his missionary theology of 'Spirit and Order'. The blending of his pneumatology and ecclesiology transcended conventional missionary methodologies of his day and with this emphasis he argued for a return to an earlier apostolic model found in the primitive Church. His integrated methodology of 'Spirit and Order' was intertwined to form the basis for his church-planting missionary theology, which he was convinced encompassed true historic apostolicity and catholicity. Allen believed in the primacy of the Holy Spirit's power to organically energize and mobilize the Church for spontaneous expansion and it was this understanding that permeated his missiology. To document the truthfulness of this emphasis, this analysis of the data from his works sets out to substantiate his concept of the apostolic Church's dependency on the Spirit's ministry to empower and send the Church into every area of life. The focus of this chapter on 'charismatic ministry' is the pervasive pneumatology that was existent throughout his writings. That said, Allen devoted himself to clarity of thought concerning the transcendence of the Spirit's work in the life of the Church and argued for a return to what he believed was a proper apostolic emphasis – Spirit and Order – as expressed through his belief in the Bible, creedal confessions, ministry gifts, and the sacramental life of the Church.

Roland Allen's Contribution towards Missiology
A Contemporary Perspective[1]

By 'charismatic ministry' I mean here a ministry which is exercised by a man who is moved to perform it by an inward, internal, impulse

---

1. A significant part of my work here was previously published in the journal *India Church Growth Quarterly*, vol.21, no. 1 (April-June 2014): 973-974, 982, Madras, India, for an issue which focused on Roland Allen's contribution to Indian Church growth and mission and was entitled 'Roland Allen's Contribution towards Missiology: A Contemporary Perspective'.

of that Holy Spirit who desires and strives after the salvation of men in Christ. I do not deny that men receive a charisma, a gift of grace, for their ministry in ordination; but I use the word 'charismatic' to express the ministry which is exercised in virtue of that direct internal impulse of the Spirit, as distinguished from the ministry which is exercised by those who have been ecclesiastically ordained or commissioned.[1]

Allen's vision for the Church encased a combination of *Spirit* and *Order* – that is, pneumatology and ecclesiology. He believed that the Holy Spirit empowers Christians to apply *apostolic principles* in any given situation through the one, holy, catholic and apostolic Church. His contribution to missiology stemmed from a Pauline understanding of an indigenously-led Church with its faith and practice rooted in the Bible, creeds, ministry and the sacraments[2] and was, therefore, 'fully equipped' with ministry to function as a 'permanent and charismatic' Church.[3] He proposed the restoration of an apostolic order to enhance evangelism, particularly through the laity, by reaching out to pioneer regions where the Church had no current witness. His ongoing contribution to *missiology* advances (1) the historical significance for what he believed were universal apostolic principles and (2) how these principles provide flexibility within a framework of Spirit-driven Church growth to deal with a changing missionary environment.[4]

When missionaries discuss Allen's writings, they typically refer to either *Missionary Methods: St Paul's or Ours?* (1912) or *The Spontaneous Expansion of the Church* (1927). While, arguably, these two books are his most famous published works, it is important to realize that he wrote extensively for over fifty years – books, pamphlets, journal contributions, articles, ecclesiastical letters, speeches, sermons and

1. Formerly an unpublished work by Roland Allen – 'The Ministry of Expansion: the Priesthood of the Laity' (1930), USPG X622, Box 3, Number 27, Oxford, Bodleian Library. In 2017, this work is published as: *The Ministry of Expansion by Roland Allen: the Priesthood of the Laity*, ed. J.D. Payne, (Pasadena: William Carey Library, 2017).

2. Allen, *Missionary Methods: St Paul's or Ours?* 91 (footnote 1), 107; Roland Allen, *The Spontaneous Expansion of the Church and the Causes Which Hinder It* (London: World Dominion Press, 1927. Repr., Grand Rapids: Eerdmans, 1997) 147-150.

3. Allen, *Missionary Methods*, 111.

4. Steven Rutt, 'An Analysis of Roland Allen's Missionary Ecclesiology' *Transformation* (July 2012) 29(3): 200-213 (201).

various unpublished works.[5] Indeed, his grandson and biographer, Hubert Allen, categorically states that his grandfather's booklet entitled *Pentecost and the World* (1917)[6] was his most characteristic work then and still 'can speak to us today as cogently as when it was written'.[7] 'My grandmother once remarked to me', recalled Hubert, 'that Roland himself believed his best piece of writing to have been his brief *Pentecost and the World*',[8] and that 'on his death, for this reason, Grannie gave bound copies to each of us, his three grandchildren.'[9]

Allen's main thesis in *Pentecost and the World* can be summarized by stating that the Pentecost story is the fulfilled promise of the Holy Spirit's coming in supremacy to baptize, fill, indwell, lead, inspire and empower the 'missionary' Church as a witness to all nations.[10] He argued that the main emphasis in Acts is that Pentecost marked the turning point in the Church's emergent juncture in 'that they were the recipients of a gift of the Holy Spirit sent upon them by Christ, and that all the labours and successes of their lives were due to the influence of that Spirit'.[11] Harry Boer agreed and was convinced that Allen was the pre-eminent 'missionary thinker of the Spirit' and that 'except by Roland Allen, a missionary theology centring on Pentecost and its continuing meaning for the Church has not been developed'.[12] Things have progressed since 1961, when Boer made that remark. Today, many books now stress a missionary theology that engages the charismatic dynamic of Pentecost within the Church's mission.[13] That

5. Deposited papers: Roland Allen, USPG X622, Boxes 1-8, Oxford, Bodleian Library.

6. Roland Allen, *Pentecost and the World: the Revelation of the Holy Spirit in the Acts of the Apostles* (London: Oxford University Press, 1917). Repr. in David Paton (ed.) *The Ministry of the Spirit: Selected Writings of Roland Allen* (Grand Rapids: Eerdmans, 1970) 1-61.

7. Hubert Allen, *Roland Allen*, 104.

8. Email correspondence from Hubert Allen (19 May 2011).

9. Hubert Allen, *Roland Allen*, 104.

10. Paton, *Ministry of the Spirit*, 3-12.

11. Ibid., 3.

12. Harry R. Boer, *Pentecost and Missions* (Grand Rapids: Eerdmans, 1961. Repr., 1964) 63.

13. See Gordon D. Fee, *God's Empowering Presence: the Holy Spirit in the Letters of Paul* (Peabody: Hendrickson, 1999); Clark Pinnock 'The Concept of Spirit in the Epistles of Paul' (unpublished PhD dissertation, Manchester, 1963); Kirsteen Kim, *Mission in the Spirit: The Holy Spirit in Indian Christian Theologies* (Delhi: ISPCK, 2003); Harvey Cox, *Fire From Heaven: The Rise of Pentecostal Spirituality and the Reshaping of Religion in the Twenty-first Century*, (Cambridge: Da Capo Press, 2001).

said, we might ask whether Allen's writings have influenced past and current trends in mainstream missionary theology. There can only be one answer. Yes.[1]

A century ago, Roland Allen envisaged a global Church emerging from indigenous Christianity. From one side, his missionary experience in China convinced him to the validity of planting the indigenous Church as self-supporting, self-governing, and self-extending. From the other, he challenged mission societies regarding their policy of establishing 'mission stations' that unconsciously created a dependency on foreign missionaries and quite often unintentionally promoted colonial hegemony. 'A mission station is indeed a contradiction in terms: mission implies movement, station implies stopping.'[2] As to why, as Lamin Sanneh puts it, 'Roland Allen protested missionary endorsement of Western political interests as a betrayal of their vocation', the reasons are not difficult to identify.[3] He argued that Pauline missiology was a better way to do mission:

(1) by transferring missionary churches to indigenous converts without going through a devolutionary process;

(2) by ordaining local ministers – stipendiary and voluntary – to direct, manage and administer the sacraments for their own churches by means of an indigenous episcopate; and

(3) by trusting the Holy Spirit to direct these churches without foreign control. Today, these are considered mainstream practices, but this was not the case a century ago.

The Contribution towards Missiology in India

In 1910, Roland and his wife visited 'Delhi, Calcutta and Madras' and he was 'invited to preach in these and several smaller places'.[4] He met with Vedanayagam Samuel Azariah and probably saw Henry Whitehead, Bishop of Madras. This visit initiated an ongoing friendship with both men over the years. In 1927, he was invited back to minister for two bishoprics: Azariah (Dornakal) and George Hubback (Assam), between 2 December 1927 and 8 March 1928.[5]

---

1. See Hendrik Kraemer, *A Theology of the Laity* (London: The Lutterworth Press, 1960) 20; Donald A. McGavran, *Church Growth and Christian Mission*, 43, 54; Schnabel, *Paul the Missionary*, 11-14, 21.

2. Allen, *Spontaneous Expansion*, 105.

3. Sanneh, *Disciples of All Nations*, 248.

4. Hubert Allen, *Roland Allen*, 86.

5. Roland Allen, 'Diary of a Visit in South India' (unpublished), USPG X622, Box 7, File N, Oxford, Bodleian Library.

Bishop Azariah's familiarity with Allen's writings in general, and his *apostolic principles* in particular, contributed to an environment for Church growth and expansion. Azariah and Allen saw that Church expansion was certain since the bishop was willing to ordain the existing teachers and catechists as fully equipped priests and to distinguish from among the pastors those who were gifted as trans-local evangelists. Azariah embraced his principles wholeheartedly and sought ways to administer diocesan adjustments wherever necessary. The time was right for Church renewal and transformation because Azariah had already 'proved to be such a competent leader and administrator'.[6] Therefore, Allen's teachings reinforced the 'clergy troops' to prepare for planting more missionary churches. According to Susan Harper, some years later, the facts reveal that

> under the leadership of Bishop Vedanayagam Samuel Azariah (1874–1945), Dornakal became the fastest growing Anglican diocese in South Asia. The total Anglican Christian population in the Dornakal diocese increased from 56,681 in 1912 to 225,080 in 1941, a number that exceeded the total number of Anglican converts for all of Japan, Korea, and China combined. In 1936 the Dornakal Church baptized over 200 converts each week, and a total of 11,400 converts that year, and sustained this general level of accession throughout the decade.[7]

The Dornakal diocese was enriched by the teaching ministry of Allen during his missionary journey in 1927. His earlier ideas, which shaped a proactive missionary theology, can still significantly contribute to missiology for the situation of the changing structures within World Christianity today. More details of Roland Allen's missionary trip to India are discussed later.

---

6. Susan Harper, *In the Shadow of the Mahatma: Bishop V.S. Azariah and the Travails of Christianity in British India*, Studies in the History of Christian Missions (Grand Rapids: Eerdmans, 2000), 132.

7. Susan Harper, 'The Dornakal Church on the Cultural Frontier', (Chapter 9), in *Christians, Cultural Interactions, and India's Religious Traditions*, J.M. Brown and R.E. Frykenberg, (eds.), (Grand Rapids: Eerdmans, 2002), 185.

5. Roland Allen's Charismatic Missiology[1]

Allen's charismatic missiology is systematically articulated in *Missionary Principles – and Practice*[2] (1913) and *Pentecost and the World: the Revelation of the Holy Spirit in the Acts of the Apostles*[3] (1917). Subsequently, this broadly pneumatological understanding is interspersed throughout his sermons, teaching notes, articles and correspondence.[4] His emphasis on pneumatology and ecclesiology – Spirit and Order – stem from his devotion to Pauline thought, especially with his instruction on spiritual gifts (I Corinthians 12-14),[5] which the apostle's concluding emphasis underscores: 'Let all things be done decently and in order' (I Cor. 14:40).

Additional disclosure of his pneumatology is located within an unpublished work entitled 'The Doctrine of the Holy Spirit'[6] which encorporates a symphonic blend of – pneumatology, ecclesiology and missiology – that shapes his overall missionary ecclesiology.

'The Doctrine of the Holy Spirit'

Allen's ecclesiology of 'Spirit and Order' resounds through his unpublished work, 'The Doctrine of the Holy Spirit', wherein he critiqued the 'difficulties' in the propagation of the faith through mission

---

1. This section (with slight modifications) is from a lecture I was asked to present at the Oxford Centre for Mission Studies on 2 July 2013 (Oxford, UK) and was followed by a question and answer format.
2. Roland Allen, *Missionary Principles – and Practice* (1st edition entitled *Foundation Principles of Foreign Missions*, Bungay, Suffolk: Richard Clay & Sons, May 1910. Repr., entitled *Essential Missionary Principles*, Cambridge: The Lutterworth Press, 1913. Repr., *Missionary Principles – and Practice*, 2006).
3. Allen, *Pentecost and the World*, 1-61.
4. Roland Allen's archives, USPG X622, Boxes 1-8, Oxford, Bodleian Library.
5. Allen: 'The Ministry of Expansion: the Priesthood of the Laity,' USPG X622, Box 3, Number 27, chapter 7: 4, (1930); see D.A. Carson, *Showing the Spirit: A Theological Exposition of I Corinthians 12-14* (Grand Rapids: Baker, 1989).
6. Unpublished work by Roland Allen, 'The Doctrine of the Holy Spirit,' USPG X622, Box 3, 13: Introduction, 1-16, Oxford, Bodleian Library.

societies when: (1) they established mission stations that resulted in 'sterility' towards evangelism; and (2) they demonstrated an 'absence of missionary policy' to deal with the continual appeal for 'men and money', thus reinforcing hegemony instead of indigenization.[7] He then provides an apologia for the significance of the Spirit's descent at Pentecost and the ongoing empowerment of the Church. The role of the Spirit is, he argues, (1) to mobilize the Church for extending the 'faith' everywhere 'from Jerusalem to the uttermost parts of the earth'[8] (Acts 1:8) and (2) to guide 'bishops' towards the recognition and ordination of indigenous Christian leadership. Such leaders, he pointed out, were already serving their communities as 'farmers . . . miners and traders', as well as being 'priests in their own houses'.[9] As such, they could quite easily serve the sacraments to 'kinsfolk perishing for lack of spiritual food!'[10] The 'ordered' Anglican framework he envisaged was a Communion which actually practises what it preaches. 'If the sacraments are necessary we ought either to send clergy or ordain men on the spot; but we do neither sufficiently.'[11] At least, prior to Vatican II, Roman Catholicism took seriously the indigenization principle, and, as Francis Anekwe Oborji states, it was Pierre Charles (1883-1954) who 'founded the Louvain school of missiology, which maintained that the aim of missionary activity should be the planting or formation of a church (with its own hierarchy, indigenous clergy, and sacraments) in non-Christian countries'.[12]

For Allen, the missionary Spirit creates, nourishes, fills and empowers 'the native apostles'[13] to plant the Church and provide sacramental spiritual food. His missiology of 'Spirit and Order' incorporates a central fostering of the faith through the sacramental means of grace. This argument for 'native clergy' presupposes the necessity of the sacramental life of the Church and demonstrates how his theology embraced the frequency of its administration. The organic nature of Church growth stems from people who have embraced the faith, he believed, and subsequently desire to share what they have received.[14] This is natural. Allen compares this with how Muslim missionaries – traders, soldiers, teachers – that is,

---

7. Allen, Introduction, 1-16.

8. Ibid., Introduction, 1.

9. Ibid., 7.

10. Ibid.

11. Ibid.

12. Francis Anekwe Oborji, *Concepts of Mission: The Evolution of Contemporary Missiology* (Maryknoll: Orbis Books, 2006) 82-83.

13. Allen, 'The Doctrine of the Holy Spirit', 12.

14. Ibid., 3.

common people who have embraced Islam, share their faith with people and eventually see that 'a mosque springs up, a school is established, a Moslem community arises'.[1] He critiques his fellow Anglicans' reluctance to share their faith in the way that Muslims do and concluded that much of the hesitancy in 'our fellow churchmen who go abroad' is due to a past reliance upon *professional clergymen* to provide for them all the ministerial services, especially the sacraments.[2] This comparison serves as his charge for them to exercise faith in the missionary Spirit's creativity. He cites how the layman, Frumentius (c. 300 -c. 380) – referred to as the 'Apostle of the Abyssinians' – evangelized Alexandria and was later consecrated bishop of Axum (Northern Ethiopia) by Athanasius.[3] 'I suppose most of our Bishops would deny that they had ever met a Frumentius. So rare a thing is it for a layman to think that as a Christian he has the right [and] duty to propagate his religion and instruct the ignorant in his faith.'[4]

The basis for Allen's ecclesiology *from below* originates in his interpretation of the way 'the universal common priesthood of Christians' functions through the presence, direction and ministry of 'the missionary Spirit'.[5] This pneumatology, which, to a large extent, anticipates John V. Taylor's pioneering 1967 Cadbury Lectures, published as *The Go-Between God: The Holy Spirit and the Christian Mission,* shaped Allen's church-planting methodology, in that it served both to advocate the oversight by missionary bishops[6] for the ordaining of a 'specialized ministry' and to support the administration of the sacraments by the 'priesthood of the body' (i.e., 'the priesthood of the laity')[7] whenever 'they were outside the range of the organized Church' due to the absence of ordained clergy. Again, his argument was always that 'the universal priesthood cannot

1. Ibid. Allen's engagement with Muslims intensified later in life. His son, John, wrote: 'My father made notes for an introduction, of which only the first part is complete. He writes, "English readers familiar with the Hebrew story [of Job] in the beautiful English of the Authorized and Revised Versions cannot help comparing that poem with this Moslem Utenzi,"' J.W.T. Allen, *Tendi: Six examples of a Swahili classical verse form with translations & notes,* (Nairobi, London and Ibadan: Heinemann, 1971. Repr., London: Richard Clay [The Chaucer Press], 1971, 373-74).

2. Ibid.

3. F.L. Cross and E.A. Livingstone, *Dictionary of the Christian Church* (Peabody: Hendrickson, 1997) 644.

4. Allen, 'The Doctrine of the Holy Spirit', 4.

5. Allen: 'The Ministry of Expansion: the Priesthood of the Laity', Box 3, Number 27, 1930, chapter 6: 7.

6. Allen, 'The Doctrine of the Holy Spirit', 14.

7. Allen, 'The Ministry of Expansion: the Priesthood of the Laity', 6: 7.

be annulled by an absent specialized priesthood'.[8] Allen's second point here clearly expresses what he believes is the *missionary Spirit's* validation for Eucharistic lay-presidency. In his formerly unpublished work from 1930 – 'The Ministry of Expansion: the Priesthood of the Laity'[9] – he insists that this 'ought properly to be addressed only to Christians who are geographically beyond the reach of any bishop. . . . '[10] Again, Allen's missiology, like Taylor's, is rooted in the conviction that the Spirit transforms cultures through the missionary work of laypeople.

Missionary Principles

Following on from the above discussion, in *Missionary Principles* (which was actually an earlier work) Allen develops his pneumatology in relation to missiology. Published a year after *Missionary Methods* (1912), *Missionary Principles* argues that 'Missionary zeal is grounded in the nature and character of the Holy Ghost . . . [and] the Holy Spirit is a missionary Spirit . . . which labours for the salvation of the world'.[11] He took very seriously the popular missiological conviction that the missionary movement does not depend upon human endeavours and techniques to accomplish the Church's task of mission. Rather he consistently sought to root his understanding of mission in a particular view of the *missio Dei.* This understanding of the 'missionary God' resonates throughout the book. Again, so central is it to his thought that he, as Brian Stanley puts it, 'anticipates the emphasis of modern theologies of mission on the *missio Dei* . . . which is now given to the Holy Spirit in Christian theology and in the churches of the majority world, so many of which are Pentecostal in emphasis'.[12] He unpacks this missional pneumatology in four chapters around the notions of 'impulse', 'hope', 'meaning' and 'reaction'.[13]

In the first chapter, entitled 'The Impulse', he describes various biblical commandments which lean towards 'external form' where the 'word' or letter of the law 'is the standard',[14] and then he distinguishes this from the 'internal life' or spiritual awakening that happens wherein

---

8. Ibid., 7: 3.

9. Recently published in 2016 by William Carey Library (Pasadena, California).

10. Ibid., 7: 13.

11. Allen, *Missionary Principles*, 26, 33, 61.

12. Ibid., *Foreword* by Brian Stanley, vi; see Bosch, *Transforming Mission*, 10, 370, 389-93.

13. Allen, *Missionary Principles*, Table of Contents.

14. Ibid., 12.

'the Spirit is the standard'.[1] He is not promoting an antinomian theology here, but rather developing a pneumatology for which 'obedience to the commands of the Gospel is a spiritual act'.[2] This spiritual act, he argues, is natural to the *missio Dei*.

> How then did the Father send the Son? By a command? Certainly by a command. Christ speaks of a command, "As the Father gave Me commandment even so I do." But not by an external command. Christ speaks more often of a community of will, "My meat is to do the will of Him that sent Me." The Father sent the Son by a command; but the command was a Procession of the Holy Ghost. The Spirit of the Father who sent was the Spirit of the Son who came. The command was an expression of the Spirit and the response was the expression of the same Spirit; because there was community of Spirit; for the Spirit proceeds from the Father and from the Son. So Christ sends His people into the world not by an external command only; but by a giving of the same Spirit, "He breathed on them."[3]

Firstly, this statement discloses his Western creedal understanding of the Spirit's procession in accordance with both Nicene and Athanasian Trinitarian theology – 'the equal ultimacy of the one and the many'[4] – which establishes no disunity within the 'community of will', as he describes the relationship within the Trinity. He superimposes this theological grid upon the mission of the Church, thereby articulating an apologia for *missio Dei*. In other words, this is, to use Stuart Murray's words, the way newcomers are inducted 'into a missional mindset by . . . introducing them to the missionary God and the scope of *missio Dei*'.[5] Again, in Stanley's words, Allen 'anticipates the emphasis . . . on the *missio Dei*'.[6] The contemporary use of the term *missio Dei* in missiological circles originated at the Willingen Conference on World Mission in 1952, at which, as David Bosch says, the Church 'began to

---

1. Ibid., 12, 14.

2. Ibid., 14.

3. Ibid., 14–15; John 14:31; 20:22 (καὶ τοῦτο εἰπὼν ἐνεφύσησεν καὶ λέγει αὐτοῖς· λάβετε πνεῦμα ἅγιον).

4. Rousas J. Rushdoony, *The One and the Many: Studies in the Philosophy of Order and Ultimacy* (Craig Press, 1971), 156; cf. Maurice, *The Kingdom of Christ*, vol. 1,133.

5. Stuart Murray, *Church After Christendom*, (Milton Keynes, Colorado Springs and Hyderabad: Paternoster, 2008), 137.

6. Allen, *Missionary Principles, Foreword* vi.

flesh out a new model'.[7] However, while this is true, it is clear that this 'new model' already existed. Indeed, not only had it been systematically developed in Allen's writings, but there is evidence to suggest that this work influenced the later ideas developed at Willingen and in the thinking of leaders within the World Council of Churches, particularly through the writings of Lesslie Newbigin[8] and David Paton,[9] both of whom acknowledge their indebtedness to Allen. In a similar way, Rousas Rushdoony argues that

> in orthodox Trinitarian Christianity, the problem of the one and the many is resolved. Unity and plurality are equally ultimate in the Godhead. The temporal unity and plurality is on the basis of equal validity. There is thus no basic conflict between individual and community. . . . Instead of a basic philosophical hostility between individual and government, believer and church, person and family, there is a necessary co-existence. Neither the one nor the many is reducible to the other.[10]

Allen's Trinitarian belief shaped the way he understood both the 'individual' and 'community' in the social sphere, as well as the 'local church' and the 'universal Church' in the ecclesiastical sphere: 'the universal is in the particular as truly as the particular is in the universal Church'.[11]

Secondly, he believed that the 'external command' and the 'community of will' which exists within the Trinity provides a framework for understanding how the *missio Dei* empowers the Church to do mission through 'the administration of the Spirit' as 'the motive',[12] which, according to his thinking, transcends doing mission out of duty to the Great Commission mandate:[13] 'the command is a missionary command, the Spirit is a missionary Spirit'[14] because 'Christ imparts the Spirit

---

7. Bosch, *Transforming Mission*, 370.

8. Newbigin, *A Word in Season*, x-6, 21-32.

9. David Paton, *Christian Missions & the Judgment of God* (Grand Rapids: Eerdmans, 1953. Repr., 1996), 49, 79.

10. Rushdoony, *The One and the Many*, 16; cf. Maurice, *The Kingdom of Christ*, vol. 2, 115.

11. Allen, 'The Priesthood of the Church', *Church Quarterly Review* (January 1933): 239.

12. Allen, *Missionary Principles*, 16-17.

13. Ibid., 23, 39; Matthew 28:18-20.

14. Ibid., 2006, 23.

from which the command emanates'.[1] Harry Boer agrees with Allen's thought at this point.[2] 'The Great Commission does not bring anything qualitatively new into being.'[3] Boer cites Wilhelm Michaelis' critique of both Harnack's belief that the Church's expansion was due 'to the universalism of Jesus' teachings'[4] and Gustav Warneck's belief that the 'Great Commission is simply the natural and unavoidable climax of Old Testament universalism and of Jesus' teaching concerning the kingdom of God'.[5] Boer agrees with the 'two dangers' that Michaelis had identified, because he believed other interpretations missed the whole point of Pentecost's significance: ' . . . that her witness did not arise from conscious obedience to it [the Great Commission], but that her witness can be understood only in terms of Pentecost'.[6]

In his second chapter, entitled 'The Hope', Allen ties together how this compelling 'missionary zeal' is internally energized because of 'the presence of Christ in the soul'.[7] Much of his thesis is devoted to an articulation of the present reality of the 'revelation of Christ' to the individual, which reinforces that 'Christ is our hope'.[8] And it is this hope which supports 'the apologetic value of Foreign Missions' – Christ's 'claim to draw all men unto Himself is a strong apology for our faith'.[9] Next he emphasizes how this revelation of Christ is expressed in three ways:

(1) through 'the conversion of individuals, in the influence of Christ over the lives of individual men and women';[10]

(2) through the 'progress of the Church' and the wisdom of God in 'bringing to us new conceptions of the manifold working of the Spirit of Christ';[11] and

1. Ibid., 2006, 18.

2. Harry R. Boer, *Pentecost and Missions* (Grand Rapids: Eerdmans, 1961. Repr., 1964) 141.

3. Ibid.

4. Wilhelm Michaelis, 'Geist Gottes und Mission nach dem Neuen Testament,' *Evangelisches Missions Magazin* (1932) 7-8; Boer, 139.

5. Gustav Warneck, *Evangelische Missionslehre*, 2nd ed., (Gotha, 1897), vol. I, 135-57, (E.T. *Outline of History of Protestant Missions*, London, 1901); Boer, 139; also, Gustav Warneck, *Allgemeine Missions-Zeitschrift* (1913): 40, 95.

6. Boer, *Pentecost and Missions*, 139.

7. Allen, *Missionary Principles*, 39, 40.

8. Ibid., 45.

9. Ibid.

10. Ibid., 46-50.

11. Ibid., 50-53.

(3) through the Church's establishment throughout the world 'we see, too, the leavening of society' where 'society is more and more influenced by Christian ideals and principles'.[12]

Allen's broadly evangelical roots become apparent as he distinguishes between (a) the revelation of Christ to individuals who then are incorporated into the Church and (b) those who are mainly concerned with Christianizing the world through the dissemination of a 'social gospel'.[13] He talks about the 'grave danger' that exists when the focus is 'upon the external conditions':[14]

> Christ is more than a Christianized world. Just as we cannot arrive at Christ by adding virtue to virtue, so we cannot arrive at Christ by adding social betterment to social betterment. . . . They see this as the end, and their imaginations are fired by the vision of a world led by many paths to the throne of God. . . . Very often they speak as if the Christianizing of the world – that is, the leavening of human thought with Christian ideas – were the supreme end. The result is that they would make missionaries, preachers of social and political righteousness more than preachers of Christ. . . . The introduction of purely Western theology into our missions is bad, the introduction of purely Western and modern sociology is far worse: for then we overlay the Gospel instead of preaching Christ.[15]

Critical to his charismatic ecclesiology is the disclosure of this 'primary concern' found in his confessional starting point through a spiritual encounter with the Gospel of Christ.[16] Any missionary focus

---

12. Ibid., 53-57; cf. Charles Kraft, *Christianity In Culture: A Study in Dynamic Biblical Theologizing in Cross-Cultural Perspective* (Maryknoll: Orbis Books, 1980), 79, 98.

13. See Ka-Che Yip, 'China and Christianity: Perspectives on Missions, Nationalism, and the State in the Republican Period, 1912-1949', *Missions, Nationalism, and the End of Empire*, Brian Stanley, (ed.), Studies in the History of Christian Missions, (Grand Rapids: Eerdmans and Cambridge: Eerdmans, 2003), 134, 140-41.

14. Allen, *Missionary Principles*, 54.

15. Ibid., 54, 55; cf. J. Andrew Kirk, *Liberation Theology: An evangelical view from the Third World* (Basingstoke: Marshall Morgan & Scott, 1985) 205; Gustavo Gutierrez, *The God of Life* (London: SCM Press, 1991) 118-39, 'The Ethics of the Kingdom.'

16. Sermons and teaching notes on 'The Knowledge of God – Knowing God'– John 17:3 (1906) Box 5: 39-40; 'The Knowledge of God' – John 17:3 (1907, Chalfont St. Peter's; 1915, St. John's Harpenden) Box 5: 41-42; 'Faith in a Person', USPG X622, Box 5: 315, Oxford, Bodleian Library; cf. Max Warren's debate with John Hick on the 'uniqueness' of Christ, Max Warren, 'The Uniqueness of Christ', *The Modern Churchman* 18 (winter 1974), 55-66.

that gave precedence to social issues which 'overlay the Gospel instead of preaching Christ'[1] Allen believed was a misplaced focus. His sermons thoroughly focus on the person and work of the crucified and risen Christ.[2] He goes on to clarify what things are of first importance within mission preaching. The Gospel of Christ is contrasted with social betterment through Christianizing and he prefers the preaching of the Gospel of Christ over social reform.[3]

Allen's opposition to contemporary aspects of social gospel teaching is similar to David Bosch's later analysis of the work of those who at the Uppsala Assembly (1968) endorsed Johannes Hoekendijk's theology and the 'received view' propagated within 'WCC circles': 'Mission became an umbrella term for health and welfare services . . . activities of political interest groups, projects for economic and social development . . . [and the] distinction between church and world has, for all intents and purposes, been dropped completely.'[4] Allen believed that any misplaced focus compromised the Church's main objective to plant churches, whereas Hoekendijk thought that the parish system was 'an invention of the Middle Ages', which caused the Church to be introverted.[5] Bosch, although recognizing Hoekendijk's 'attacks on the institutional church' as 'pertinent', responded by saying that 'Paul, who knew so much about the weaknesses of the churches to which he wrote his letters, began nearly every time by thanking God for their existence, their faith, their loyalty'.[6] Allen's argument for ecclesial mission is reinforced in Bosch's analysis of the 'Hoekendijkian position' that by 'the mid-1970s the euphoria that had characterized the 1960s had evaporated' and how the 'same

---

1. Allen, *Missionary Principles*, 54, 55; cf. Kirk, 205; Gutierrez, 118-39.

2. Sermons on 'The Cross: Vicarious – Christ must needs suffer' – Acts 17:3 (1909, including notes from Prof. Moberly and Bishop Westcott's *Victory of the Cross*); Box 5: 424-25; Good Friday sermons on Mark 10:32 and I Peter 2 (1921 and 1927 Beaconsfield), Box 5: 422-23; Sermons on Romans 5:6 (1923, Beaconsfield; 1929, Hedgerley), USPG X622, Box 5: 421, Oxford, Bodleian Library.

3. Sermon on 'Charity is the Curse of the Reformer' which is Allen's assessment of the Socialist's cry at the 'great appeal for Charity in the winter of 1905-06, USPG X622, Box 5: 509, Oxford, Bodleian Library; also, Allen, *Missionary Principles*, 2006, 54, 55.

4. Bosch, *Transforming Mission*, 383.

5. Quoted in William R. Hutchison, *Errand to the World: American Protestant Missionary Thought and Foreign Missions* (Chicago and London: The University of Chicago Press, 1987) 185; see Bosch's analysis in *Transforming Mission*, 384.

6. Bosch, *Transforming Mission*, 385.

theologians who criticize the empirical church now hold firmly to the view that it is impossible to talk about mission as responsibility towards and solidarity with the world unless such mission is understood also in ecclesial categories'.[7] Michael Goheen believed Hoekendijk's influence in time caused 'the life of the church and evangelism' to be set aside and 'receded from view as mission was swallowed up by social activity',[8] which misrepresented Karl Hartenstein's understanding of *missio Dei*.[9] Francis Oborji pointed out that Hartenstein's definition – rooted in Barthian theology[10] – set out to 'protect mission against secularization and horizontalization, and to reserve it exclusively for God'.[11] Not everyone at the Uppsala Assembly, however, agreed with the new direction that had evolved. Certain evangelical voices emerged. Arthur Glasser, Donald McGavran, and John Stott[12] all 'stressed evangelism, conversion, church growth, and the Christian community as God's agent in mission',[13] thereby confirming Allen's earlier concerns.[14] This clarification eventually was articulated in the Lausanne Covenant (1974):

> We affirm that God is both the Creator and the Judge of all men and women. We therefore should share his concern for justice and reconciliation throughout human society and for the liberation of men and women from every kind of oppression. . . . Here too we express penitence both for our neglect and for having sometimes regarded evangelism and social concern as mutually exclusive. Although reconciliation with man is not reconciliation with God, nor is social action evangelism, nor is political liberation salvation, nevertheless we affirm that evangelism and socio-political involvement are both part of our Christian duty. . . .[15]

---

7. Ibid., 384–85; cf. J.M. van Engelen, 'Missiologie op een keerpunt,' *Tijdschrift voor Theologie*, vol. 15, 1975: 291–312 (309).

8. Goheen, '*As the Father Has Sent Me*,' 69.

9. Bosch, *Transforming Mission*, 392.

10. Oborji, *Concepts of Mission*, 146.

11. Ibid.; see Bosch, *Transforming Mission*, 392.

12. John R.W. Stott, *Christian Mission in the Modern World* (Downers Grove: InterVarsity, 1975) 96–101.

13. Goheen, '*As the Father Has Sent Me, I Am Sending You*,' 72.

14. Allen, *Missionary Principles*, 90.

15. Lausanne Covenant, 1974. (International Congress on World Evangelization, Lausanne, Switzerland, 1974), section 5, cited from J.I. Packer and Thomas C. Oden, *One Faith: The Evangelical Consensus* (Downers Grove: InterVarsity, 2004) 177–78.

He was not at odds with the concept of Christian care for the whole person, as expressed later in the *missio Dei* model. Obviously, he believed that God loves humanity. That said, as a traditionalist, he believed that God's salvific connection with humanity functioned through the Church 'that called for [personal] repentance and that gathered folk into the church by means of baptism' without calling this 'objectionable "proselytism"' and mission wholly understood in an instrumental way as participation in various social, economic, and political programmes', as the WCC (1967) advocated.[1] Allen's understanding was, therefore, a God-Church-world sequence, *not* a God-world-Church order, as promoted in the WCCs Geneva Conference.[2] In light of how the *missio Dei* engages with the care of the whole person, his pneumatology necessitates and reinforces holistic mission that stems from an *ecclesiocentric* understanding. And, this missionary ecclesiology was nourished by a sacramental belief and practice.

Church as a Sacramental Community

In the third chapter, entitled 'The Means', Allen logically surmises that if the goal or 'end' of mission is 'spiritual' then the 'means also must be spiritual'.[3] In hindsight, this thesis shows that he quickly grasped the missiological milieu of the late nineteenth and early twentieth centuries during which a major proportion of missionary work was based upon a 'task' orientation wherein the Mission Station became the central headquarters for health, education and welfare. This form of 'mercy' mission often began with good intentions, which were 'spiritually' based, yet in time had the tendency to develop into an operational system that minimized the 'spiritual' dimension and maximized the 'programme' structure.

These mission compounds inadvertently created for their indigenous converts a context of hegemonic enslavement through dependency. J.D. Payne argues that during 'the missionary practices of Allen's day, he believed that Western missionaries interfered with the work of the Spirit' and that 'contemporary methodologies erected unnecessary barriers

---

1. World Council of Churches (*WCC*), 1967. *The Church for Others and the Church for the World: A Quest for Structures for Missionary Congregations. Final Report of the Western European Working Group and North American Working Group of the Department on Studies in Evangelism.* Geneva: World Council of Churches: 75, as cited in Goheen, '*As the Father Has Sent Me, I Am Sending You*', 70.

2. World Council of Churches, 1967, 16, 69f, as cited in Goheen, '*As the Father Has Sent Me, I Am Sending You*', 70-71.

3. Allen, *Missionary Principles*, 59.

between the converts and the Spirit's work, thus hindering the expansion of the Church'.[4] Allen's answer, however, specified 'that in missionary work everything depends upon the spiritual state of the Church which sends the mission'.[5] His assessment did not leave him to only theorize but to address what he understood to be the primary problem – lack of trust in 'the Divine Missionary'.[6]

> Christ is the source, the end, the worker. . . . All that we can do is to bring to Christ surrendered wills and hearts and minds to cooperate with Him. He is the only source of spiritual power. Missionary life begins with an act of reception; missionary zeal grows upon knowledge of the Spirit so received; missionary work is the expression of that Spirit in activity.[7]

It was during this first decade of the twentieth century that pneumatology began to inform his missionary ecclesiology. But another area of his theology was also developed in line with his pneumatology during this period, namely his sacramental theology. This 'harmonious' theological blend in Allen's work marked him as a missiologist of 'Spirit and Order'. The key for Allen is that 'the Spirit works through the material'.[8] But what is actually meant by this? Three points can be identified:

(1) 'The power of making material things into the vehicles of spiritual force' is accomplished sacramentally. For example, when a groom places a ring on his bride's finger this ring 'conveys a meaning, a power, which is not its own', thereby becoming something 'more' than just a piece of metal but in actuality 'it is a sacrament'.[9]

(2) There is a strong emphasis on Jesus' incarnation. This provides the sacramental basis for Christianity, because it indicates that 'matter' *does* matter to God. The incarnation, by drawing matter towards the centre of theology, thereby 'instituted a religion of sacraments'.[10] Indeed, because, in Christ, there can

---

4. Jervis David Payne, 'An Evaluation of the Systems Approach to North American Church Multiplication Movements of Robert E. Logan in Light of the Missiology of Roland Allen', PhD diss., (The Southern Baptist Theological Seminary, 2001) 34.

5. Allen, *Missionary Principles*, 67.

6. Ibid., 59.

7. Ibid., 59.

8. Ibid., 69.

9. Ibid., 69.

10. Ibid., 69.

be 'no ignoring of the outward material form', the 'whole world
is sacramental . . . Christ is sacramental . . . the religion of
Christ is sacramental'[1]and, 'mission work [is] sacramental in
character', as expressed from his handwritten comment in his
first edition of this work.[2]

(3) Therefore, 'the missionary spirit which Christ brings into our
souls' takes a hold of all material items, such as, 'money . . .
bricks . . . mortar . . . paper . . . ink . . . and gives to them a new
character, a spiritual character, and makes them the instruments
of spiritual force'.[3]

He then builds upon this sacramental understanding to explain the
usefulness of form and Spirit together. When he speaks of 'form' he is
basically referring to 'method'.[4] He is not opposed to methods/forms, but
does make the qualification that 'the form is subject to the Spirit, not the
Spirit to the form'.[5] Hence, he explains that whenever the form/method
is yielding to the Spirit, the missionary efforts stemming from sacrificial
and 'wholehearted devotion'[6] finds more substantial effectiveness.
Indeed, 'Men who have the Spirit can use any method'.[7] He makes sure
that no one misunderstands this emphasis, in that he insists on using 'the
best methods'. Any refusal 'to study the best methods, refusal to regard
organization as of any importance, is really not the denial of matter, but
the denial of the Spirit'.[8]

---

1. Ibid., 69; Francis Paget, 'Sacraments' in *Lux Mundi: A Series of Studies in the
   Religion of the Incarnation*, Charles Gore, (ed.), (London: John Murray, 1890),
   402-33 (p. 422): 'The consecration of material elements to be the vehicles of
   Divine grace keeps up on earth that vindication and defence of the material
   against the insults of sham spiritualism which was achieved forever by the
   Incarnation and Ascension of Jesus Christ.'
2. Roland Allen, 1st edition [*Missionary Principles* 2006] entitled *Foundation
   Principles of Foreign Missions*, (Bungay, Suffolk: Richard Clay & Sons, May
   1910), 37.
3. Allen, *Missionary Principles*, 69; cf. from a Roman Catholic understanding,
   see Susan K. Wood, *Sacramental Orders*, *Lex Orandi* Series, (Collegeville: The
   Liturgical Press, 2000) 8-9, 66-67: 'Sacramental realism exists on several
   levels: the body of Christ is truly present in the Eucharist and so is the
   ecclesial body, the Church.'
4. Allen, *Missionary Principles*, 74.
5. Ibid.
6. Ibid., 72.
7. Ibid., 75.
8. Ibid., 76.

Towards a Trinitarian Missiology

Allen confronts the Church of England as an institutional failure because it seemed to understand itself as primarily 'a Church *for* England'[9] and not as a missionary Church to the entire world. This, of course, was a concern shared by Archbishop William Temple, who, as is well known, memorably insisted that 'the Church is the only society on earth that exists for the benefit of non-members'.[10] For Allen, this was a systemic problem within the English context because the 'spiritual and social needs of the people' were being attended to but there was little recognition of the Holy Spirit's ministry as 'the Spirit of Missions' beyond its shores.[11] This bothered him, as it later bothered Temple, for he was convinced that 'once a man has admitted the all-embracing Spirit of Redeeming Love he can no longer look upon the Church as an institution' and can be 'delivered from the twin demons of parochialism and pauperism'.[12]

His criticisms of the Church of England suggest that he was a frustrated churchman, who, because of his global view of Christianity, was willing to venture beyond Anglicanism in order to engage with leaders from other denominations. As he did so, his criticisms turned to affirmations as he witnessed the 'extraordinary feeling of unity and harmony present then and there' at the 'Pan-Anglican Conference, the Edinburgh Conference and the recent Conferences held in different parts of the East under the Presidency of Dr Mott'.[13] Allen now divulges what appears to be an incipient form of ecumenical missiology within his ecclesiology. Firstly, after referring to Mott's influential leadership,[14] he quotes J.N. Farquhar's observation that the 'frankness of the discussions astonished many, and, above all, the fact that such frankness could co-exist with such complete unity of spirit'.[15] Secondly, he draws attention to

---

9. Ibid., 80.

10. William Temple, quoted in Judith A. Muskett, 'From Vicarious Religion to Vicarious Social Capital: Information and Passive Participation in Voluntary Associations', in Ralph L. Piedmont and Andrew Village (eds.), *Research in the Social Scientific Study of Religion*, vol. 23 (Leiden: Brill, 2012) 29-52 (39).

11. Allen, *Missionary Principles*, 77, 81.

12. Ibid., 81.

13. Ibid., 82.

14. See John R. Mott, *The Decisive Hour of Christian Missions* (New York: Educational Department Board of Foreign Missions of the Presbyterian Church in the USA, 1910. Repr., Charleston: BiblioLife and Milton Keynes, 2010).

15. J.N. Farquhar in the *International Review of Missions*, April 1913, as cited in Roland Allen, *Missionary Principles*, 82-83.

the bishop of Madras and Maclean's comments on these conferences, in order to reinforce the extraordinary display of 'unity' amongst diversified Christian denominational leaders.[1] Thirdly, he rejoices at the significance of these events, for 'this union was something that they discovered, not something that they made'.[2] What actually was discovered within these conferences in India and Scotland, he believed, was due to the 'internal, spiritual, essential' characteristics of the life of Christ within the universal Church.[3] The 'pressure of circumstances'[4] alone cannot provide the context for genuine unity.

> The vital unity recognized must issue eventually in agreement, an agreement not necessarily of uniformity, but quite reasonably of diversity. It is in this way that missions make for unity, and it is in this way, I believe, unity will be attained. It will be by discovery not by creation. The discovery has begun to be made. The more it is discovered the more it will find expression in harmony of feeling of mind, and of will.[5]

Such 'internal' characteristics transcend 'external circumstances'.[6] That which the delegates experienced at the missionary conferences was exactly what he had begun to articulate. Indeed, his 'discovery' of the pneumatological presence and impetus within the Church became central to his understanding of 'unity in diversity' within his missionary ecclesiology.[7]

Again, the foundation for missiology stems directly from his Trinitarian theology.[8] Allen's unflinching belief in the catholic creeds, as

1. Allen, *Missionary Principles*, 82-83.
2. Ibid., 83.
3. Ibid.
4. Ibid., 84.
5. Ibid.; cf. Allen, 'Educational Principles and Missionary Methods,' *The English Church Review*, vol. IV, no. 37 (January 1913) 21: 'The child trained in the school of Pestalozzi was capable of teaching others. There is nothing the child mind more delights in than announcing its discoveries . . . St Paul's converts were manifestly the children of discovery.'
6. Allen, *Missionary Principles*, 83-84.
7. Roland Allen, a letter to the editor entitled 'The Unceasing Appeal for Men for Foreign Missions', *The Guardian* (23 July 1902). See also Allen, *The Guardian* (18 June 1902 and 25 June 1902); Allen, 'The Churches of the Future' (23 July 1902).
8. Refer to Allen's sermons on the Trinity, and also the Unity in the Church: 'The Athanasian Creed' – Hebrews 12:28, 29 (Beaconsfield, July 1927), USPG, Box 5: 43; 'The Creed as a Confession of Faith' – Acts 8:37, Box 5:

evidenced in his systematic creedal teachings and sermons, provide the backdrop for understanding why he emphasized the 'internal' nature of unity. Christians are united into one body because this unity stems from the unity that exists within the Trinity:[9] 'we worship one God in Trinity and Trinity in Unity . . . the whole three Persons are co-eternal together; and co-equal. So that in all things, as is aforesaid: the Unity in Trinity, and the Trinity in Unity is to be worshipped. . . . '[10] In Cornelius Van Til's words, 'diversity and the unity in the Godhead are . . . equally ultimate'.[11] In summary, Allen did believe that: (1) an adherence to a Trinitarian faith was essential for all Christians; (2) the unity and diversity in the Triune God is the basis for unity and diversity within the Church; and (3) this catholic doctrine emerged from within 'the experience of Christians'.[12]

To look at this from another angle, on one hand, Alistair Mason argued that Schleiermacher's *The Christian Faith* (1821)[13] placed 'the doctrine of the Trinity' at the conclusion of his book because he had difficulty seeing 'how it related to direct religious experience'.[14] Mason's critique of Schleiermacher's compares it with that of H.H. Kelly, a close friend of Allen's: 'Father Kelly, on the other hand, loved the Athanasian Creed, with its Trinitarian incomprehensibilities, the stumbling block to English liberal thinkers, and claimed it was central to Christian teaching.[15] Indeed, both Allen and Kelly were not only friends but they tended to embrace similar theological positions, especially when it related to creedal confessionalism. In summary, Allen did believe that:

44-45; 'The Doctrine of the Trinity Sprang from Experience of Christians' – John 3:16 (Chorley, May 1921), Box 5: 46; 'St Paul on Unity in the Church' – Acts 11:17, Box 5: 49; on the Athanasian Creed (1928), USPG X622, Box 5: 317, Oxford, Bodleian Library.

9. Allen's teaching notes on 2 Thessalonians (5 pages) USPG X622, Box 3: Acts – Revelation, Oxford, Bodleian Library.

10. *Quicunque Vult* (Athanasian Creed) 1662 Book of Common Prayer, Cambridge: Cambridge University Press, Measure (1968) 27-30.

11. Cornelius Van Til, *Apologetics* (Philadelphia: Presbyterian and Reformed Publishing, 1953) 8.

12. Roland Allen's sermon: 'The Doctrine of the Trinity Sprang from Experience of Christians' – John 3:16 (Chorley, May 1921), USPG X622, Box 5: 46, Oxford, Bodleian Library.

13. Friedrich Schleiermacher, *The Christian Faith*, Conclusion: The Divine Trinity (1821. Repr., London: T & T Clark, 1999. Repr., 2004), 738-751.

14. Alistair Mason, *History of the Society of the Sacred Mission* (Norwich: The Canterbury Press, 1994), 89.

15. Ibid.

(1) an adherence to a Trinitarian faith was essential for all
    Christians;
(2) the unity and diversity in the Triune God is the basis for unity
    and diversity within the Church; and
(3) this catholic doctrine emerged from within the experience of
    Christians.'[1]

In the remainder of *Missionary Principles*, he calls the Church to
return again to the principle of trust in the Spirit's internal work for 'a
renewal of the mind' and the freedom to give 'a truer presentation of
the Gospel'.[2] On the last page of this book he reinforces his argument
that the Church of England at home needs to apply the 'missionary
principles . . . which have a wider application than to Foreign Missions'
and consider how to accept that these 'principles applied to any work
anywhere' will find relevance because intrinsically 'they are worldwide'.[3]
He concludes that when the Church in England adopts these missionary
principles there will be 'a reaction, and that reaction is inevitable, certain,
and of incalculable value to us at home'.[4]

Pentecost and the World: the Revelation of the Holy Spirit in the Acts of the Apostles[5]

The earlier discussion of *Pentecost and the World* established how Allen's
main thesis highlighted the nature of the Holy Spirit's supremacy
at Pentecost in empowering the Church to witness. He notes how the
account in the Acts of the Apostles does not begin 'with a command'
towards mission, but rather 'with a promise of the Spirit',[6] similar to the
way the Gospel of Luke ends: ' . . . but tarry in the city of Jerusalem until
you are endued with power from on high' (Luke 24:29).[7] The promise was
fulfilled at Pentecost, which marked the pivotal change that empowered

---

1. Roland Allen's sermon: 'The Doctrine of the Trinity Sprang from Experience
   of Christians' – John 3:16 (Chorley, May 1921), USPG X622, Box 5: 46,
   Oxford, Bodleian Library.
2. Allen, *Missionary Principles*, 90.
3. Ibid., 94.
4. Ibid.; cf. Lesslie Newbigin, *Foolishness to the Greeks: The Gospel and Western
   Culture* (London: SPCK, 1984. Repr., March 1986) 147: The Benjamin B.
   Warfield Lectures given at Princeton Theological Seminary.
5. Allen, *Pentecost and the World*, 1970, 1-61.
6. Ibid., 4-5; cf. Acts 1:8; 2:2.
7. Ibid., 4

the apostles – and *all* believers – for missionary service to all nations.[8] He argued that the 'apostles did not confound the gift which they received with the manifestation of the grace and power of the Holy Spirit in the Old Testament'.[9] The reason for the clarification hinges on his Christology. For Allen, there was 'a sharp distinction drawn between the prophets and forerunners of Christ inspired by the Holy Spirit' under the Old Covenant order in comparison to 'the apostles and followers of Christ baptized with the Holy Spirit'[10] within the New Covenant order. This 'different order' now incorporates 'only Christians', he argued, because 'this gift was Christ's gift'.[11] This, of course, was a distinction made by Geerhardus Vos, who, on one hand, referred to the Holy Spirit's ministry under the Old Covenant as 'the Spirit of the theocratic charismata', while on the other hand, of 'this charismatic Spirit Jesus has received the fullness, [and] dispenses of it to His followers . . . in greater fullness by way of fulfillment at Pentecost'.[12] The difference between Babel's language diaspora (Gen. 11:9) and Pentecost's language reunion (Acts 2:1-11) was that 'the Father and the Son'[13] put the *curse in reverse* by sending the Holy Spirit – i.e., Pentecost trumped Babel. Adolf von Harnack describes this new order as 'an "evangel" and that it was felt to bring blessing and joy'.[14]

A foretaste of Allen's pneumatology is unpacked when describing how 'the Pentecostal gift' was given to Cornelius, his 'relatives and close friends' after 'Peter taught him [and the others] to believe in Jesus Christ'.[15] His pneumatology centred on the uniqueness of Christ. For Allen, therefore, his Trinitarian thought was always thoroughly Christocentric. Both Gerrit Berkouwer and Lesslie Newbigin – both of whom were indebted to the theological work of Barth – developed

---

8. Ibid., 11-12; cf. Andreas J. Kostenberger and Peter T. O'Brien, *Salvation to the Ends of the Earth: A Biblical Theology of Mission*, NSBT 11, (Downers Grove: InterVarsity Press, 2001) 165-66; Schnabel, *Paul the Missionary*, 124.

9. Allen, *Pentecost and the World*, 9.

10. Ibid., 6.

11. Ibid., 9.

12. Geerhardus Vos, *Biblical Theology: Old and New Testaments* (Grand Rapids: Eerdmans, 1948. Repr., Grand Rapids: Eerdmans, 1971) 413.

13. Book of Common Prayer (1662) Western version of the Nicene Creed: 'And I believe in the Holy Ghost, the Lord and giver of life, Who proceedeth from the Father and the Son . . .'

14. Adolf von Harnack, *What is Christianity?* 'Sixteen Lectures delivered in the University of Berlin during the Winter-Term 1899-1900', (New York: G.P. Putnam's and Sons, 1901) 50.

15. Acts 10:1-48 (vs. 43-48); Allen, *Pentecost and the World*, 11.

similar missiologies to Allen and argued their version of *missio Dei* from
a Trinitarian perspective that was also Christocentric.[1]

Allen begins his third chapter by drawing attention to the 'gift of
tongues' as the 'first gift' which was evidenced at Pentecost and how
the people marvelled when they heard 'the wonderful works of God'
spoken in their native languages.[2] Although he mentions this glossolalia
phenomenon he avoids any comment other than leaving it to biblical
scholars 'to explain what exactly happened'.[3] He felt the discussions
on this matter were 'curiously uninteresting and unprofitable, and
their conclusions equally dubious and barren'[4] when he wrote this in
1917. Lesslie Newbigin identifies that 'Allen was not a prototype of
the contemporary evangelical charismatic – much as I think he would
have welcomed the charismatic explosion'.[5] Firstly, Newbigin's accurate
analysis of Allen's thinking is disclosed in the charismatic dynamic of the
missionary Spirit emphasis located in his ecclesiology as 'the Pentecostal
gift'.[6] However, this does not imply that he was a 'charismatic' in the sense
of the modern understanding of speaking in tongues; neither does it
suggest that he was opposed to this grace (*charis*). Instead he emphasized
it, in a primary sense, of 'charismatic ministry' for the equipping of the
Church through 'that direct internal impulse of the Spirit';[7] and also, in
a secondary sense, for her empowerment from 'a spiritual illumination'[8]
through the gifts of the Spirit: '*charismata, diakonia* and *energemata*'.[9]

Secondly, his 'charismatic' understanding was articulated through
his belief in the abiding validity of apostles, prophets, and teachers –
'wandering evangelists'[10] as he called them – who demonstrated significant

---

1. See Gerrit C. Berkouwer, *The Church* (Grand Rapids: Eerdmans, 1976) 395;
    and, Lesslie Newbigin, Reply to Konrad Raiser, *International Bulletin of
    Missionary Research*, (1994) 18, 2, 51-52.
2. Allen, *Pentecost and the World*, 22; cf. Gordon Fee, *God's Empowering Presence: The
    Holy Spirit in the Letters of Paul* (Peabody: Hendrickson Publishers, 1999) 193-94.
3. Ibid.
4. Ibid.
5. Hubert Allen, *Roland Allen*, Foreword by Lesslie Newbigin, xiv.
6. Allen, *Pentecost and the World*, 11.
7. Allen: 'The Ministry of Expansion: the Priesthood of the Laity', 1930, 3: 1.
8. Allen, *Pentecost and the World*, 46.
9. Arnold Bittlinger, *Gifts and Graces: A Commentary on I Corinthians 12-14*
    (Grand Rapids: Eerdmans, 1974) 20.
10. Allen: 'The Ministry of Expansion: the Priesthood of the Laity' (1930) 3:6
    and 4:5.

trans-local ministry 'ascension' gifts.[11] These he believed to be foundational to what Arnold Bittlinger calls 'inter-congregational ministries' as differentiated from 'congregational ministries (overseers, elders, servants)'.[12] This became an integral part of his Church growth missiology and today is what Murray identifies as 'the Ephesians 4 model of a healthy church'.[13] For Allen, he did not believe that the ministry 'ascension' gifts of apostles and prophets functionally disappeared at the end of the first century, but rather interpreted them as abiding ministries throughout Church history. John Calvin also argued that 'the Lord . . . now and again revives them as the need of the times demands. . . . I do not deny that the Lord has sometimes at a later period raised up apostles, or at least evangelists in their place, as has happened in our own day'.[14] The historical validity of this 'charismata', he believed, generally referred to a pneumatological 'grace' given to individuals, including 'native apostles',[15] specifically for service in the Church by the means of the laying on of the hands,[16] or by divine sovereign action and 'not commissioned by any ecclesiastical body'.[17]

That said, he chose rather to focus on the 'point of real significance and importance', that being how the apostles and other disciples immediately began to evangelize people 'of every nation and language'.[18] He regarded this impetus as rooted in the Holy Spirit's 'nature as a Spirit who desired the salvation of all men of every nation'[19] or, what Donald McGavran refers to as, 'not a man-initiated activity but *missio Dei*, the mission of God, who Himself remains in charge of it'.[20] Allen believed that God's intention

---

11. See Ephesians 4:8 (ἔδωκεν δόματα).

12. Bittlinger, *Gifts and Graces*, 67.

13. Stuart Murray, *Church After Christendom* (Milton Keynes: Paternoster, 2008) 170, 189.

14. John Calvin, *Institutes of the Christian Religion* (two volumes), The Library of Christian Classics: vol. XXI: Books III.xx-IV.xx, John T. McNeill, ed., Translated and Indexed by Ford Lewis Battles (Philadelphia: The Westminster Press, 1960) 1056-1057 (IV. iii. 4).

15. Allen, 'The Doctrine of the Holy Spirit', 12.

16. See 2 Timothy 1:6 (τὸ χάρισμα τοῦ θεοῦ, ὅ ἐστιν ἐν σοὶ διὰ τῆς ἐπιθέσεως τῶν χειρῶν μου).

17. Steven Rutt, 'Roland Allen's Apostolic Principles: An Analysis of his "The Ministry of Expansion" ' *Transformation* (July 2012) 29(3): 234; cf. Allen, 'The Ministry of Expansion: the Priesthood of the Laity', Chapter 3: 2; Sanneh, *Disciples of All Nations*, 197-200.

18. Allen, *Pentecost and the World*, 22.

19. Ibid.

20. Donald McGavran, *Understanding Church Growth* (Grand Rapids: Eerdmans, 1980) 23.

was to have a people emerging from all 'people movements'[1] in response to the Holy Spirit's work.[2] Likewise, the Barthian thinker, Hendrik Kraemer, describes how the Church 'lives by *charismata*', that being by 'gifts worked by the Spirit' for its edification, citing Paul's teaching on 'spiritual gifts and business ability in connection with the Church'. The 'divinely willed theocentric fellowship' is enhanced through the gifts of 'apostles, prophets, teachers, workers of miracles, healers, helpers, *administrators* and those speaking in tongues'.[3] Both Kraemer and Allen focused on the planting of the Church as their primary emphasis though, and then, secondarily, underlined the Church's mission to evangelize the unreached regions.

Similarly, Jürgen Moltmann (1926-present) would detect in Allen's thought an ecclesiology of the Orthodox churches which 'understands the history of Jesus itself pneumatologically [where the] incarnation, his mission, his anointing and his resurrection are the works of the Holy Spirit. . . . For that reason the Son of God is also present in and through the Spirit in his church. . . .'[4] This is interesting, in that Moltmann's indebtedness to Orthodoxy in his articulation of the view that 'pneumatological Christology leads to a charismatic ecclesiology',[5] highlights a similar line of influence in Allen's thought. That is to say, it is highly probable that Allen's ecclesiology was influenced by one whom he called 'my friend the Rev F.E. Brightman, of Pusey House, Oxford',[6] a leading scholar 'on the liturgies and the spirituality of the Eastern Orthodox Churches'.[7] He further elaborates this 'first recorded action in the Gospels of the Holy Spirit's activity in Christ's incarnation whereby the Holy Spirit's 'expression of redeeming love' is revealed and therefore gives impetus for the Church reaching out 'towards others . . . for the

---

1. Alan R. Tippett, *People Movements in Southern Polynesia: Studies in the Dynamics of Church-planting and Growth in Tahiti, New Zealand, Tonga, and Samoa* (Chicago: Moody Press, 1971) 198-200.

2. See Acts 2:14-36; 2:38-40; 3:12-26; 5:30-32; Allen, *Pentecost and the World*, 1970, 22-23.

3. Kraemer, *The Christian Message in a Non-Christian World*, 418 (original emphasis).

4. Jürgen Moltmann, *The Church in the Power of the Spirit: A Contribution to Messianic Ecclesiology* (1st edition in German 1975. Repr., London: SCM Press, 1977) 36.

5. Ibid.

6. Roland Allen, *Gerbert, Pope Silvester II*, repr. from 'The English Historical Review' vol. VII, London: Spottiswoode & Co., 1892, 46. A copy is located in the Pusey House Library, Oxford, S:59.00.c2, Miscellania: Hagiology.

7. Talltorp, *Sacrament & Growth*, 11; see Frank Edward Brightman, *Liturgies Eastern and Western*, 1896.

salvation of men everywhere'.[8]

Turning to the work of the Spirit in the individual, he goes on to argue that, unlike John the Baptist's message of repentance and baptism which emphasized a turning away from sin, he emphasized the Pauline focus on turning to Christ. 'What men turn to is more important than what they turn from.'[9] The motive for 'missionary zeal' is positioned in neither 'intellectual beliefs' nor 'theological arguments', but rather in 'love' because Allen recognized the positive side where theological proclamation has answered the 'real need of the world' through the redeeming act of love in 'the Spirit of the Incarnation and the Passion' and subsequent outpouring of 'the Spirit given at Pentecost'.[10] Francis Anekwe Oborji speaks similarly of this love in affirming redemptive terms:

> Love is to animate the work of proclamation and the witness to the Gospel involved in preaching. . . . Proclamation and preaching, however, are to serve the aim of implanting the church through which people enter into the new household of God. . . . Thus, in proclamation we have the call to conversion, anticipation of the forgiveness of sins and regeneration in the Spirit. . . . Such love for the faith and others has been described as an evangelization that is new in fervour, new in expressions and new in methods.[11]

Oborji and Allen recognize the positive side on which theological proclamation has answered the 'real need of the world through the redeeming act of love' in 'the Spirit of the Incarnation and the Passion' and subsequent outpouring of 'the Spirit given at Pentecost'.[12] Redemptive love has created an emerging apostolic ministry of evangelism and church planting that was rooted in the experiential 'administration of the Spirit' which Allen identifies as the 'key' in all 'apostolic work'.[13] This focus discloses how the pneumatological dynamic within the apostles' experience likewise empowered them to administer the Spirit.[14] And, this principle of reciprocity incited to action an incipient apostolic ministry, which then produced vision and mission for evangelizing frontier regions. 'What was not familiar, what was indeed peculiar to the new dispensation,

---

8. Allen, *Pentecost and the World*, 27-28.

9. Ibid., 31.

10. Ibid., 38.

11. Francis Anekwe Oborji, *Concepts of Mission: The Evolution of Contemporary Missiology* (Maryknoll: Orbis Books, 2006) 208-09.

12. Allen, *Pentecost and the World*, 38.

13. Ibid., 39, 42.

14. Ibid., 39.

was the communication of the Spirit to the whole body of Christians.'[1] This emphasis from below – a grassroots movement – where all Christians were equally valued by the apostles as they began to 'lay hands on common men that they might be filled with the Spirit for their common daily life' was a new direction.[2] He discloses how the primitive Church embraced this apparently 'universal practice' of the laying on of hands upon everyone who was baptized 'that they might receive the Holy Spirit'[3] and experience union with Christ and fellow members:

> It exalted the common life of common men to heights before held only by some special and important service of God. It exalted men occupied in humble tasks of daily toil to the position before peculiar to prophets and kings and priests. Christians all became kings and priests (Rev. 1:6; I Pet. 2:9); the Church became a kingdom of priests.[4]

Later on, this apologetic is further developed in 'The Priesthood of the Church'[5] in which, by deductive reasoning, he argues for more lay participation within the life of the faith community due to the Holy Spirit's empowerment of the laity, especially if Christians 'meet far from any episcopally ordained cleric'.[6] He contended that in churchless regions 'where the Christians are whether few or many in number', he encouraged them to gather together for worship 'even if only one household' assembles.[7]

Allen's analysis of Acts concluded that the recipients of the Holy Spirit were 'all members of the Christian body'[8] and that the apostles' general practice was to lay hands on those who believed and were baptized.[9] Then, he points out that there were two examples where 'the laying on of hands by one of the twelve was definitely excluded': (1) Ananias – 'not one of the inner circle of apostles' – laid hands on Paul who then received the Holy Spirit after his conversion;[10] (2) Cornelius'

---

1. Ibid., 40.
2. Ibid.
3. Ibid.
4. Ibid.
5. See Roland Allen, 'The Priesthood of the Church', *Church Quarterly Review*, January 1933, 234-244.
6. Ibid., 241.
7. Ibid., 239.
8. See Acts 2:1-4; 2:37-39; Allen, *Pentecost and the World*, 41.
9. Cf. Acts 6:6; 8:14-17; 19:5-6; Allen, *Pentecost and the World*, 40.
10. Cf. Acts 9:17; Allen, *Pentecost and the World*, 41.

household received the Holy Spirit 'without any laying on of the hands'.[11]
He surmises that Luke 'was far more profoundly concerned with the
reality and universality of the gift than he was with the mode of the
administration of the gift'.[12] This was not a denial of normality for
ecclesial order, since Allen advocated Anglican ethos and order, yet he
did believe that the supremacy of the Holy Spirit's ministry trumps
normal ecclesiastical order and custom. Why? The title of his book says
it all: *Pentecost and the World*. Kraemer agrees and argues in *The Theology
of the Laity* that 'the inner meaning and scope of God's self-disclosing
and saving dealing with the world as a whole, the Church . . . should be
always conscious of this basic fact that it primarily exists on behalf of
the world and not of itself'.[13]

The 'key of the apostolic work', according to Allen's analysis of Acts,
was the 'administration of the Spirit'. This, he contends, explains the
following:

(1) the apostles preaching the reality of the 'remission of sins';
(2) the converts experiencing 'the assurance of forgiveness';
(3) the Holy Spirit imparting new power for the Church;
(4) 'the certainty of the hope of eternal life' which anchored the
    Church to embrace 'persecution and martyrdom';
(5) the Church's 'new sense of the value and dignity' which
    produced 'purity of life' and the formation of 'hospitals for the
    care of the diseased'; and
(6) the zeal to bring people to 'salvation' by proclaiming 'the Gospel
    of Christ throughout the then known world'.[14]

Particularly interesting to Allen is the 'remarkable' and 'most curious
change' as the apostles significantly shift from 'the influence of an
intellectual theory' to the reality of Pentecostal empowerment where
they were 'acting under the impulse of the Spirit' and began boldly
to proclaim the 'Gospel' to those whom they previously feared.[15] C.H.
Dodd explained this apostolic *kerygma* as rooted in the 'divine event'
and articulating a 'realized' kingdom where the 'open manifestation of
the power of God is the overthrow of the powers of evil'.[16] Within this

11. Cf. Acts 10:44-48; 11:15; 15:8; Allen, *Pentecost and the World*, 41-42.

12. Ibid., 42.

13. Hendrik Kraemer, *A Theology of the Laity* (London: The Lutterworth Press,
    1958. Repr., 1960), 130.

14. Allen, *Pentecost and the World*, 42-43.

15. Ibid., 44-45.

16. C.H. Dodd, *The Apostolic Preaching: and its Developments* (Lectures at King's

new context the 'charismatic' apostles immediately spread this faith abroad because 'the New Testament writers are clear that history is henceforward qualitatively different from what it was before Christ's coming'.[1] Allen repeatedly draws attention to this 'way of the Spirit'[2] that drove the apostolic ministry to rely more upon 'the impulse of the Spirit' rather than their pre-Pentecost 'exigencies of any intellectual theory'[3] or methodologies about how to evangelize frontier regions.

This understanding for 'the impulse of the Spirit' is principal in his charismatic missiology. Throughout this chapter he explained how the 'impulse of the Spirit' was experienced by the apostles in general, and Philip, Peter, Paul, John and the Jerusalem Council, in particular.[4] Allen does not refer to any sources while developing this charismatic missiology except for his hermeneutic of the Acts of the Apostles. And yet, his constant emphasis on sovereignty and divine providence disclose the theological backdrop for how he understood 'the revelation of a Spirit governing, guiding, controlling, directing men in the acts here recorded', because in his understanding of the Spirit's sovereignty he believed that in Acts 'it is the guidance and government of the Spirit which is constantly recalled to mind'.[5]

Obviously, this understanding is not new. An argument can be made for an earlier Protestant explanation through John Calvin's pneumatology, especially articulated within his *Institutes*:[6] 'we ought to seek our conviction in a higher place than human reasons, judgements, or

---

College, London, 1935; 1st edn 1936; Cambridge: 1938. Repr., New York: Harper & Brothers Publishers, 1954) 86-87.

1. Ibid., 88.

2. Allen, *Pentecost and the World*, 49.

3. Ibid., 46-47.

4. Ibid., 44-51.

5. Ibid., 3; cf. Alistair Mason, *SSM: History of the Society of the Sacred Mission* (Norwich, UK: The Canterbury Press, 1994) 102. Allen's friend H.H. Kelly commented at a conference in Swanwick, after being told that his 'high doctrine of God [was] "the finest Calvinism he had ever heard preached". Kelly commented, "Of course it was Calvinism, though we call it predestinarianism at Kelham (Nottinghamshire, UK). Those old rascals did believe in God, if they believed in nothing else"', SCM/Report on Swanwick, 9-16 July 1912, 237.

6. John Calvin, *Institutes of the Christian Religion* (two volumes), The Library of Christian Classics: vol. XX: Books I:i-III.xix, John T. McNeill, ed., Translated and Indexed by Ford Lewis Battles (Philadelphia, Pennsylvania: The Westminster Press, 1960).

conjectures, that is, in the secret testimony of the Holy Spirit';[7] 'reason itself teaches us to climb higher and to examine into the secret energy of the Spirit, by which we come to enjoy Christ and all his benefits';[8] 'without the illumination of the Holy Spirit, the Word can do nothing';[9] 'it will not be enough for the mind to be illumined by the Spirit of God unless the heart is also strengthened and supported by his power';[10] 'as we cannot come to Christ unless we be drawn by the Spirit . . . we are lifted up in mind and heart above our understanding . . . the Spirit, as the inner teacher, through his illumination makes entry for it';[11] 'to sum up: Christ, when he illumines us into faith by the power of his Spirit, at the same time so engrafts us into his body that we become partakers of every good'.[12] Calvin's pneumatology of the 'secret testimony' and 'secret energy' of the Holy Spirit, is very similar to Allen's belief in the 'impulse of the Spirit'[13] for enabling the mind and heart of Christians to rise above human methods. Moreover, both Calvin and Allen advanced their charismatic ecclesiologies to also embrace the Spirit's influence within the sacramental life of the Church because ' . . . the sacraments profit not a whit without the power of the Holy Spirit'.[14]

Finally, Allen provides an examination of the tension that ensued following the Jewish Christians' adjustment to the *newer* covenantal transition as Gentiles became 'members of the body'.[15] He carefully unpacks the Hebrew Bible's concept of covenant theology (e.g., 'covenant' is mentioned twenty-three times in this chapter) and how it pervaded Jewish thought and practice.[16] His main point in explaining the difficulty for Jews to accept Gentiles into the Church, especially those connected with the Judaizer problem discussed at the Jerusalem Council, was accepting the fact that 'God gave them the Holy Spirit'.[17] He argued that the 'Mosaic teaching had been a preparation for the Gospel' so that 'the Gentiles' would eventually be 'received into a church within the

---

7. Ibid., Book I. vii. 4: 78.

8. Ibid., Book III. i. 1: 537.

9. Ibid., Book III. ii. 33: 580.

10. Ibid., Book III. ii. 33: 581.

11. Ibid., Book III. ii. 34: 582.

12. Ibid., Book III. ii. 35: 583.

13. Allen, *Pentecost and the World*, 44–47.

14. Calvin, *Institutes*, vol. XXI: Book IV. xiv. 9: 1284.

15. Allen, *Pentecost and the World*, 52.

16. Ibid., 52-58.

17. See Acts 15:1-29 (cf. 15:8); Allen, *Pentecost and the World*, 56-57.

covenant'.[1] The Jewish Christians were challenged to address their elitist opinions upon hearing the apostles' narrative that the Holy Spirit was poured out upon the Gentiles.[2] His concluding chapter reaffirms how his charismatic missiology was shaped – not designed out of duty – but recognizing that it was caused by the missionary impulse of the Holy Spirit.[3] For Allen, the 'missionary Spirit' is the *missio Dei* who inspires the missional Church to 'embrace the world because Christ embraces the world'.[4]

When foreign missionaries successfully plant a church, they are then called to trust the pneumatological dynamic to nurture and sustain what Allen's missiology inculcates, that being, 'faith in the Holy Ghost in our converts'[5] for the Church's spontaneous growth. Oborji agrees. 'According to Allen, the basic difference is that Paul had founded "churches" while modern missionaries founded "missions" in the sense of *dependent* organizations.'[6] In order to free indigenous converts from 'prevailing dependency structures', Oborji engages with Allen's understanding of 'Paul's success' by saying 'he trusted both the Lord' and 'the people to whom he had gone'.[7] In this respect, Pauline apostolic ministry of 'Order' is realized when missionaries impart – the Scriptures, a basic creed, the ministry and the sacraments – all necessary when joined with the 'missionary Spirit's ministry' to form a charismatic ecclesiology of 'Spirit and Order' for empowerment 'to extend the kingdom of Christ to the uttermost limits of the earth'.[8]

---

1. Ibid., 56.

2. Ibid., 56–57; see Acts 10:45–47; 11:15, 17; 15:8.

3. Ibid., 60–61.

4. Ibid., 61.

5. Allen, *Missionary Methods*, 152.

6. Oborji, *Concepts of Mission*, 92.

7. Ibid.; see Allen, *Missionary Methods*, 1956, 90, 107–90.

8. Roland Allen's handwritten (unpublished) notes on 'The Doctrine of the Holy Spirit', USPG X622, Box 3, 13: 14, Oxford, Bodleian Library.

6. The Influence of Roland Allen's Missiology in India

A Case Study on Bishop Vedanayagam S. Azariah and Bishop George C. Hubback[1]

An analysis of the ecclesiastical conversation between Allen and several Indian bishops – both critical and complimentary – discloses the relevancy of his thought for leadership issues. In general, attempts to carefully analyze the significant contribution he made to missionary ecclesiology as he engaged with various bishops who embraced his teachings, and conversely, with other bishops who refused to adapt to changing structures within the Church of England are highlighted in this study. The following is a case study of two such bishops in India, Vedanayagam Samuel Azariah of Dornakal and George Clay Hubback of Assam. Through an analysis of the reception of his ideas by these two men, we will be able to see how, on one hand, his thought was able to facilitate Church renewal and transformation significantly without costly infrastructural apparatuses, while, on the other, this renewal was inhibited by leadership inflexibility and a lack of missional foresight.

One might assume that Allen, like many Anglican priests, was passively submissive or uncritical of bishops when they personally disagreed with episcopal decisions, methodologies or plans. Nothing could be further from the facts. Firstly, although he recognized episcopacy as divine order, he never shied away from confronting bishops who, in his opinion were elitist, lazy, lacking missional foresight or disobedient to what he believed was biblical truth. Archival evidence discloses two letters from Bishop Henry Whitehead (Madras)[2] to himself in appreciation of his

---

1. This case study derives from a paper I was invited to present at the *Yale-Edinburgh Group* on the History of the Missionary Movement and World Christianity – 'Religious Movements of Renewal, Revival, and Revitalization in the History of Missions and World Christianity' (28-30 June 2012) New College, Edinburgh, Scotland.

2. Azariah's mentor, Bishop Henry Whitehead (Madras), was the person who introduced Allen's writings to Azariah. Whitehead wrote two letters to

defence of V.S. Azariah's consecration process as Anglicanism's first indigenous bishop in India. Secondly, as a missionary methods analyst, his confrontational style with various bishops could be misinterpreted as that of some independent radical, who, although an Englishman reared within the Victorian era, seemed to set aside good manners and to 'take on' the Church of England's institutional leadership whenever he concluded that some custom was hindering the spontaneous growth of the Church's mission. With these points in mind, we turn to his relationships with Bishop Azariah and Bishop Hubback.

Allen's Account of the Two Bishops

The leadership dynamic of the Church incorporates a wide range of areas of service within its organic mission and institutional maintenance. Whether its mission is local or international, ecclesiastical politics is inescapable. The reality is that the Church tends to have the most intense form of internal politics because its members seek to obey a particular interpretation of God's will and the *missio Dei*. Likewise, its leaders hope to direct the community towards a particular interpretation of faith and practice, which may not enjoy a consensus. Such issues are compounded by certain tensions, which need to be maintained between mercy and truth, freedom and order, activism and conformity, innovation and curating. One way forward is to determine a person's unique gift to the Church, which enables one to live somewhere on a spectrum between 'elitist' clericalism and 'leader-less' egalitarianism. It was Allen's catholicity that guided him through the maze of these tensions to engage with bishops concerning how they might lead and equip the Church for the work of the ministry.

Allen's visit to the Diocese of Dornakal
(2 December 1927 – 28 February 1928)

The central part of this episcopal story can be understood through the examination of Allen's unpublished *Diary of a Visit in South India* (an 85-page handwritten document),[1] which contains details of his missionary journey to India (2 December 1927 to 8 March 1928)[2] in response to the

---

Allen regarding the consecration of Azariah, USPG X622, Box 1, File A (7 June 1912 and 11 June 1912) Oxford, Bodleian Library.

1. Roland Allen, *Diary of a Visit in South India* (unpublished) USPG X622, Box 7, File N, Oxford, Bodleian Library.

2. David Paton, *Reform of the Ministry: A Study in the Work of Roland Allen* (London: The Lutterworth Press, 1968) presents a brief section from Allen's *Diary of a Visit in South India*. Paton published the events in *Reform of the Ministry*, 106-

invitation by Azariah and Hubback to minister within both dioceses. To begin with, his missionary work within the dioceses of Dornakal and Assam needs to be understood within the context of his communication with both bishops prior to his arrival. Firstly, an analysis of this early communication will provide the background for this visit. Secondly, an examination of archival letters discloses the ecclesiological discussions between these men and how this engagement prepared the groundwork for him to address various issues during his visit. Thirdly, his *Diary of a Visit in South India* discloses the personal analysis of his discussions with Azariah, Hubback and other clergy and laity during this visit. This section closely examines the dynamic of leadership empowerment of the laity, as well as encountering ecclesiastical power struggles among insecure leaders whom he taught, consulted, analyzed and charged with mission. The primary apostolic principles that he was asked to address while in India were: (1) that self-supporting indigenous voluntary priests and bishops should not be financed by foreign sources, and (2) that the spontaneous expansion of the indigenous Church should be based upon an apostolic model.

The archives disclose two letters between Allen and Azariah (in which Azariah also refers to an earlier letter).[3] The context for this correspondence revolved around his recent book *Voluntary Clergy* (1923),[4] which Azariah thanked him for sending to him. Azariah refers to the earlier letter, in which Allen states that 'a Bishop who accepted the arguments of the book and acted on it will be more or less martyred'.[5] Azariah disagreed and assured him that the bishops in India have already approved the 'order of permanent Deacons and Voluntary Permanent Deacons'.[6] Furthermore, Azariah assures him that the principle of

---

119, which covered only 4–11 December 1927, which is only the first part of the missionary journey in South India in the diocese of Dornakal (Diary: 1-18) without any information of his journey to North India in the diocese of Assam (Diary: 18-85). The complete diary begins with 4 December 1927 which includes his arrival in Bombay on 2 December and concludes with the events of 8 March 1928. The diary's length is eighty-five handwritten pages. According to my research this current thesis contains the *first* complete analysis of Allen's *Diary*.

3. Azariah's letter to Allen, Box 6, File K: 12, 29 December 1923, USPG, and Allen's draft letter to Azariah, Box 6, File K: 15 (30 January 1924). An earlier letter of Allen's dated 13 July 1923 which Azariah refers to in his letter of 29 December 1923. Cf. Whitehead to Allen, USPG X622, Box 1, File A (7 June 1912 and 11 June 1912) Oxford, Bodleian Library.

4. Allen, *Voluntary Clergy* (London: SPCK, 1923).

5. Allen's letter is missing in his archives (dated 13 July 1923).

6. Azariah's letter to Allen, Box 6, File K: 12 (29 December 1923).

voluntary ministry will eventually incorporate the practice of the 'Voluntary Priest'[1] and discusses such a movement within the Dornakal diocese. In addition, Azariah conveys hope for a possible restructuring of ministerial training and placement from the general criteria of a university education, Latin learning and 'a Title to a living',[2] which he thought could eventually change if given the liberty to implement the adjustments. This was based on Azariah's assessment of what would work best in his diocese. Secondly, additional information from his grandson discloses how a friendship began to develop between Azariah and himself approximately a decade earlier when he and his wife spent a few months visiting various mission workers in India (1910-11).[3] The ongoing friendship between these men continued after he published *Missionary Methods: St Paul's or Ours?* (1912), a book that sparked Azariah's vision and mission for Dornakal. His influence on Azariah's ministry, as Susan Harper observed, came in a letter from Azariah to Bishop Whitehead's wife, Isabel, in April 1912:

> I have been enjoying Mr Roland Allen's volume immensely. I like his fearless conclusions – I may say reckless – it thoroughly suits my militant spirit! . . . I wish someone would send a copy of this book to all South India's Church of England missionaries. . . . You know how practical the book is to me.[4]

The previous evidence provides a brief introduction to Allen's missionary journey to India in 1927. To understand the events of this journey, we will now unpack his recorded ministry activities, beginning with Azariah in Dornakal and continuing with Hubback in Assam.

Diary of a Visit in South India
(2 December 1927 – 8 March 1928)

An entry on 4 December 1927 discloses that, upon arrival on 2 December in Bombay,[5] a letter was given to him from Hubback, welcoming him to India. Hubback advised him to postpone his visit to the diocese of Assam and instead visit the diocese of Madras and subsequently speak for 'a big

---

1. Ibid.
2. Ibid.
3. Hubert Allen, *Roland Allen*, 86 and 129 (photo taken in Murhu, India in 1910). Ongoing interviews with Hubert Allen disclose additional information concerning Roland and Beatrice Allen's visit in India.
4. Harper, *In the Shadow of the Mahatma*, 210 (letter from V.S. Azariah to Isabel Whitehead, 17 April 1912, Sundkler Collection, Uppsala, Sweden).
5. Allen, USPG X622, Box 7, File N, Diary: 1, Oxford, Bodleian Library.

meeting of Indian Christians' later in February. He was given another letter upon his arrival which came from Azariah's diocese inviting him to speak on a daily basis 'for an hour or an hour-and-a-half' with interpretation, beginning on Monday and ending on Saturday'[6] at Ellore (Eluru). As he analyzed the two opportunities before him, he chose first to go to Dornakal.

Arriving at Ellore, he was greeted by George Azariah, the bishop's second son.[7] George informed him that the bishop and his elder sister, Mercy, were anticipating his arrival. Mercy had read his recent book *The Spontaneous Expansion of the Church and the Causes Which Hinder It*[8] (which Allen referred to as *Sponx*) as soon as it was published in 1927 and fully supported its thesis, including the chapter on 'Morals' which Azariah said offended him.[9] Mercy's perceptiveness on *Sponx*'s missionary theology is indicative of her theological astuteness. George Azariah took him to Bezwada's 'Church Bookhouse', where the manager said that *Sponx* had already 'sold out'.[10] Differences of opinion already existed how to implement what he called the 'voluntary clergy principle' within an organizational structure, which depended so heavily upon foreign finances.

Allen addressed the clergy conference (5-7 December) by first of all referring to his earlier paper on the Liberian preaching ministry of William Wade Harris,[11] whom Lamin Sanneh refers to as 'another charismatic figure'[12] by contrasting the 'Native movement' practising the voluntary clergy principle with the existing Western 'Mission' model of clerical professionalism. What caused him to emphasize the practice of voluntary clergy? His answer, simply stated, was the frequent availability to the sacramental life of the Church from self-supporting clergy authorized to administer. For him, this was central to 'the bond of fellowship, and stamps the Church'[13] within any culture in which people

---

6. Ibid.

7. Ibid., 2.

8. Allen, *Spontaneous Expansion* (1962).

9. Allen, Box 7, File N, Diary: 2.

10. Ibid.

11. Allen, Box 7, File N, Diary: 3. See Sanneh, *Disciples of All Nations*, 198-200; W. J. Platt, *From Fetish to Faith: The Growth of the Church in West Africa* (London: Cargate, 1935), 87; also, R. Allen, 'The Ministry of Expansion', Ch. 3, 2. These sources disclose how those affected by William W. Harris' ministry in the Gold Coast (Ghana) and the Ivory Coast in the early twentieth century called him 'the Prophet Harris'.

12. Sanneh, *Disciples of All Nations*, 189.

13. Roland Allen's letter to the editor of the *East Africa Standard*, Nairobi, Kenya (24 May 1932) USPG.

feed – on Word and Sacrament – for their spiritual health and growth. He believed any congregation that was dependent on their spiritual food to come from outside their local community was (1) not a Church and (2) functioned as a 'mission' welfare system which has not grown up yet. His Tuesday morning teaching focused on the relationship between money and evangelism. He began with these questions:

> How many paid agents had Gandhi to preach his doctrine? How many unpaid? Has any doctrine spread widely by the employment of paid agents? Do people ask "How much are you paid for preaching to us?" Is the effect of that question good? How many men would be needed to Evangelize this diocese? Is it conceivable that we can pay them?[1]

In order to contextualize these questions, he spoke of three specific forms of evangelistic work:

(1) preaching bands;
(2) an example of a conversation which he had with African students at Umtata; and
(3) how Christian outcastes evangelized the Sudras.[2]

Allen's main point was 'voluntary service breeds voluntary service: the more paid, the less [*sic*] voluntary workers'.[3] His audience responded with a consensus of approval. Bishop Azariah was pleased to see his clergy positively respond to Allen's theology of mission.

His reference to whether Gandhi had any paid agents to further his cause is indicative of the Allenic tactic designed to challenge the standard 'professionalism' generally practised since medieval times. On one hand, some of the clergy present wondered if Azariah arranged for him to discuss the issue of 'paid agents' as a precursor to an 'abolition of their salaries',[4] which they thought the bishop planned to impose. On the other hand, most of the 70-90[5] clergy who, were in attendance, agreed with Allen's thesis.

During his next session with the leadership of these churches, he again refers to the non-establishment independent 'Harris Churches' of the Ivory Coast (West Africa)[6] and explained how they seemed to be

1. Allen, Box 7, File N, Diary: 5.
2. Ibid.
3. Ibid.
4. Ibid., 6.
5. Ibid., 3.
6. Sanneh, *Disciples of All Nations*, 59, 194.

'complete in themselves' to administer the rites and successfully multiply newer churches, as, he concluded, was the apostolic practice of the early Church.[7] His diary reveals that the clergy 'all agreed'.[8] He continued to challenge their current practice, by which numerous teachers were given responsibility to oversee districts consisting of many churches evidently incomplete due to a lack of spiritual authorization – ecclesiastically and socially – even though, in practice, he said, did they not function as 'Pastors of their flocks?'[9] In his diary, he records how they were doing pastoral work in immense districts where they had limited contact with individual members: 'Are you not really bishops, without the authority of bishops?' And yet, he asks, were they not attempting to be pastors, when in reality they were evangelists who ought to go with what they 'feel all the time', in terms of their desire to evangelize the villages?[10] He immediately moved the conversation towards his missionary experiences in Yung Ching, China (1895-1903),[11] where he first began to realize the inefficient leadership training models used by various missionary societies.[12] His experience in China was pivotal for understanding this need for a paradigmatic shift from paternalism to *local* empowerment. He continued to challenge the Dornakal clergy to honestly assess their possible vocational misplacement. There were frustrated evangelists, who, being misplaced in pastoral roles, were given hope when he encouraged them with a solution to consider appointing voluntary self-supporting evangelists, who would be authorized to evangelize and teach the 'true Pastors' within villages.[13] Overall, his ecclesiological solutions were persuasive as evidenced even by Gledstone, the director of Dornakal's Training College, and, of course, Azariah.[14] Allen's missionary principle of leadership emphatically argued that, 'We must not throw away the gift of the leader to the Church which God gives us.'[15] Theological training in and of itself does 'not make leaders',[16] he pithily told them, because leaders are spiritually formed by divine charisma. He unpacked this idea of leadership for these Indian Christians by making

7. Allen, Box 7, File N, Diary: 6.

8. Ibid., 7.

9. Ibid.

10. Ibid.

11. Allen, *The Siege of the Peking Legations, Being the Diary of the Rev Roland Allen* (London: Smith, Elder, 1901) 13, 56, 59.

12. Allen, *The Spontaneous Expansion*, 1997.

13. Allen, Box 7, File N, Diary: 8.

14. Ibid.

15. Ibid., 9 (8-11 December 1927).

16. Ibid.

two points. Firstly, he reminded them how Paul appointed presbyters who had already acquired 'most of their training [in life-skills], before they became Pastors' . . . whereby their pastoral skills would come 'by being Pastors'.[1] Azariah agreed with this teaching. This emphasis – gifting and experience – permeated his missionary ecclesiology. Both Allen and Azariah were convinced that the spontaneous expansion of the Church has its origin in organic experience and precedes theological training for its leaders. Again he cited the phenomenal growth of the West African indigenous churches through Harris' ministry. Eventually the 'people wanted teaching'.[2] The Africans' emerging need for teaching stemmed from a missional spontaneity which produced home-grown teachers.[3] Secondly, he believed the most effective way to train evangelists was by 'taking men with him'[4] on itinerant mission trips. The significance of an evangelist's itinerant ministry, he argued, both within the established order and outside the existing order, served Christianity as an integral function to challenge the Church to be mission *rather than* maintenance orientated.

The next morning, he presented a series of questions about self-support. Firstly, he asked the clergy if any of the village churches within the diocese could 'give you a sympathetic hearing' if they discussed with them the issue of self-support. Secondly, he reasoned with them how, in nature, wild animals support themselves. That is to say, he continued to press the point that 'natural laws [are] the laws of God'.[5] Then he strategically enquired about the natural way for offspring to propagate itself and become self-sufficient. He asked why a religion expands, 'if those who preach it and those who hear it think that they cannot support and carry out its forms for themselves'.[6] Thirdly, he asked whether 'the Gospel [is] such a religion' and whether 'the Church [is] the holder of such a religion'.[7] This led to a series of other questions regarding whether or not the indigenous Church could financially manage its affairs. Fourthly, Allen proposed what he believed was the apostolic criteria for the establishment of the Church – Bible, Creed, Sacraments, Ministry. Thus, he argued, the Church could exist without any need for 'Church buildings, and furniture, and cassocks, and stoles, and surplices, and paid officers'.[8] Fifthly, he argued for the

---

1. Ibid.
2. Ibid.
3. Ibid.
4. Ibid.
5. Ibid., 10.
6. Ibid.
7. Ibid.
8. Ibid., 11.

legitimacy of showing charity and asked the clergy whether entertaining 'wandering Evangelists and Prophets' is more of an important form of charity than purchasing cassocks.[9] Sixthly, in anticipation of a reaction to misplaced priorities, he addressed these fears by saying that when the apostolic principle of charity takes pre-eminence in established churches, two things transpire, namely, churches multiply freely[10] and 'the needs of the diocese as a whole [are] amply supplied'.[11] Seventhly, he addressed two hindrances: (1) the hindrance of envy over certain village churches being helped while others were neglected; and (2) the premature hindrance of placing money before the establishment of churches.[12] What was his answer to these hindrances? He gave them a charge to go plant churches and 'say as little as possible about money' and then, by organic means, 'the spiritual growth of the churches' will produce its own support.[13] Although some of these points challenged the current practice in Dornakal, Azariah was not deterred from building on them.

Many of the clergy were becoming more convinced concerning the validity of Allen's apologetic for implementing the voluntary clergy principle. This caused Azariah to be 'very pleased'.[14] Indeed, it was a reversal of events, for months earlier 'they were all against it'.[15] Azariah's handwritten notes – which Allen had access to – disclosed how seven of these clergymen brainstormed ways to apply what he was teaching. Firstly, 'G. Daniel' suggested that instead of teachers overseeing the village churches, there ought to be a 'central school',[16] where teachers could teach and delegate the 'pastoral charge' in each village to the 'voluntary clergy'.[17] Secondly, 'Bunyan Joseph' suggested the separation of education from the work of the Church by incorporating retired teachers to be the 'voluntary pastorate'.[18] Thirdly, 'A. John' suggested subdividing the current pastorates and then appointing 'honorary priests'.[19] Fourthly, 'Devasahayam' emphasized how self-supporting elders ought to be in every village and authorized to administer the sacraments.

9. Ibid.
10. Ibid., 12.
11. Ibid.
12. Ibid.
13. Ibid., 13.
14. Ibid., 15.
15. Ibid.
16. Ibid.
17. Ibid., 16.
18. Ibid.
19. Ibid.

Fifthly, 'Anga Samuel' argued for a policy of abandoning the practice of removing literates from their villages and suggested that they and their educated sons ought to return to these villages as 'voluntary clergy'.[1] Sixthly, 'Elias Simon' introduced compulsory 'retirement' after specified duration of service.[2] And, seventhly, 'Andrew' (Roland Allen's interpreter) believed that officially ordained evangelists ought to be free to serve within villages for 'one or two months' in order to train a few leaders to 'read and conduct' liturgical services. He also suggested that, if the villages wanted teachers for their children, 'they' were responsible for administering those teachers' salaries.[3] This feedback from the clergy supported Azariah's 'hopeful view'. Likewise, others told Allen that he had definitely 'planted seeds which would grow'.[4]

The six-day clergy conference ended on Saturday (10 December 1927) and left Allen with the knowledge that Azariah had embraced his missionary ecclesiology. Nevertheless, he went on to say that 'we [he and Azariah] have not threshed out anything together. He is a little apt to say as other bishops say: "I do not want to argue about it, but I think . . ." and end there, as if that ended the matter'.[5] His reflection on the bishop's words was recorded in the diary:

> One thing the Bishop said interested me: "If you were to talk to the clergy in Madras or Tinnevelly diocese as you have talked here, you ought first to make sure that no one in the hall had a pistol."
> I answered, "Get me the opportunity to speak, and I will risk the pistol." I do not believe that anywhere in the world I should not find some support.[6]

Communication between Hubback and Allen[7]

Archival evidence reveals that a series of thirty-four letters originally existed between Allen and Hubback over the space of five years.[8] The

---

1. Ibid.
2. Ibid.
3. Ibid.
4. Ibid.
5. Ibid., 17.
6. Ibid., 18.
7. Allen was in Assam from 17 December 1927 to 28 February 1928.
8. Allen, USPG X622, Box 6, File L: 3-22, 24, 28-29, 36-37, 46, 49, 53, 55, 57-58, 62, 83, from 13 June 1925 – 11 June 1930. According to the archival evidence two letters are missing (1) Hubback's letter dated 13 June 1925 has a handwritten comment from Allen disclosing "I did not keep a copy of my

essence of their correspondence dealt with the principle of voluntary clergy practice and whether it would work in Assam's diocese. From one perspective, he sought to convince Hubback that this episcopally delegated authority would enhance holistic sacramental ministry, thus enhancing an overflow of laity service to their neighbouring communities. From another, while various men approached Allen during his visit to Assam to tell him they would serve as voluntary clergymen if asked by the bishop,[9] Hubback insisted that only those he 'considered fit'[10] would be allowed to serve. Firstly, Allen's missionary ecclesiology was rooted in an ecclesiology 'from below' (organic) – focusing on those chosen from within the local church – while Hubback's ecclesiological model was shaped by an autocratic emphasis 'from above' (i.e., elitist) which focused on selection from outside the indigenous churches by the established *magisterium*. This distinction between 'from below' and 'from above' was vital in Roland Allen's understanding of spontaneous expansion of the indigenous Church in India, as seen in his earlier letter to Azariah (1924).[11] And yet, for whatever reason, Hubback hesitated to embrace the voluntary clergy approach, as disclosed within the next section.

Secondly, after a month of ministering within Assam's diocese, he began to question Hubback's willingness to cultivate a context where the principle of voluntary clergy could emerge. His comments disclose a discussion he later had with Hubback which reveal how he wanted him to visit his diocese in order to see for himself 'the actual conditions'. This he hoped would lead Hubback to 'act now' by incorporating a voluntary clergy practice within the diocese. Hubback simply replied 'that he was not going to be rushed'.[12] Allen reminded him that, for the past two years, they had corresponded by letters and that he had already had plenty of time 'to think about it'. Again, Hubback responded 'that he had not thought' about it enough and if 'the people said that they wanted it and put up men whom I considered fit'[13] then he might consider it.

---

first letter written after I heard the Bishop speak at Church House.' Original letter written 10 June 1925; and (2) a letter written sometime from 19-22 June 1925. See Paton, *Reform of the Ministry* (1968) where Paton published all but five (5) of these letters, that being, 4 September 1926; 1 May 1928; 9 August 1928; 29 November 1928; and 11 June 1930.

9. Allen, Box 7, File N, Diary: 51.

10. Ibid., 55.

11. Allen's draft letter to Azariah, USPG X622, Box 6, File K: 15, 30 January 1924, Oxford, Bodleian Library.

12. Allen, Box 7, File N, Diary: 55.

13. Ibid.

The diary discloses how they both argued with each other about various questions and that Allen 'got rather tired of him'.[1] 'I find it hard to hold my peace and say nothing. He has no idea what he is doing.'[2] This overview provides the context of the tension between Allen and Hubback and also serves as a backdrop for the following details of Allen's missionary visit to Assam.[3]

Allen's visit to the Diocese of Assam
(17 December 1927 – 28 February 1928)

Allen arrived in Dibrugarh, Assam, on 17 December, where Hubback greeted him.[4] His diary records '*the Bishop* gave me an extremely warm welcome. He *talks with delightful frankness* . . . is afraid of nothing; but is face to face with very serious difficulties. In general he agrees with what I say. . . . '[5] (original emphasis). His diary entry alludes to a conversation with Hubback where he told him about his son, John Allen, and his willingness to celebrate the Eucharist for himself in the Sudan whenever ordained clergy were not available.[6] Allen submitted his thinking to Hubback concerning what he thought about this practice and whether he had given his son good advice or not. He said that Hubback approved. 'I did that,' wrote Allen, 'to see what he would say because I may possibly strike an individual case out here. Now I know what to say.'[7]

His entry focuses on the events of 19-25 December, explaining how stressed Hubback was with episcopal oversight over a large area and he noticed Hubback's pastoral frustration concerning limited sacramental services in many of the village churches. Both men engaged in conversation concerning the issue as to why many village churches were without priests but did have catechists who served for 'personal position'.[8] When Hubback reiterated his episcopal concerns about those who had fallen away from Church life, feeling that it was his fault, Allen reminded him that one 'cannot be *pastor* to the whole diocese'[9] (original emphasis). He thereby indicated the necessity for a bishop to authorize voluntary clergy in all the villages.

---

1. Ibid., 56.
2. Ibid.
3. This part of Allen's diary does *not* appear in Paton's *Reform of the Ministry*.
4. Allen, USPG X622, Box 7, File N, Diary: 18 (18 December 1927).
5. Ibid.
6. Ibid. See Hubert Allen, *Roland Allen*, 152.
7. Allen, Box 7, File N, Diary: 18.
8. Ibid., 19.
9. Ibid., 20.

He worried about the bishop overextending himself, but tried to determine whether this service was out of a perceived sense of duty or a desire to control. He was certainly discouraged after his analysis of Hubback's work and this compelled him to tell the bishop that 'he could not be pastor himself of a diocese like this and care for each individually'.[10] Hence, Allen continued, he needed to 'make up his mind either to go on as he is or to cut that out', suggesting that 'he could not afford to run hospitals and to burden himself with finance if he was to do the other'.[11] He said, 'The [Bishop] constantly barked back . . . that the present position was impossible.'[12] Hubback decided to give Allen his list of the various mission stations and districts in Dibrugarh, Sibsagar, Silchar, Chittagong, Tezpur and Shillong for analysis.[13] On 27 December, he gave him feedback, which did not please Hubback:

> Perhaps it was unwise, but I do not like going about a man's [diocese] saying things and hearing things which I dare not tell him. Anyway he was jolly sick about it. . . . Thereafter he listened with such pain that twice I stopped and suggested that we should talk of something else. He would not have that . . . and told him what Corner said about the [Bishop] hammering in my nail; he broke out, "I am not going to do anything in a hurry," and I felt that he had got on the track that I was trying to force his hand. He went on, "If I urged the . . . (Metropolitan) to appoint you [Bishop] and me go, would you accept?" and he pursued that line till I broke it off by saying, "This is silly talk." I protested that he had as a matter of fact acted as if his mind were made up when he made appeals to England for men, because the presence of the men put a great stumbling block in the way of any [voluntary clergy]. And he again got off, "I am not going to sack all my clergy." I was not quite happy about our conversation.[14]

Later, Hubback and a few other clergy intended to implement a scheme which he said enabled the bishop to 'put off the . . . [question] of ordaining to the indefinite future and yet [enabled] him to say that he is doing his utmost'.[15] The subject of church planting methods in India, Allen believed, would be helped by using John Wesley's methodology. 'I prefer Wesley. When he went and spoke something remained. When

---

10. Ibid.
11. Ibid., 21.
12. Ibid.
13. Ibid., 32–33 (26 December 1927).
14. Ibid., 34–35.
15. Ibid., 35–36 (28–31 December 1927).

he went away, [the] people . . . did *do* something'[1] (original emphasis). He liked Wesley's missiology because it was simple, apostolic and it emphasized church-planting by trans-local evangelists.[2]

A few years later, Allen noted how, in India, he had 'found these charismatic ministers outside the limits of the regularly organized congregations, in the hills of Assam',[3] whom he believed were divinely called and equipped for ministry. His missionary ecclesiology envisioned the Church's growth and development from the grassroots level – bottom up, not top down. Two things provide the context here: (1) he perceived the bishop to have 'come to the crossroads' and that he 'must begin at the bottom'[4]; (2) if the bishop chooses not to empower the laity, 'as he can',[5] then these existing churches will diminish. Allen traced the problem of missionary hegemony in Assam back to Hubback's hesitancy to think beyond the conventional methodology of Western theological training. During his itinerant ministry throughout the Assam diocesan churches, he noticed that many of the men had 'the trained intellect which sees difficulties and says that it cannot be done'.[6] He concluded that this passive attitude was an extension of Hubback's unwillingness to see ministry potential among the locals. Allen's proactive posture was to present the Gospel to 'the derelict and the simpler folk who feel the need'[7] and then gather together this community because they desire to and are not troubled with 'purely ecclesiastical objections'.[8] He concluded that he wished he could just go and investigate the diocese as a 'wandering stranger' who, as 'a private individual', might assess diocesan problems better.[9]

The next week in Bordubi Dum Duma, a woman, 'Mrs Corner',[10] approached Allen and conveyed that her husband was willing to serve as a voluntary clergyman and said 'that if the [Bishop] accepted gladly he would get his man'.[11] His diary entry recorded that 'I am certain that the [Bishop could] establish [voluntary clergy] at once, if only he

1. Ibid., 39 (2-7 January 1928).

2. Ibid.

3. Roland Allen, 'The Ministry of Expansion: the Priesthood of the Laity', USPG X622, Box 3 Number 27, Chapter 4: 1, Oxford, Bodleian Library.

4. Allen, USPG, Box 7, File N, Diary: 42.

5. Ibid., 42.

6. Ibid., 43.

7. Ibid.

8. Ibid.

9. Ibid.

10. Ibid., 50 (8-13 January 1928).

11. Ibid.

would go straight at it. And this is the dio [diocese] where it was said to be quite impossible!'[12] Another man within this diocese approached him with the same desire to serve but felt that Hubback's definition of ministerial 'fitness' emerged from a 'kind of ideal standard' which eliminated every possible indigenous candidate from serving voluntarily, and Allen concluded, the bishop 'instantly and inevitably faces that he cannot take the risk of ordaining anyone'.[13] He commented on what constituted Hubback's criterion for priestly service as: (1) a theological college education where '[he] has been through the set course'[14] or (2) that local people look for a pastor from among them 'who know his life'[15] and fits St Paul's qualification criteria for pastoral ministry.[16]

Although Hubback gave him complete access to analyze and comment on the ministerial potential within the diocesan churches, Allen was frequently frustrated with Hubback's reactions to his observations and feedback, such as, firstly, when a tea planter told him that he and other tea planters had criticized Hubback's attempt to 'try to create the want'[17] [for episcopal leadership] and that they were not interested in his leadership role among them that Hubback took offence by repeating the sentence over and over 'as if it had been a *personal* attack on him'[18] (original emphasis).

Secondly, after he asked Major Wright if the proposal on voluntary clergy from the Sadiya people was actually given to the bishop, Wright responded that Hubback 'was definitely opposed to it'.[19] Hubback's vacillation on applying the principle caused him to conclude that the bishop was unwilling to take missional risks from these villages, even though Allen observed the willingness among various indigenous men to take holy orders.

Thirdly, after speaking on two occasions to approximately 200 Christians in Chabua, Dibrugarh, his diary records that he again began to reflect on Hubback's episcopal indecisiveness. 'The [Bishop], as far as I can judge, has settled down definitely to the position, "What other and better men than I have refused to do I cannot, will not do."'[20] His

---

12. Ibid., 51.

13. Ibid., 66 (16-28 January 1928).

14. Ibid.

15. Ibid.

16. Ibid.

17. Ibid., 74-75 (29 January – 19 February 1928).

18. Ibid., 75-76.

19. Ibid., 76 (23-25 February 1928).

20. Ibid., 77.

frustration with the bishop appears to stem from the previous years of communication between both men, especially Hubback's willingness to implement the principle if a definite desire emerged within the churches. However, when Allen presented the data from his survey to the bishop, he retreated from his earlier position. He wrote:

> Please remember that before I came I told the [Bishop] that the difficulty which I had met in other lands was that when I spoke of [voluntary clergy] to men they always asked me "But will the [Bishop] do it?" and that he wrote to me that I should find no such difficulty here; the difficulty here was that the men would not serve. The moment that I proved that that was a mistake and that men did welcome the idea, he began to suggest to me that it was time for me to go home. His present attitude is one only too familiar to me: "I cannot, will not do what other wiser [Bishops] have not done."[1]

This reinforces within his mind the common problem of 'visionless' and 'inflexible' risk-taking bishops who appear to be more concerned with maintenance than mission. Hubback's leadership style, he believed, lacked episcopal dependability and missional foresight, as seen in the following extract from a proposed letter, which he decided against posting:

> Remember that he has been familiar with the suggestion [for voluntary clergy] for over two years . . . saying that he only wished men ready to serve were to be found in his diocese. Remember that when I first arrived in the diocese, he repeated to me that if the men ready to serve were found, he would ordain. Perhaps then you will understand that I was surprised when he began to raise difficulties upon difficulty till he ended in the familiar "I cannot act alone". . . . When I see these things I get sick at heart and I cannot *easily* sit down to wait till Bishops learn that it is their duty to establish the Church rather than to leave Christ's children to wander [original emphasis].[2]

Although Roland Allen chose not to send the letter, he summarized his concerns to him in person. His diary discloses the following: 'If I had known that the [Bishop would] take up this attitude, I certainly should never have come to Assam; but I am glad that I have come.'[3] Allen's analysis continued to demonstrate his frustration when he wrote this in his diary: 'I told him that he was not a [Bishop] but only a big

---

1. Ibid., 78-79.
2. Ibid.
3. Ibid.

padre trying to supplement the work done badly by little padres who, if good, ought to do the work which he does.'[4] Obviously, this was not well-received, he wrote, for the Bishop 'really was badly shaken'.[5]

He left Dibrugarh and during this time sent a letter to Hubback.[6] He then visited with Chakrabarti while travelling by boat and asked him questions about his evangelistic work. He responded that he 'had read *Sponx* [The Spontaneous Expansion of the Church] and evidently agreed with it but he said we can do nothing with English [Bishops] in the position of the Metropolitan; we can make no progress'.[7] Chakrabarti identified the impact of Bishop Hubback's hegemony when he told Allen that he could not approach the bishop with his ideas because 'if I say anything they will think that I want to be made a [Bishop]. So I can do nothing. The [Bishop] of Assam said to me: "I have been trained to obey, and I can only obey." '[8]

Conclusion

Roland Allen's *theoretical* missionary ecclesiology and Bishop Azariah's *practical* diocesan ecclesiology, on one hand, overlapped in terms of *vision* and *mission*. On the other hand, no such overlap happened between Allen and Bishop Hubback. Azariah and Allen engaged in creative ways to empower the laity for Christian service, which, for Azariah, was extremely beneficial. And yet, Hubback struggled to try to understand Allen's vision for empowering the indigenous laity.

In terms of Azariah and Allen, firstly, both men recognized their need for each other's ministry partnership – Allen's innovative ideas and Azariah's apostolic ministry – to enhance the spontaneous growth of the diocese of Dornakal. Both men agreed in their interpretation of the Pauline model for establishing churches, central to which was a particular understanding of the relationship between the *Holy Spirit* and *Order*. An example of how their complementary ministries foundationally enhanced and challenged local churches is seen in Allen's perceptive analysis of Azariah's proposed procedure to implement 'village curate priests' within the diocese. This innovation was based upon good intentions, Azariah believed. However, Allen argued against it on the grounds that these curates would not be 'fully equipped', as the proposed plan limited their responsibilities by *not* authorizing them for administration and discipline.

---

4. Ibid.

5. Ibid.

6. Ibid., 83 (28 February to 8 March 1928).

7. Ibid., 84–85.

8. Ibid.

Azariah's proposal for the forthcoming *Synod of Bishops in Calcutta*[1] was analyzed by Allen to be a chink in his diocesan leadership approach. Allen wrote this about Azariah:

> I think that he is an ass to go to the [Episcopal Synod] of India with this matter. He alone knows what he is doing and I think that "no responsibility for administration and discipline – the work of [Holy Communion] *only . . .* " is both unwise and impossible [original emphasis].[2]

Allen's 'donkey' analogy to describe Azariah's proposal is not only pithy, but informative. Although Azariah was not only his longtime friend, but also a bishop whom he respected, it still did not prevent him from questioning a procedure which he believed had ecclesial difficulties. This demonstrated how Allen was *doing theology* within an indigenous ecclesiastical framework. He argued that all priests – including 'village curate priests' – ought to be fully equipped to exercise all necessary rites pertaining to the vocation. He thought it made no sense for Azariah to stray from his original policies and procedures. His trans-local prophetic gift enhanced Azariah's *local* apostolic methodology, in a similar way that experienced consultants are called in to supplement business corporations.

Secondly, Azariah's familiarity with Allen's writings in general, and his *apostolic principles* in particular, created an environment for Church growth expansion for its clergy, laity and diocesan boundaries. Azariah assessed the willingness of his clergymen to expand their mission base for the sake of developing new dioceses. It was evident to both Azariah and Allen that Church expansion was certain since the bishop was willing to authorize the existing teachers and catechists as fully equipped priests to ordain new voluntary clergy in all the churches and to distinguish from among the pastors those who were gifted as trans-local evangelists rather than resident priests. Azariah embraced his principles wholeheartedly and sought ways to administrate diocesan adjustments wherever necessary. The time was right for Church renewal and transformation. Since 1912, and even earlier before his consecration, Susan Harper said that Azariah had already 'proved to be such a competent leader and administrator that, within a decade, the Synod extended his diocese to cover an area roughly the size of England'.[3] Allen's teachings in Dornakal reinforced

---

1. Ibid., 47–48.
2. Ibid.
3. Susan Billington Harper, *In the Shadow of the Mahatma: Bishop V.S. Azariah and the Travails of Christianity in British India*, Studies in the History of Christian Missions (Grand Rapids: Eerdmans, 2000), 132.

the 'clergy troops' to prepare for planting more missionary churches. According to Susan Harper, some years later the facts reveal:

> Under the leadership of Bishop Vedanayagam Samuel Azariah (1874–1945), Dornakal became the fastest growing Anglican diocese in South Asia. The total Anglican Christian population in the Dornakal diocese increased from 56,681 in 1912 to 225,080 in 1941, a number that exceeded the total number of Anglican converts for all of Japan, Korea and China combined. In 1936 the Dornakal Church baptized over 200 converts each week, and a total of 11,400 converts that year, and sustained this general level of accession throughout the decade.[4]

The Dornakal diocese was prophetically enriched by the teaching ministry of Roland Allen during this missionary journey in December 1927. His ministry was accepted within this diocese by Azariah, and therefore experienced greater freedom in church planting and ministry expansion. In terms of Allen's ministry in Hubback's diocese, it is easy to recognize that it had its good and bad points. His assessment of Hubback's leadership skills disclosed episcopal immaturity, especially after probing questions provoked various reactions in the bishop. The proverb states that 'as iron sharpens iron so a man sharpens the countenance of his friend',[5] which describes the unique nature of dialogue between these two men. Hubback's hesitance to put into effect certain apostolic principles and his perception that Allen lacked pastoral astuteness concerning diocesan difficulties reveals the tension between both men. It is interesting to note that eventually Hubback became the Metropolitan of India, Burma and Ceylon in 1945. Is it possible that Allen contributed to Hubback's episcopal maturity while engaging in 'iron sharpening iron' dialogue? It seems to be the case.

When comparing the episcopal leadership of Hubback with Azariah concerning character, integrity, vision and mission it is not surprising that Hubback's legacy is recorded in Church history as an *institutional* Metropolitan; whereas, Azariah – the indigenous Indian bishop – stands out as the *empowering* 'Church growth' bishop who led by example in India and is still admired today. Furthermore, the missionary ecclesiology articulated by him still has relevance to contribute to the changing structures within post-Western and non-Western Christianity today.

---

4. Susan Harper, 'The Dornakal Church on the Cultural Frontier,' (Chapter 9) in *Christians, Cultural Interactions, and India's Religious Traditions*, eds. J.M. Brown and R.E. Frykenberg, Studies in the History of Christian Missions (Grand Rapids: Eerdmans, 2002) 185 (see footnotes 3-5).

5. Proverbs 27:17.

7. Spontaneous Church Growth: Catholicity, Sacramentalism and Volunteerism[1]

Allen's Ecclesiastical Catholicity: 'E Pluribus Unum'

Allen understood the relationship between particular churches and the universal Church as follows: 'The Church is a Body, the Sacraments are the rites of the Body, and the Priesthood is in the Body. The universal is in the particular as truly as the particular is in the universal Church.'[2] First of all, the prevailing ecclesiology, according to Allen, was that there is only *one* Church which contains all particular or local Christian churches – *e pluribus unum*. This conception of the one, holy, catholic and apostolic Church, he believed, was biblically rooted in an understanding that the apostles, prophets and teachers – 'wandering evangelists'[3] – were the gifted missionaries that planted and equipped the local churches and were responsible for establishing the foundation of the Church and expressing its *Catholicity*. He argued that these 'wandering evangelists' were basically itinerant missionaries who frequently operated 'outside' the established order,[4] even though they were capable of functioning 'within' the established structure if the resident elected leadership (i.e., bishops and deacons)[5] accepted their vocation to function within their churches. Interestingly, a similar line of reasoning has recently been developed by Stuart Murray: 'Apostles are trans-local rather than local leaders, and their focus is on mission rather than maintenance.'[6] Murray's belief in

---

1. The first portion of this chapter is taken from a section of my published article 'An Analysis of Roland Allen's Missionary Ecclesiology', *Transformation*, July 2012, 29(3) 200-213 (205-209).

2. Roland Allen, *Church Quarterly Review*, 'The Priesthood of the Church', 239.

3. Roland Allen, 'The Ministry of Expansion: the Priesthood of the Laity', Ch. 3, 6 and Ch. 4, 5 (1930, unpublished). See also Allen, *Spontaneous Expansion*, 76.

4. Allen, 'The Ministry of Expansion', Ch. 3, 3.

5. Ibid., Ch. 4, 5.

6. Stuart Murray, *Church Planting: Laying Foundations* (London: Paternoster Press, 1998) 242.

apostolic ministry, i.e., his 'Ephesians 4 model of a healthy church'[7] is similar to Allen's apologia for this gift.[8] For both men, the apostolic ministry focuses on, firstly, the short-term establishment of the pioneer church (i.e., mission) with the intention to, secondly, delegate authority as soon as possible to locally authorized leaders who will govern the new church plant (i.e., maintenance). By retiring from the young church plant the apostolic ministry can remain devoted to their primary calling of mission to plant other churches. This is a critical point in understanding Allen's missionary ecclesiology.

Secondly, he believed that since the Church is one, Christian unity is inescapable. In his day, especially during the conferences in Edinburgh and Calcutta, along with the Pan-Anglican Conference at which 'Christians met and felt not simply that they must find a way out of their divisions, but that they were much more united than they expected'[9] he rejected sectarianism and embraced Christian unity. He argued against the idea of 'national' churches if it meant that these churches were somehow viewed as not united to the universal Church. That would mean, for instance, that there is no mandate for an 'American' Church or 'British' Church as separate or distinct from an 'African' Church or 'Asian' Church. Allen's arguments for 'indigenous' bishops in Africa meant that these 'African' bishops would be peers in full standing with fellow bishops in America and Britain in the *one* Church. In other words, he argued against ethnic identities that asserted patronizing characteristics and hegemonic customs, as evidenced in Paul's refutation of the Judaizers' practices outlined in his epistle to the churches of Galatia. Allen said:

> We have seen that St Paul did not set out on his missionary journeys as a solitary prophet, the teacher of a solitary individualistic religion. He was sent forth as the messenger of a Church, to bring men into fellowship with that body. His converts were not simply united one to another by bonds of convenience arising from the fact that they lived in the same place, believed the same doctrine, and thought it would be a mutual assistance to form a society. They were members one of another in virtue of their baptism. Each was united to every other Christian everywhere, by the closest of spiritual ties, communion in the one Spirit. . . . He constantly spoke of the churches of Macedonia, of Achaia, of Galatia, of Syria and Cilicia, of Asia as unities.[10]

---

7. Murray, *Church After Christendom*, 170, 189.

8. Allen, *Missionary Methods*, 85.

9. Allen, *Missionary Principles*, 82.

10. Allen, *Missionary Methods*, 126. Allen footnotes this statement by citing the

He argued that Paul and Peter emphasized the equal forsaking of ethnic identity for the sake of their common or non-culturally mediated identity in what he believed was the holy nation (I Peter 2:9-10), that being, the Church (Galatians 3:26-29). To illustrate Allen's argument here, consider the sophisticated marginalization by the Archbishop of Canterbury over the past decade of 'fellow' African bishops and archbishops, who, although they numerically represent the highest percentage of Anglican membership, were treated as though Canterbury's leadership knows best (papal or paternalistic?). This inequality among fellow Primates was addressed by the Primates of Nigeria (Nicholas Okoh) and Kenya (Eliud Wabukala), who, speaking to the Fellowship of Confessing Anglicans (FCA) in London on 6 April 2012, where delegates – representing some 55 million 'churchgoing Anglicans' from 30 countries in Africa – said:

> It seems that the Church of England is not carrying along everybody in the Communion, and that is why you can see there is a crisis; if we solve the problem, we have to change the system. . . . We have to go back to the basic principles and develop new structures while remaining firmly within the Anglican Communion. Our Communion has come of age, and it is now time that its leadership should be focused not on one person or one Church, however hallowed its history, but on the one historic faith we confess.[1]

Roland Allen could not have said it any better than what was said by these two African archbishops. Two fundamental phrases came through their statements: (a) 'we have to change the system'; and, (b) 'we have to go back to the basic principles and develop new structures'. This succinctly argues his case concerning the Church as one.

Thirdly, he spoke of the distinction and unity between the Church and churches. 'For him the Church was prior to the churches. The churches did not make up the Church, but the Church established the churches.'[2] A similar line of reasoning is found in the writings of the Anglo-Catholic, Charles Gore. Bishop Gore's contribution to the World Missionary Conference in Edinburgh (1910) had a specific impact on this catholic understanding of the Church's existence within all nations. Brian Stanley, in his discussion of Gore's influence as chairman on Commission III and

---

text: 'Macedonia: II Cor. 8.1; Achaia: Rom. 15. 26; 2 Cor. 1.1; 9.2; Galatia: Gal. 1.2; I Cor. 16.1; Syria and Cilicia: Gal. 1.21; Acts 15.23, 41; Asia: I Cor. 16.19; Judaea: I Thess. 2.14.'

1. Ed Thornton, *Church Times*, 'We should elect our chair, say Primates' and 'Wabukala: "Get back to basics"' no. 7780, London (27 April 2012): 5.

2. Allen, *Missionary Methods*, 127.

the Commission's report regarding the education of Asian indigenous leaders, draws attention to the problem of how the Church might avoid 'appearing as an "exotic" European implant while still maintaining the demands (so important to Gore) of catholicity'.[3] Gore argued for a clear Gospel contextualization by indigenous leadership whereby

> all Churches hold the same faith, use the same Scriptures, celebrate the same sacraments, and inhere in the same universal religion; each local Church should from the first have the opportunity of developing a local character and colour. . . . In this way can "the glory and honour of all nations" – that is, their own distinctive genius and its products – best be brought within the circle of the Holy City.[4]

Stanley correctly recognizes Gore's eschatological allusion to Revelation 21,[5] which discloses how representatives – 'the kings' (οἱ βασιλεῖς) – from all nations bring distinct gifts to the Holy City. Gore's catholicity presupposed an eschatological Church – the Holy City – or what the Apostle Peter called a 'holy nation' (I Peter 2:9) which consists of Christians from every ethnicity. Gore's ecclesiological belief embraced an 'interracial catholicity'.[6] Gore's contribution to the Conference seemed to generate an incipient vision of World Christianity even though only small percentages from non-Western nations were represented. The next century would tell a different narrative.

In 1920, ten years after the World Missionary Conference in Edinburgh, the Anglican Communion's encyclical letter for the Lambeth Conference of 1920, addressed 'Missionary Problems'[7] as follows:

> No community of Christians has a right to attempt to produce a replica of itself in a foreign country which it evangelizes. . . . Foreign missionaries should set before themselves one ideal, and one only: to plant the Catholic Church needs the fullness of the nations. . . . He must leave to the converts the task of finding out their national response to the revelation of God in Christ, and

3.   Brian Stanley, *International Bulletin of Missionary Research*, vol. 34, no. 1, 'From "the poor heathen" to "the glory and honour of all nations": Vocabularies of Race and Custom in Protestant Missions, 1844-1928' (January 2010): 7.

4.   Ibid., 8.

5.   Ibid.

6.   Ibid.

7.   *The Lambeth Conferences (1867-1948): The Reports of the 1920, 1930 and 1948 Conferences, with Selected Resolutions from the Conferences of 1867, 1878, 1888, 1897 and 1908* (London: SPCK, 1948), 32.

their national way of walking in the fellowship of the Saints by the help of the One Spirit. Thus will the glory of the nations be brought into the Holy City.[1]

The evidence of the Lambeth Conference of 1920 appears to point to Gore's influence earlier, especially his specific 'theme of global catholicity'[2] and eschatological understanding of the 'one' Church from all the nations which was also Allen's ecclesiology.

A Missionary Ecclesiology which Extends the Church's Sacramental Life

Allen's credo was 'I believe in "the Church"',[3] which, when it is unpacked even further meant that in 'the beginning the Church was a missionary society'.[4] Allen said:

> But there is another view of missionary work. Some people have sometimes been inclined to believe that the duty of the missionary is not to reproduce Anglican parties and English manners and forms, but rather to plant amongst the people the principles of the Gospel. Some have dreamed of native churches united to the Anglican body by unity of faith, creeds, orders, sacraments, charity, rather than by outward organization and external form; that the churches of the future shall be infant daughters of the older body, not slavish copies of a full-grown society and stereotyped institution.[5]

Hubert Allen believes that his grandfather's ecclesiology was influenced by the idea of 'handing over to people what F.D. Maurice called the "Signs of the Kingdom" – the Creed, the Bible, the Ministry and the Sacraments – and then leaving the Church's further growth to the Holy Spirit, without seeking constantly to train and to control. . . .'[6] Is there any evidence to suggest that Allen's use of Maurice's 'Signs of

---

1. Ibid.
2. Brian Stanley, *International Bulletin of Missionary Research*, 8.
3. Allen, *Missionary Methods*, 7.
4. Allen, *Spontaneous Expansion*, 117.
5. Roland Allen, letter to the editor entitled 'The Unceasing Appeal for Men for Foreign Missions' (23 July 1902). See also *The Guardian* (18 June and 25 June 1902); 'The Churches of the Future' (23 July 1902), USPG X622, Oxford, Bodleian Library.
6. Hubert Allen, *Roland Allen*, 107.

the Kingdom' comes as a direct influence of him engaging with Maurice's ideas? After examination of his archives the only evidence to make this assertion is seen in two specific emphases which both writers use: (1) as mentioned already, the Creed, the Bible, the Ministry and the Sacraments, and (2) the constant use of 'principles' in contrast to 'systems'. Both of these emphases permeate Maurice's magnum opus *The Kingdom of Christ*.[7] Apart from Maurice's assumed influence on Allen's ecclesiology it is necessary to make the following distinction. It would be inaccurate to say that Maurice's 'quasi-universalism'[8] with a liberal interpretation of eternal damnation had any impact on Allen's theological formation. Allen's belief relied upon the Pauline eschatological Day of Judgement. He said Paul

> proclaimed that the man who was "in Christ" was "in the way of salvation", "saved" and the man who was not in Christ was perishing. . . . One day I think we shall return to these stern doctrines, realizing in them a truth more profound than we now know; and then we shall preach them with conviction, and being convinced ourselves we shall convince others. "Knowing the terror of the Lord" we shall persuade men to the great advancement of the Kingdom of God.[9]

These are the words of a Biblicist, not a universalist. For example, Susan Harper argues that St Paul's influence on Roland Allen's thought encouraged Bishop Azariah and the diocese of Dornakal to embrace 'the ancient church as a model' to follow and subsequently calls Allen 'a biblical primitivist'.[10] For Allen, everything was critiqued through the grid of a traditionally apostolic and catholic understanding of the Bible, Church tradition and reason. How did Allen incorporate these principles within his missionary ecclesiology?

The Signs of the Kingdom as a Framework for Missionary Ecclesiology

After years of training indigenous leadership in North East China (1895-1903), Allen recognized the dilemma between supervising a well-intentioned institutional ministry and planting 'the principles of the Gospel' among indigenous leadership. As early as 1901 he made reference

---

7. Maurice, *Kingdom of Christ*.
8. Brian Stanley, *Bible and the Flag*, 66.
9. Allen, *Missionary Methods*, 72-74.
10. Harper, *In the Shadow of the Mahatma*, 210.

to these four 'fundamental principles concisely articulated by the Lambeth Conference of 1888'.[1] These essential principles are located throughout Allen's writings though quite often contextualized and modified for indigenous use and define his understanding for the 'core' requirements of catholic Christianity, previously discussed by Maurice but later articulated at Lambeth. Due to the significant nature for Allen's use of these fundamental principles, it is incumbent to articulate these points which are rooted within the historical context of nineteenth century Anglican thinking, originally proposed by the Protestant Episcopal Church's earlier work drawn up at *The Chicago-Lambeth Quadrilateral* (1886) and subsequently submitted at the *Lambeth Conference* (1888) as *Resolution 11*. Upon examination of the preface to the *Chicago-Lambeth Quadrilateral* the evidence points to certain core beliefs that the House of Bishops believed were the essentials of Catholic unity, that being,

> the Christian unity can be restored only by the return of all Christian communions to the principles of unity exemplified by the undivided Catholic Church during the first ages of its existence. . . . As inherent parts of this sacred deposit, and therefore as essential to the restoration of unity among the divided branches of Christendom. . . .[2]

The substance of this *Quadrilateral* was submitted to *Lambeth* (1888) and resulted in accepting the following:

(a) The Holy Scriptures of the Old and New Testaments, as "containing all things necessary to salvation" and as being the rule and ultimate standard of faith.

(b) The Apostles' Creed, as the Baptismal Symbol; and the Nicene Creed, as the sufficient statement of the Christian faith.

(c) The two Sacraments ordained by Christ Himself – Baptism and the Supper of the Lord.

(d) The Historic Episcopate, locally adapted in the methods of its administration to the varying needs of the nations and peoples called of God into the Unity of His Church.[3]

In what way did Allen's ecclesiology stem from these four principles? Firstly, upon analysis of *Missionary Methods: St Paul's or Ours?* (1912) he

---

1. Roland Allen, 'Church in Japan' in *Church Missionary Intelligencer* (April 1901), USPG X622, Box 2, File J 2: 1, 3, draft copy, Oxford, Bodleian Library.

2. *The Chicago-Lambeth Quadrilateral*, Article III, Part IV, The Reformed Episcopal Church (2002), 121.

3. *The Lambeth Conference of 1888, Resolution 11*, Article III, Part IV, Reformed Episcopal Church (2002), 122-23.

understood these principles to be rooted in Pauline ecclesiology when he said 'Four things, then, we see St Paul deemed necessary for the establishment of his churches. . . . A tradition or elementary Creed, the Sacraments of Baptism and the Holy Communion, Orders, and the Holy Scriptures.'[4] The substance of *Resolution 11* underpins Allen's thought – seen through his prescriptive Pauline lens – with few exceptions: (1) *Resolution 11* emphasizes the Apostles' and Nicene Creeds, whereas Allen specifies that only a basic 'tradition or elementary Creed' is necessary for the planting of an indigenous church; and (2) *Resolution 11* necessitated the 'undivided' Church's practice where the 'Historic Episcopate' provided oversight, whereas Allen generally makes reference to 'Orders'. However, one cannot assume a non-episcopal ecclesiology here due to Allen's references to the necessity for and responsibilities of bishops within the Church.[5]

Secondly, some years later (1927) when discussing how the missionary ought to relate with the diocesan bishop concerning a network of indigenous churches, Allen says the 'little group must be fully equipped with spiritual power and authority; and *the bishop* (emphasis mine) ought to deliver to them the Creed, the Gospel, the Sacraments and the Ministry by solemn deliberate act'.[6] In terms of differences Allen's catholic ecclesiology necessitates (1) the episcopal office to deliberately oversee the affairs of the diocesan churches as a senior father and defender of the Christian faith; (2) the bishops intentionally administer the 'Orders' even though here Allen used the interchangeable word 'Ministry' to describe the offices of deacon, presbyter and bishop; and (3) the bishops' calling for delivering to the diocesan churches what Allen here calls 'the Gospel' – not negating *Resolution 11*'s emphasis on the 'Holy Scriptures' – but rather alluding to the Anglican Ordinal. During the consecration of a bishop the archbishop prays 'Grant, we beseech thee, to this thy servant such grace, that he may evermore be ready to spread abroad thy *Gospel*, the glad tidings of reconciliation with thee.'[7] (Emphasis mine). Here is Anglican order describing the bishop's responsibility to spread the 'Gospel'.

---

4. Allen, *Missionary Methods*, 107.

5. Cf. Allen's letter to the Bishop of Central Tanganyika, Box 6, letter 137A (10 June 1930); also, Allen, 'The Work of the Missionary in Preparing the Way for Independent Native Churches' for the *Federation of Junior Clergy Missionary Associations*, John Rylands Library, Manchester, (November 1903), USPG X622, Oxford, Bodleian Library.

6. Allen, *Spontaneous Expansion of the Church*, 147.

7. *The Book of Common Prayer*, 1662, Cambridge: Cambridge University Press (2002), 593.

Allen's ecclesiology maintains a distinct episcopal order which assumed the bishop's pastoral nature of service and guardianship. According to Allen this concept for enormous diocesan jurisdictions is contrary to early Church practice. For example, he said, 'When Ignatius wrote "Do nothing without the bishop," the bishop was not a remote person who might, or might not, be able to visit the place once or twice in his lifetime.'[1] The 'professionalism' in episcopacy which negates the relational 'spiritual' shepherding presence and interaction with 'the flock', Allen argued, is an abdication of the nature of the episcopal office.

'Volunteerism within Islam and Christianity' (1920)

In 1920 Roland Allen examined the growth of Islam within the Sudan and concluded that its spontaneous growth was due to what he thought was an interesting strategy: *volunteerism*. In an article entitled 'Islam and Christianity in the Sudan' he wrote:

> Islam is advancing in the Sudan in some parts rapidly, in others more slowly, and it is advancing by peaceful propaganda. It is this peaceful penetration which Christian missions must meet . . . Islam is advancing more rapidly than Christianity, and if that advance is to be checked it must be understood.[2]

Allen observed how Muslims in the Sudan implemented a practice of volunteerism, in terms of the extension of their faith. This influenced him to address the issue within this article by setting out to compare and contrast Diedrich Westermann's[3] portrayal of Islam's growth in light of Edward Wilmot Blyden's theory, who, as an African Christian, more correctly disclosed the real causes of its advancement.[4] Firstly, Allen interacts with some basic questions posed by these men concerning the growth of Islam in the Sudan and asks the question: 'What is there in Islam which so powerfully attracts the African? Is it something which Christianity cannot or will not offer?'[5] Secondly, he argued how Blyden believed 'that Islam offered the African social advancement', whereas

1. Allen, 'The Priesthood of the Church' *Church Quarterly Review* (January 1933): 235.
2. Roland Allen, 'Islam and Christianity in the Sudan' *International Review of Missions*, vol. 9, (1920): 531-543 (531).
3. Diedrich Hermann Westermann, *International Review of Missions* (1912).
4. Edward Wilmot Blyden, *Christianity, Islam and the Negro Race* (London: W.B. Whittingham, 1887).
5. Allen, 'Islam and Christianity', 532.

Westermann declared that 'Islam advances because it makes no moral demand'.[6] Thirdly, he does point out how Westermann did recognize that when an African becomes a Muslim he is acknowledged to be 'a member of a higher social class' which Allen does not disagree with.[7] Allen does agree with Blyden's understanding how Islam advanced due to the way its faith was promoted through *volunteerism*, especially by Muslim 'missionary' traders.[8] Of course, this voluntary principle approach reaffirmed Allen's belief in the universality of volunteerism and the apostolic principle of indigenous ministry. Blyden's Christian world view contained the principles of self-reliance and dignity for the African but he observed that among his contemporaries the Muslims were more successful than the Christians in advancing their faith.

> There was among the native Christians none of that natural progress, that independence and self-respect that native learning and original thought, that free natural expansion, which he so much admired in the Mohammedans. Missionaries, he said, made imitators rather than disciples. And he said all this not only repeatedly, but rather bitterly; and missionaries who in their hearts knew that they were doing their utmost to uplift the natives resented it, and refused to listen to him.[9]

For the African, Islam enabled them to develop a level of self-reliance and self-respect. Allen believed that the Church needed to *stop enabling* their African converts through its mission station system. The dependency model produced enslavement to missional inactivity and thus hindered the Church's advancement towards indigenous 'dignity, self-respect and self-reliance'.[10] Allen concludes by encouraging a 'free native church conscious of its royal prerogatives [which] might beat back Islam: a dependent one cannot . . . [so] that they can advance the Church by their own unaided efforts'.[11]

'Deconstructive Devolution' (1927)

Advocates of the 'three self' indigenous model generally practise some level of devolution when it comes to transferring the ministry over to the

---

6. Ibid., 537.

7. Ibid., 532.

8. Ibid., 533.

9. Ibid., 532, 538-39.

10. Ibid., 532.

11. Ibid., 541-43.

younger faith communities. This process frequently views the younger churches as 'daughter' churches versus 'sister' churches. On one hand, a 'daughter' church makes sense if it stemmed from a 'mother' diocesan church – the cathedral – where the bishop's seat is located. On the other hand, among the non-episcopal 'independent' churches, a change in terminology is in order when referring to the new churches as 'sister' churches. However, is there a time when a diocesan 'daughter' church matures to the status of 'sister' church to the diocesan cathedral? This question begs a response by Allen and he did address this idea in his article 'Devolution and its Real Significance'.[1]

The article begins in typical Allenic style with him seeking clarity to define the term 'devolution' due to its frequent use by 'missionary statesmen' and within 'missionary magazine articles'.[2] He compares, firstly, how the terminology of 'devolution' and 'mission agent' were commonly used by missionaries 'without thinking what it really meant'.[3] He argued that the practice of employing mission agents – which he predicted would eventually 'disappear'[4] – implicitly assumed the mission station to be 'the Master for whom they work',[5] and, as the indigenous agents were entrusted with more managerial responsibilities, the missionaries decided that the implementation of the process of 'devolution' could placate any potential rebellion. His thinking was probably influenced by John Nevius' comments on the 'injurious effects of the paid-agent system' as it was practised in China where criticisms emerged among the Chinese to their 'countrymen' who now, as confessing Christians, were 'propagating a foreign religion' which they saw to be 'a mercenary one'.[6] He believed this 'creation of a class' – mission agents – had no Pauline precedent for its practice and that the 'devolution' process had roots in secular government and not apostolic order.[7] Robert Dann states that both Watchman Nee (China) and Bakht Singh (India) were 'convinced that by paying local believers to serve their Lord, the denominational missions had started out on the wrong

---

1. Roland Allen's 'Devolution' and Alexander McLeish's 'The Real Significance of "Devolution"' Repr. in *World Dominion*, 'Devolution and Its Real Significance' (London: World Dominion Press, April 1927): 5-31.

2. Ibid., 5.

3. Ibid.

4. Ibid., 6.

5. Ibid., 5.

6. John Nevius, *The Planting and Development of Missionary Churches* (1st edition [1886] in Shanghai, China. Repr., Hancock: Monadnock Press, 2003), 27.

7. Allen, 'Devolution,' 6.

foot'.[8] In China, Watchman Nee believed and taught that the local elders were to be unpaid and that evangelists should be self-supportive.[9] John Herman Bavinck agreed with Allen and Nevius by arguing how the missions needed to 'be on guard against playing Santa Claus'.[10] Bavinck goes on to say that Allen stressed how 'Paul had no money to pay co-workers' but instead looked for 'voluntary help . . . to proclaim the name of Jesus spontaneously'.[11] Allen's definition for devolution referred to any authoritative body which possesses power to choose the timeline when there will be transfer of power and 'we begin by leaving portions or details of duties to subordinate Committees'.[12] He did not have a problem with secular governments acting in this way, but he did argue that this was not a Pauline model for church-planting practice. The rejection of this idea of paid 'mission agents' was also argued in *Rethinking Missions*[13] where ecclesiastical leaders started to develop remedial measures by releasing 'a larger burden of church ministry on unpaid lay workers',[14] for the purpose of encouraging indigenous self-support.

Secondly, devolution, according to Allen, 'is primarily imperialistic',[15] as the 'economist Adam Smith' understood 'this kind of imperial devolution'.[16] He regarded it legitimate that secular government would possess the authority to practise devolution with its subjects, but on the contrary, he argued that the Church possessed a different kind of authority. His missionary ecclesiology was *not* imperialistic. And, in

---

8. Robert Bernard Dann, *Father of Faith Missions: The Life and Times of Anthony Norris Groves* (Milton Keynes: Authentic Media, 2004), 464; see Daniel Smith, *Bakht Singh of India, a Prophet of God* (Washington: International Students Press, 1959); also, T.E. Koshy, *Brother Bakht Singh of India: An Account of 20th Century Apostolic Revival* (Secunderabad, Andhra Pradesh, India: OM Books, 2003) and Watchman Nee, *Concerning Our Missions* (1939. Repr. as *The Normal Christian Church Life*, Anaheim: Living Stream Ministry, 1980), 40, 109-110.

9. Watchman Nee, *The Normal Christian Church Life*, 171.

10. John Herman Bavinck, *An Introduction to the Science of Missions* (Grand Rapids: Baker Book House, 1961), 212.

11. Bavinck, *Science of Missions*, 212-13.

12. Allen, 'Devolution', 7.

13. William Ernest Hocking, Chairman of The Commission of Appraisal, *Re-Thinking Missions: A Laymen's Inquiry After One Hundred Years* (New York and London: Harper & Brothers Publishers, 1932).

14. Ibid., 89.

15. Roland Allen 'Devolution,' *World Dominion* (April 1927), 7.

16. Niall Ferguson, *Empire: The Rise and Demise of the British World Order and the Lessons for Global Power* (New York: Basic Books, 2004), 74-75.

terms of mission stations he believed they could not officially practise devolution since they did not possess any ecclesiastical authority in the first place. Mission stations viewed their ministry as if 'it is a conception of the Church as a Committee' and he intensely disagreed with this idea.[1] For him, the Church is *not* a committee but rather a united body of members (local and universal) with appointed officers who are 'first' among 'equals' – *not* elitist autocrats but 'servant leaders' – within what Stuart Murray calls 'a harmonious church'.[2]

Thirdly, Allen raised three questions that he believed were necessary to ask when addressing the issue of mission devolution: (1) 'whether a mission has properly any authority of which it can devolve; (2) what is the nature of the authority which it claims; [and] (3) what is the conception of the Church implied in the claim?'[3] His argument for the first question contends that the generally accepted mission policy – 'devolution in our sense of the word'[4] – was sadly lacking any New Testament basis for its practice. He argued that when Paul established the Church he 'devolved' all authority and powers to it immediately 'by a spiritual act' that being, by the apostolic ordination practice of 'the laying on of hands with prayer'.[5] He thought that the mission societies' practice of mission devolution had to do with 'grants of money' and totally misunderstood how Paul's devolutionary method of ordination within the Church – not the mission station – was applied before his departure and had nothing to do with grant money.[6] The imposition of delayed devolution within the mission system was not only hegemonic to the core, but it also, he concluded, lacked ecclesiastical authority to devolve.[7] Why? The apostolic order for planting the Church,[8] according to Allen's hermeneutic of Pauline ecclesiological practice, was summarized by him saying: 'When St Paul had once established a Church there was nothing left to devolve.'[9]

In terms of the second question concerning the 'nature of the authority' that foreign missions claim, his analysis discloses their

1. Allen, 'Devolution,' 14.

2. Stuart Murray, *Church After Christendom* (Milton Keynes: Paternoster Press, 2008), 189.

3. Allen, 'Devolution,' 8.

4. Ibid.

5. Ibid., 9.

6. Ibid., 8-9.

7. Ibid.

8. See Lesslie Newbigin, *The Gospel in a Pluralist Society* (London: SPCK, 2000), 146-47.

9. Allen, 'Devolution', 9.

practice of devolution to be a misplaced focus on the 'control of funds . . . between Committees', delegation of evangelistic responsibilities and the transference of 'mission' churches to 'the native church'. Firstly, the mission's management of the finances was conducted by committees and the mission converts were mentored in the foreigners' administrative image. He said this procedure confused 'the Church with a financial Committee' and that the practice 'is not far from blasphemy'.[10] His concern was that the indigenous converts were getting the wrong impression as to the nature of the Church and that there was a misplaced emphasis on money: 'The Church is not the Temple of Mammon, but of the Holy Ghost.'[11] This practice only caused him more frustration with the mission station system. However, not everyone viewed this as a problem the way he did. After David Livingstone's expedition in Africa, Scotland's established Church and Free Church began to get involved in mission. James Stewart and others believed 'the mission stations from the 1870s were developed essentially as secure, self-supporting and independent settlements'.[12] According to Stewart these settlements were practical expressions of industrialized progress.[13] Although Allen would agree that these mission stations were secure settlements he still argued that they had misplaced priorities concerning the indigenization 'of a spiritual Church'.[14] Oborji describes McGavran's view of this system as that which 'arrests the development of wider mission'.[15]

Finally, the third question emphasizes what is the mission's idea of the Church in light of devolution. He categorically says 'without a doubt it is a conception of the Church as a Committee'.[16] Most articles in his day that dealt with the indigenization of the Church and devolution said that 'the idea of a Committee is always prominent . . . and is spoken of as the Church for the purposes of devolution'.[17] But this does not constitute what the Church is, he argued, because it elevates the committee system as an elitist group, who, quite often does not represent the members of the laity. This system sets up the potential for a revolt similar to 'what has happened in India', he said, where the 'educated Indians want to hold

---

10. Ibid., 10–11.

11. Ibid., 11.

12. Andrew Porter, *Religion versus empire?*, 269.

13. Ibid.

14. Allen, 'Devolution', 13.

15. Oborji, *Concepts of Mission*, 95; McGavran, *Understanding Church Growth*, 373–86.

16. Allen 'Devolution', 14.

17. Ibid., 15.

the strings by which all mission work and all mission institutions are controlled'.[1] This article ends by pointing out 'two serious defects' of devolution: (1) that it 'proclaims' how the 'mission is first lord over the Church . . . with authority to give or to withhold the ordinary rights of the Christians at its will';[2] and (2) that it 'tries to make a coping stone of the Church what Christ made a foundation'.[3] His forthrightness continued when he declared that this system 'sets up a Committee in the place of Christ' and without realizing it 'creates a new prelacy of Committees in the place of the old prelacy of autocratic clergy . . . which Christ never gave to it'.[4] It is obvious that Allen had issues with committees, especially when it related to how it was being used in a paternalistic context. At the end of the day, devolution, he says, 'shouts aloud the lesson of foreign domination broken down'.[5]

'The Spontaneous Expansion of the Church and the Causes which Hinder it' (1927)[6]

The focus of this section sets out to highlight significant apostolic principles within Allen's second most well-known book – *The Spontaneous Expansion of the Church*. The first chapter lays the foundation for defining, defending and equipping indigenous churches 'in the soil from the very first seeds planted'.[7] He argues that the Church's 'spontaneous expansion must be free' from the control of domineering foreign bishops and 'superintending missionaries' who are unwilling to ordain indigenous leadership.[8] Then he goes on to explain the nature and 'charm' of spontaneous expansion when the Church's life emanates naturally from faith and practice, even if it appears unorganized and disorderly. He believed that the Church's charisma through a 'native episcopate'[9] actually opens the door for expansion more than its dependency on foreign aid. The thesis continues by contrasting the difference between the way Christ trained his disciples in three years and then wonders why the general practice of foreign missionaries took 'more than two

1. Ibid., 16.
2. Ibid., 16-17.
3. Ibid., 17.
4. Ibid.
5. Ibid.
6. Allen, *Spontaneous Expansion*, 1997 (first published 1927).
7. Ibid., 2.
8. Ibid., 2-5.
9. Ibid., 16.

or three generations' to train its indigenous leaders.[10] This reasoning penetrated into the heart of the problem of paternalistic missionaries who had difficulty accepting the fact that they are not indispensable after authorizing and equipping the indigenous churches. He believed that empowering local leadership, as previously stated, was the Pauline practice for Church expansion.[11] His argument essentially distinguishes between the apostolic way to 'contend for the faith which was once for all delivered to the saints' (Jude 3) and of 'an imperial attitude' which had set 'a standard' that must be maintained by 'the exercise of authority'.[12] He understood this difference as two opposing systems: (1) the system of 'Christianity' which generates gospel ministry to reveal a person – Christ; and (2) a system of 'fear for the doctrine' being misrepresented by the converts – 'the besetting sin of Western people' – who do not want to lose 'control and government'[13] of their missions.

Later, he addresses 'two ways of maintaining a standard of morals': (1) to focus on the ideal presented to us in Christ before 'ourselves and our converts'; and (2) to 'define a standard' and then enforce 'that definition as a law'.[14] In one sense, he argues that the New Testament does not legislate morality. He states that the 'only Christian standard' is 'Thou shalt love the Lord thy God with all thy heart, and with all thy soul and with all thy mind and with all thy strength, and thy neighbour as thyself' (Matthew 22:37, 39).[15] Hans Wolfgang Metzner observed that it took German missiologists four years after its publication to finally critique Allen's work.[16] Metzner commented that Wilhelm Oehler's review (1931) declined to offer any negative criticisms, but Oehler did focus on Allen's significant and courageous contributions[17] to contemporary mission thought concerning issues of African polygamous practices.[18]

---

10. Ibid., 21–22.

11. Ibid., 24–25.

12. Ibid., 44–45.

13. Ibid., 43–59.

14. Ibid., 60.

15. Ibid., 68.

16. Hans Wolfgang Metzner, *Roland Allen Sein Leben und Werk: Kritischer Beitrag zum Verstandnis von Mission und Kirche*, Gutersloh: Gutersloher Verlagshaus Gerd Mohn (1970), 108.

17. Roland Allen, 'Kenya Contrasts: The Missions and Polygamy', letter to the editor, *East African Standard* (1 May 1936).

18. Wilhelm Oehler, 'Rezension von The Spontaneous Expansion of the Church and the Causes Which Hinder It, *Evangelisches Missions-Magazin*, 75 (1931): 383–85, ' . . . auch nicht vor der schwierigsten Frage unserer Missionstheorie

Further on in chapter six, entitled 'Civilization and Enlightenment', he does *not* take issue with whether or not the indigenous converts should or should not abandon 'their native customs'.[1] He believed the 'real problem is not whether we should encourage or discourage any particular custom, but whether we should be the judges of what is fitting; not whether we should retain or revive this or that native custom, but whether we should touch these things directly at all'.[2] Allen expresses a somewhat 'libertarian' position that each individual should take personal responsibility to govern their own behaviour and lifestyle without outward coercion. He goes on to say: 'We must begin with positive teaching, not with negative prohibitions, and be content to wait and to watch . . . as the Spirit of Christ gradually teaches them to transform what today is heathen, and tomorrow, purged of its vice, will appear as a Christian custom. . . .'[3] This is exactly the line of argument he takes when missionaries were legislating against polygamy in their African missions and churches. Allen referred to these actions as similar to the problems Paul confronted with the Judaizers. He engaged with this issue through the press by writing in the *East African Standard*:

> An African has answered Archdeacon Owen. That is a sign. Native Christians are criticizing missionaries; they are asking questions which must be answered. Can Archdeacon Owen answer the questions? (3) Is Christ revealed to us in the Gospels the kind of person who refused to accept and help men who appealed to Him because they had bad habits which they did not and could not see to be bad at all? Is the casting off of wives the way of approach which Christ would approve? (4) Did not the gift of His Holy Spirit gradually teach Christians that things which they at first thought good were not good? And is not that the way of the Spirit? (5) Did the missionaries who first came to the West of Europe refuse to baptize polygamists? Do we deny that Charlemagne was a Christian because he had more than one wife?[4]

zuruckschreckt, der afrikanischen Polygamie'; Hans Wolfgang Metzner, *Roland Allen Sein Leben und Werk: Kritischer Beitrag zum Verstandnis von Mission und Kirche*, Gutersloh: Gutersloher Verlagshaus Gerd Mohn (1970): 108; Allen, *Spontaneous Expansion*, 66-67.

1. Allen, *Spontaneous Expansion*, 78-79.
2. Ibid., 78-79.
3. Ibid., 79.
4. Roland Allen, 'Kenya Contrasts: The Missions and Polygamy', letter to the editor, *East African Standard* (1 May 1936), USPG X622, Box 8: 25, Oxford, Bodleian Library.

Allen's missiology was to be 'fishers of men' not 'cleaners' of men. Therefore, his missionary ecclesiology inculcated to evangelize the unconverted, bring them to faith in Christ, baptize them and trust that the Holy Spirit would enlighten their understanding as they were received into the Church, in which they would gradually hear and read the Bible, learn the creeds, receive the sacramental food and obtain instruction from the ministerial leadership. His theology was deeply rooted in the pneumatological dynamic that empowers Christians towards sanctification.

He revisits this issue of 'social reform' but what stands out in this section is the clarity he expresses as to why he thought the way he did. Retrospectively he argues that all attempts to uplift the societal condition after many years of activities have already evidenced that 'the great mass of those who have used them have not drawn nearer to the Church or to Christ'.[5] He chose not to question the motives behind the 'Christian men with the most serious Christian intention' who were 'thrown into this social work presupposed',[6] but rather he questioned whether the essence of the Gospel was being communicated by bringing transformed lives into the faith community. This concerned Allen. In the section entitled 'Missionary Organization', he presents his *apologia*: (1) that every Christian is a missionary; and (2) that the Church is a missionary body.[7] All throughout this section of *The Spontaneous Expansion of the Church* he unpacks what this means.

Another important issue that he addressed stemmed from this statement: 'mission implies movement, station implies stopping'.[8] This distinction is critical to understanding his missionary ecclesiology. And, it is this missiological emphasis that continued to permeate his thinking the rest of his life. This chapter now shifts from 'Missionary Organization' to an emphasis on the Church's organization.[9] He commenced with this understanding that 'in the beginning the Church was a missionary society'.[10] Then he questions the validity of mission societies that function outside the authority of appointed ecclesiastical representatives, that being, the episcopate. For him this type of separation from episcopal leadership is likened to what he calls a 'divorce' for he says 'the organization of missionary societies was permitted for the hardness of our hearts, because we had lost the power to appreciate and to use the divine organization of the Church

---

5. Allen, *Spontaneous Expansion*, 81.

6. Ibid.

7. Ibid., 96–116.

8. Ibid., 105.

9. Ibid., 117–142.

10. Ibid., 117.

in its simplicity for the purpose for which it was first created'.[1] Obviously, his Anglo-Catholic belief that bishops serve a necessary function within the life of the Church, not for political or hegemonic reasons, as evidenced within aspects of the Christendom model, but for 'pastoral' purposes of caring, guiding and protecting. Rather his ecclesiological apologia argues for the practice of the Church as 'family'[2] – what Francis Oborji calls 'the universal church-family'[3] – in contrast to 'councils' who 'advance on the pure autocracy of foreign missionaries' and who function by making critical decisions in committee. He argues that the current policies of the mission societies 'further misled the native Christians' from understanding the 'true character of church organization'.[4]

In the concluding chapter entitled 'The Way of Spontaneous Expansion' he begins, firstly, with a rehearsal of the earlier emphasis on how the early Church expanded because of 'the spontaneous activity of individuals' who shared their 'new-found joy' of conversion to their friends, family and strangers.[5] Secondly, he unpacks the significant influence of 'a charismatic ministry' within the Church which he believed is 'rooted as it is in a universal instinct, and in a Grace of the Holy Spirit given to all Christians, is not peculiar to any one age or race'.[6] Next he argues for the 'inalienable rights' of baptized Christians.[7] He begins with a question: 'What are those rights?' and then states that they are: (1) the 'right to live as Christians in an organized Christian Church where the sacraments of Christ are observed';[8] (2) the 'right to obey Christ's commands, and to receive His Grace';[9] and (3) the 'right to be properly organized with their own proper ministers'.[10] These he said are 'the inalienable rights of Christians' and that once baptized they ought to have access to the Church as individuals 'fully equipped with spiritual power and authority . . . the bishop ought to deliver to them the Creed, the Gospel, the Sacraments and the Ministry by solemn and deliberate act'.[11] Then he unpacks what this all means according

---

1. Ibid., 117.
2. Unpublished (1943) work by Roland Allen 'The Family Rite', USPG, Rhodes House, Oxford University Library Services, Box 7.
3. Oborji, *Concepts of Mission*, 97.
4. Allen, *Spontaneous Expansion*, 122.
5. Ibid., 143.
6. Ibid., 144–45.
7. Ibid., 146–47.
8. Ibid., 147.
9. Ibid.
10. Ibid.
11. Ibid.

to his understanding of a framework of apostolicity and catholicity. At the conclusion he reaffirms the need to establish the 'organization of a little church'. [12] These 'little churches', he believed, are to be fully capable of producing leadership of their own within the context of smaller diocesan units which could then expand spontaneously. [13] Basically, when it comes to diocesan territorial size – less is more.

'Jerusalem: A Critical Review of "The World Mission of Christianity"' (1928)

By 1928, Roland Allen had a reputation for annoying bishops and mission societies because in his estimation they had not always critically analyzed their missionary methods and plans of action. When the International Missionary Council Conference met in Jerusalem in 1928, he had deep concerns about the concluding report from this conference. He responded by writing 'Jerusalem: A Critical Review of "The World Mission of Christianity"'. [14] As a methods analyst, he immediately criticized what he believed was John R. Mott's extravagant language in the *Foreword* of the report, which claimed to have God-given mandates whereby Allen argued that he 'claims . . . that the findings are "discerning, timely and prophetic" and that they represent the united judgement of a "truly creative gathering . . . which it became possible to receive fresh mandates from the ever-creative God" '. [15] His immediate retort: 'What exactly does that mean?' [16] He believed that Mott's comments and the report's wording disclosed the 'social gospel' doctrinal ethos:

> at the back of all this undoubtedly a doctrine of "the Kingdom" . . . which occurs repeatedly in this volume, with which some of us profoundly disagree . . . that the idea of "the Kingdom" here accepted is that popular modern idea that Christ's Kingdom comes here upon earth by the gradual improvement of human social arrangements. . . . [17]

---

12. Ibid., 156.

13. Ibid.

14. Roland Allen, 'Jerusalem: A Critical Review of "The World Mission of Christianity"' (London: World Dominion Press, 1928), 38 pages.

15. Ibid., 7. See John R. Mott, *The Decisive Hour of Christian Mission* (New York: Educational Department Board of Foreign Missions of the Presbyterian Church in the USA, 1910), 230-36.

16. Ibid.

17. Ibid., 11.

Allen was chagrinned. Firstly, his theology of the kingdom conveyed a belief in, the already and the not yet,[1] a distinction that this kingdom advances *not* through 'social arrangements' but through the pneumatological impetus which accompanies the evangelistic mission through the Church and its sacraments. Secondly, his eschatological view implies a contrast between a 'liberal' postmillennial – social gospel – emphasis from a 'classical' postmillennial – missionary Spirit[2] – emphasis of that day.[3] His books, pamphlets, articles and sermons disclose an eschatological understanding and belief in the *present* reality of the kingdom of God, not only a futuristic view. His belief emphasized Christ's words that 'the Kingdom cometh not with observation . . . the Kingdom of God is within you. . . . My Kingdom is not of this world'.[4] Fundamentally he argued that all Christians are missionaries called to permeate every area of life *not* because of an innate ability to 'bring in the Kingdom by influencing Governments to take action which will tend towards social improvements',[5] but rather that their missional task was pneumatologically ordained, driven and sustained. The promoters for the 'social gospel', he believed, placed too much emphasis on influencing 'non-Christian Governments' to develop some type of socio-religious civilization through the means of 'social workers and welfare associations' in order 'to improve conditions' which he said 'are suggested throughout this report'.[6] Robert Dann similarly argues that this was a misplaced emphasis on 'technological progress and social justice [and] should not be confused with faith in Christ'.[7]

For Allen, this was not the original missionary call either by Christ, the Church mission societies, or their donors who sent them in the first

1. Roland Allen's sermons and teaching notes support this view: 'The [Christian] life [is] a life expectant of [the] 2nd Advent', sermon for Trinity 20, evensong second lesson, Luke 12:35-36 (16 October), USPG X622, Box 5; 'Acts Analysis', teaching notes on Acts 20:13-28, 'preaching the *kingdom*', USPG X622, Box 3: 29; 'I Corinthians' (teaching notes on I Corinthians 3:21 'the whole world order is subordinated to [Christians]'), USPG X622, Box 3, Oxford, Bodleian Library.

2. Allen, *Missionary Principles*, 2006.

3. Iain Murray, *The Puritan Hope: Revival and the Interpretation of Prophecy* (Edinburgh: Banner of Truth Trust, 1971), Introduction, 129-83; Milton S. Terry, *Biblical Hermeneutics* (New York: Eaton & Mains, 1890), 382.

4. Allen, 'Jerusalem: A Critical Review', 12.

5. Ibid., 11.

6. Ibid.

7. Robert Bernard Dann, *The Primitivist Missiology of Anthony Norris Groves: a radical influence on nineteenth-century Protestant mission* (Chester: Tamarisk Books/Oxford: Trafford Publishing, 2007), 227.

place. On one hand, throughout this review he recognizes that this type of alliance with non-Christian governments was a 'purely rational' approach for improving the human condition, and yet, according to his analysis he tersely concluded that 'Nationalism is presented in place of the Holy Ghost'.[8] On the other hand, J.H. Oldham and Luther A. Weigle, in their paper on 'Religious Education' for the Jerusalem Meeting Report (1928)[9] upheld the significance of a pneumatological emphasis in their educational work by stating '[the] reality of the presence and work of the Holy Spirit is the ground of our confidence in undertaking the task of Christian education [and] He works through us, but the results are not from us but from Him. . . .'[10] Likewise, John Mott's earlier work *The Decisive Hour of Christian Missions* (1910) suggests that 'three great laws of God' function within 'mission fields' as: (1) 'the law of sowing and reaping' which is a 'Kingdom' principle; (2) 'the law of intercession' where the focus on prayer significantly extends 'the limits of Christ's Kingdom among the peoples who have not known Him': and (3) 'the law of sacrifice' which Mott believed centred on 'the deepest principle underlying the spread of His Kingdom', i.e. Christ's words concerning 'a grain of wheat' dying but eventually bearing 'much fruit' (John 12:24).[11] Although, on one hand, Allen's concerns about Mott's theology of the kingdom of God through human initiative is to misrepresent Mott's earlier hermeneutic.[12] On the other hand, Mott's understanding of 'Nationalism' in the context of the Jerusalem Conference (1928) appears to represent a different theological emphasis. Firstly, Mott spoke of nationalism in the sense that 'corporate life and responsibility was being created by "world forces"'.[13] Allen believed this made no sense: 'Put words like that into any of the epistles of St Paul, and see what happens,' he said, because what 'he wrote was built upon a very different foundation'.[14] Of course it was not that he disbelieved in a statist

---

8. Ibid., 11, 23.

9. J.H. Oldham and Luther A. Weigle, *Religious Education*, Volume II, 'Report of the Jerusalem Meeting of the International Missionary Council March 24th – April 8th', 1928, 'Preliminary Paper for the Council' (London, Melbourne, Cape Town, Bombay, Shanghai, Humphrey Milford: Oxford University Press, October 1928).

10. Ibid., 57-58.

11. John R. Mott, *The Decisive Hour of Christian Mission* (New York: Educational Department Board of Foreign Missions of the Presbyterian Church in the USA, 1910), 231-32.

12. Ibid., 231-32.

13. Allen, 'Jerusalem: A Critical Review', 23.

14. Ibid.

right to govern the affairs of its people, but rather he meant that 'world forces' should be limited. And then, when it comes to the government of the local church it ought to be understood that the local body should govern its own affairs. Rather he promoted a 'separation' of Church and State in the sense that each institution had its own sphere of authority to govern its duly appointed affairs. But to say that 'we rejoice that the world forces operating in recent years have created in these younger Churches a new sense of corporate life and responsibility' is, according to Allen, to confuse the matter.[1] That said, for whatever reason, he chose not to commend a significant theme at Jerusalem 1928, that is, in what Howard Hopkins recognized: 'Jerusalem also produced a fresh definition of a living and indigenous church that marked a real shift from mission-centred to church-centred thinking'[2] which categorically ought to have encouraged Allen. Also, Henrik Kraemer spoke of the conference as demonstrating 'a quite different atmosphere' than Edinburgh 1910, saying that 'the mood is more introspective and observant than strategical' with a decline in 'fervour of missionary interest'.[3] Kraemer discussed how the introspectiveness this time created realistic expectations to be distinguished from the earlier 'natural Western self-confidence' as evidenced at Edinburgh.[4] That said, he continued to explain the 'unequivocal disavowal at Jerusalem of all spiritual imperialism' as evidence of 'the clearest symptoms of this change' and explained how the 'laymen's report' in time would disclose this new theological attitude to 'rethink missions', which, on one hand, revealed 'sincere devotion to the missionary cause, but, on the other exposed 'a very weak sense of apostolic consciousness'.[5]

Secondly, he asks whether the report's definition of 'younger Churches' refers to 'local Churches' or was it referring to some type of organizational body such as 'Provincial or National Churches, or bodies like the National Christian Councils of India or of China?'[6] He splits ecclesiological hairs with this question. Why? He believed the New Testament authors documented 'only two uses of the word Church, the local Churches and the Church universal'.[7] He then digressed by arguing against any

---

1. Ibid.; see Allen's response to page 32 of the report.
2. C. Howard Hopkins, *John R. Mott: 1865-1955, A Biography* (Grand Rapids: Eerdmans, 1979), 660.
3. Henrik Kraemer, *The Christian Message in a Non-Christian World* (1st edition [1938]. Repr., Grand Rapids: Kregel Publications, 1969), 36.
4. Kraemer, 36.
5. Ibid.
6. Allen, 'Jerusalem: A Critical Review', 22.
7. Ibid., 23.

idea for a 'Church of England',[8] as a New Testament definition for the Church. He did not believe the Church was to be 'provincially' defined but rather 'locally' and 'universally' defined with all rights to govern. Of course, when he referred to 'local Churches' he meant 'diocesan Churches' managed by diocesan bishops and *not* independently governed congregational churches. The report spoke of 'these younger Churches' as bodies of Christians loosely united as National Councils which had been set up. He disagreed and argued that they in theory obscure and in practice deny the full Church life of the local Churches. He believed that this practice cripples the local Churches.[9]

Thirdly, he systematically critiques the meaning behind various claims recorded in the report, but in particular argues against the Conference's definition of 'self-support'.[10] He identifies the mission societies' system of self-support as 'purely financial' and kept within the hands of the Western missionaries as the very 'mark of the imperialistic spirit of which Eastern peoples accuse them'.[11] Allen's use of the phrase 'the imperialistic spirit'[12] is later used within another article he wrote entitled 'The Imperialism of Missions in China'.[13] The thesis of the article addresses the Chinese impression of foreign missionary hegemony: 'But so long as we hold all spiritual authority in our own hands, imperialism is branded on our every action.'[14] On one hand, Peter Leithart argues this very point within *Between Babel and Beast* where he states that over the past few decades there has been 'an explosion of cultural analyses of imperialism, especially in postcolonial theory, which, unlike earlier politically focused studies, give detailed attention to the religious aspects of imperialism'.[15] On the other hand, the rhetoric of certain postcolonial theorists[16] – seemingly

---

8. Ibid.

9. Ibid., 22, 23.

10. Ibid., 27.

11. Ibid.

12. Ibid.

13. Roland Allen, 'The Imperialism of Missions in China' in *The Living Church* (Milwaukee: 26 January, 1929): 435-36.

14. Ibid., 436.

15. Peter J. Leithart, *Between Babel and Beast: America and Empires in Biblical Perspective*, Theopolitical Visions 14 (Eugene: Cascade Books, 2012), 'Studies of globalization, especially those inspired by the Frankfurt School, have likewise focused on cultural power', 160.

16. E.g. Frantz Fanon, *The Wretched of the Earth* (1st edition [1961], France. Repr., London: Penguin Books, 2001). See also, Edward W. Said, *Culture and Imperialism* (New York: Vintage, 1993) and *Orientalism* (London: Penguin

influenced by an anti-Western Civilization agenda – tend to advance a narrative of *postcolonial guilt* upon the Church by demonizing the 'white' colonial missionaries as religious imperialists. Arguably, there is evidence of imperialistic tendencies within colonial mission societies of the past few centuries. However, to stereotype 'all' Western Christian missionaries as imperialists is intellectually dishonest. The current shift within much of Christian missiology today tends towards the prioritization of social justice issues *over* the advancement of Gospel ministry through church planting. This seems to be a knee-jerk reaction to much of the *postcolonial guilt* rhetoric evidenced today, and, therefore, tends to be a denial of Christ's commission to disciple the nations (Matthew 28:18-20). Recently, there appears to be an unwillingness among advocates of postcolonial theory to address the problems of cultural hegemony, as evidenced through the actions of Islamist imperialism. The hesitancy among postcolonial theorists to confront 'the imperialistic spirit' of Islamic jihadism is academic hypocrisy (or fear). Both the Christian faith and the Islamic faith seek to advance their mission globally. The question is: How does a religion advance its faith mission without being imperialistic?

Roland Allen addressed this when he engaged with Paul Monroe's *China: A Nation in Evolution* (1928) by summarizing five main marks of what he thinks 'an imperialistic spirit' entails: (1) the presence of foreign civilization; (2) how mission schools require education to include religious studies; (3) the foreign hegemony disclosed as an unwillingness to entrust the Chinese to serve on school boards; (4) the withholding of administrative positions from Chinese; and (5) the continual promotion of the 'English way' or the 'American way' instead of 'the Chinese way'.[1] He obviously agreed with Monroe's points. Consequently, at the conclusion of this article he provides a solution to the 'foreign' element by applying the principle of trans-local *apostolic* missionaries – missionary bishops – who are sent on 'short term' church planting missions within the regions and commissioned to consecrate 'unpaid native bishops' duly appointed to manage and empower the dioceses.[2] When the missionary bishops enact the principle of authorizing indigenous leaders with all 'spiritual authority' then they can leave that region.[3] In this way his missiology for applying the apostolic principle is central to his missionary ecclesiology and discloses signs of an anti-imperialistic spirit.

Books, 2003).

1. Allen, 'The Imperialism of Missions in China', 436.
2. Ibid.
3. Ibid.

This article sheds light on the apostolic presupposition which shapes his overall 'Spirit and Order' emphasis. This missiological blending of pneumatology and ecclesiology undermines ecclesiastical hegemony by (1) restraining trans-local leadership – apostolic, evangelistic, prophetic – from creating 'mission station' bases and instead places trust in the pneumatological charismatic dynamic for (2) cultivating an indigenous culture where local leadership – deacons, presbyters, bishops – from below naturally emerge within the community, what David Bosch calls 'the primary bearer of mission'.[4] Allen's belief in the pneumatological dynamic did not negate the ecclesiastical order for he believed both worked in harmony to nurture an emerging Church where 'the missionary Spirit' empowers all members for 'missionary action'.[5]

Book Review: Kenneth Scott Latourette's 'A History of Christian Missions in China' (1929)[6]

Allen prefaced his comments with admiration for Latourette's 'most admirably arranged and carefully documented account' of how Christians evangelized China between the initial missionary efforts until 1926.[7] He recognized the significance of the book when dealing with the 'various methods employed by different missions and missionaries', while also describing Latourette's propensity towards expressing chronicle minutiae.[8] That said, he then shifts from conducting a regular book review and sets out to analyze Latourette's understanding of 'Church' and 'Mission' by posing two questions: (1) 'What were these Missions; and (2) what was the conception of their work held by those who carried them on?'[9] He takes Latourette to task by correcting what he believed is his misunderstanding of distinguishing between 'writing the History of the Church in China' and how that is different from 'Missions in China'.[10] He concludes this

---

4. David Bosch, *Transforming Mission: Paradigm Shifts in Theology of Mission* (Maryknoll: Orbis Books, 2002), 472.

5. Allen, *Pentecost and the World*, 61.

6. Kenneth Scott Latourette, *A History of Christian Missions in China*, SPCK (New York: MacMillan, 1929).

7. Ibid., 317-23.

8. Roland Allen (book review) of Kenneth Scott Latourette, *A History of Christian Missions in China* in *Church Quarterly Review* (January 1930): 317; see Latourette, *A History of the Expansion of Christianity: Advance through Storm A.D. 1914 and After* (London: Eyre & Spottiswoode, 1947), 328-78.

9. Allen's book review of Latourette's *A History of Christian Missions in China*, 317.

10. Ibid., 323.

article by disagreeing with Latourette's statement: 'The Church might be in process of disappearing' in China due to the 'Nationalist sentiment'[1] where there was increasing elements of 'Anti-Christian agitation . . . and persecution'.[2] Instead, his response was: 'No, the Missions might be in process of disappearing: the Church could not disappear, because it had never yet appeared.'[3] He thought in terms of ecclesiocentric idealism, which he argued was Pauline ecclesiology, and that it transcended all missiological attempts to marginalize the Church by giving it a secondary status behind mission practice. When Allen wrote this article in 1930 he had already clearly articulated his apologia against the 'mission station system' and its ultimate dissolution for almost thirty years. His inelasticity to accept Latourette's statement is no surprise for his unyielding stance that whenever the indigenous Church is planted – anywhere and at any time – the Church will spontaneously grow and extend. This was principal in his missionary thinking as he understood Pauline practice.

Allen did highlight some sections in the book that he found quite helpful, for example the information of the 'early Nestorian and Franciscan Missions in China'.[4] Also, he mentioned Buddhism and Islam – which he calls 'Mohammedanism' – as 'foreign' religions which were imported into Chinese culture[5] and had an established presence within the nation. At different times in history these two religions were 'despised and rejected by the older and more conservative leaders of their nation' yet because these religions did not have any 'external authority to control and guide' their converts during times of persecution, these religions still continued to exist because their followers had embraced and internalized the religion's faith.[6] On one hand, he shifts from book review analysis of Latourette's historical information and begins to contrast Christianity's 'higher Truth' with that of Buddhism and Islam. On the other he reprimands Christian missionaries for denying the Christian 'faith' and charismatic 'power' because of their unwillingness to entrust the indigenous people to manage their own churches.[7]

> They taught that the Holy Ghost was given to His disciples; but they could not believe that the Holy Ghost could direct and keep

---

1. Ibid., 322.
2. Ibid.
3. Ibid., 323.
4. Ibid., 317.
5. Ibid., 318.
6. Ibid.
7. Ibid.

His own. They could not commit the Truth and the rites of the Church to the Chinese. That is the fundamental fact . . . but the fact remains; and it is that fact which marks the character of the Christian Missions, and distinguishes them from other religious missions.[8]

In response to this contradiction, Allen *cynically* argues that missionaries must 'establish themselves within the country as professional teachers' in order to supervise, direct and train the Chinese after they had purchased property and then they could 'rely upon the power of their governments to secure them the right to hold the property and to reside'.[9] His sarcasm continues when confronting various missionary societies concerning their hesitancy and slowness to devolve their missions without first admitting the Chinese 'to membership of committees which', he argues, 'is the Protestant form of prelacy'.[10]

He then engages with Latourette's discussion about the differences between Roman Catholic and Protestant mission.[11] Allen agreed with Latourette's description how the 'Roman system' provided a good structure for their missions 'to establish a Christian community in China', even though this system 'presents an appearance of unity' it actually 'conceals and mitigates divisions'.[12] He offers what is the Protestant response to Rome's system: 'they ran after any alluring idea which for the moment was popular', that being, what Latourette called 'social betterment'.[13] The Protestants' pragmatic response for the furtherance of 'civilization as gospel' to the changing situation in China was not enough to stop the missionary departure 'out of the interior and a majority had left the country'.[14] Latourette concluded that the missions of both Roman Catholicism and Protestantism had declined and that 'the missionary could not expect to recover his former status in the Church nor his privileged position in the country'.[15] He disagreed with Latourette's perception of the missionary situation due to his concept of missionary ecclesiological 'retirement' – as practised by Paul in Galatia, Macedonia, Asia and Achaia – in order to

---

8. Ibid., 318-19.

9. Ibid., 319.

10. Ibid., 320.

11. Ibid., 321-22.

12. Ibid., 321.

13. Ibid., 322.

14. Ibid.

15. Ibid.; see David M. Paton, *Christian Missions & the Judgment of God* (Grand Rapids and Cambridge: Eerdmans Publishing, 1996), 63-108.

advance the indigenous Church. He thought that Latourette's pessimistic overview was based on his criteria for 'mission success' and that it was contingent on 'the amount of money . . . scientific attainments . . . and their democratic institutions'.[1] He also disagreed for: 'some of us believe that that conception of Missions is wrong [and] that success does not depend at all upon money or prestige or our education' because it distracts from 'the Truth' which he explained to be – 'Christ'.[2] He tenaciously argued for the 'Gospel of Christ' to take the pre-eminent place in mission. For Allen, once the Chinese internalize the principles of the Christian faith for themselves they will not need the supervision of foreign missionaries and Chinese Christianity will plant and maintain its own churches,[3] schools, hospitals and other institutions. In summary, this is what he believed Pauline mission encompassed: evangelism, church planting, apostolic principles, deposit of the faith tradition, appointment of indigenous leadership and foreign missionary displacement from the region.

'The "Nevius Method" in Korea' (1930)[4]

Within the 'Indigenous Church Series' the editor of *World Dominion*, Thomas Cochrane, proposed the reason behind Allen's article 'The "Nevius Method" in Korea' (July 1930), by saying that Allen 'shows how the "Nevius Method" falls short of the Apostolic Method'.[5] Cochrane's point is accurate. However, not only does he engage with the similarities and dissimilarities between his and John Nevius' missionary principles,[6] but he also occupies most of his time critiquing Charles Clark's *The Korean Church and the Nevius Method*.[7]

Firstly, he examines Nevius' basic 'foundation stone' in his system of 'self-support from the very beginning',[8] which, although he agrees

1. Latourette, *A History of Christian Missions in China*, 322.
2. Ibid., 322-23.
3. See Philip Jenkins, *The Next Christendom: The Coming of Global Christianity* (New York: Oxford University Press, 2002), 23, 26, 30-38, 69-70, 125, 223, 239.
4. Roland Allen, 'The "Nevius Method" in Korea', *World Dominion* (London: World Dominion Press, July 1930), 11-16.
5. Thomas Cochrane, editor, Indigenous Church Series, *World Dominion* (London: World Dominion Press, 1930), editorial comment on inside cover.
6. See Kraemer, *The Christian Message in a Non-Christian World*, 413.
7. Charles Allen Clark, *The Korean Church and the Nevius Method* (Fleming H. Revell, 1930).
8. Allen, 'The "Nevius Method" in Korea', 11.

with this emphasis in principle he disagrees with Nevius' interpretative approach, and therefore, says the 'system is broken' because of the way he identified it only to refer to money: ' . . . all Apostolic principles are subordinated to money. Dr Nevius' "Self-support" broke down here'.[9] This echoes both Allen's and Sidney Clark's argument that the principle of 'self-support' is broader in its application since it is 'spiritual as well as material',[10] and especially in reference to the Church's ability to 'supply' its own internal leadership that is fully capable to stand and act on its own. Interestingly, he owes much of his preliminary understanding of this principle to Nevius. Even Talltorp rightly argues that Nevius' thoughts about indigenous churches were probably communicated to Allen through Bishop Scott, that being, 'possibly the contact was mediated through his missionary Bishop and friend C.P. Scott of North China'[11] during the first years of his missionary experience in China. But it is obvious that over time he began to question the way 'self-support' was understood and applied in the missionary situation.

Secondly, he sets out to 'enquire what is the "Nevius plan", and wherein its strength lies'[12] by examining the 'plan' through the eyes of Charles Clark. He cites Clark's summary of 'the Nevius principles' into a framework of 'nine heads' but thinks that Clark has not gone far enough.[13] On one hand, he agrees that 'every new group of Christians' who implemented Nevius' plan by demonstrating 'spiritual' independence by doing 'more for themselves' in supplying local leadership to manage their own affairs was a proper way of understanding 'self-support' from its inception.[14] On the other hand, he disagrees with how Nevius' plan broke down and was deficient in that it 'lost sight of the self-support which is spiritual in their emphasis on the material', and also, that he believed and argued how Clark missed the whole point of indigenous self-support when he succumbed to a belief that 'money is prominent' when engaging this subject.[15]

---

9. Ibid., 13.

10. Roland Allen, 'Business Man and Missionary Statesman: Sidney James Wells Clark: An Appreciation', *World Dominion*, (London: World Dominion Press, December 1928): 3, 7.

11. Ake Talltorp, 'Sacraments for Growth in Mission: Eucharistic Faith and Practice in the Theology of Roland Allen' in *Transformation: An International Journal of Holistic Mission Studies*, vol. 29, no. 3, July 2012, London: SAGE Publications, 217.

12. Allen, 'The "Nevius Method" in Korea', 10.

13. Ibid., 11.

14. Ibid., 12.

15. Ibid.

Thirdly, he agrees with Nevius' belief that the appointment of elders authorized to administer all ecclesiastical rights is truly an 'Apostolic example'[1] and is 'the constitution of a local Church'.[2] And yet, he disagrees with Nevius' methodology where small 'groups' of Christians could select 'Leaders' and unite to form Sunday services 'without the rites of the Church inherent in the body' and can only administer the sacraments if the district missionary is present.[3] Allen found this bifurcation to be confusing and 'a strange relationship . . . to the "Church" of its creation'.[4]

Finally, he wrote this article some thirty years after he first became acquainted with Nevius' Presbyterian missionary work in China and Korea. When Allen arrived in China in 1895, he did not get the opportunity to meet Nevius since he had already died two years earlier. However, his bishop, Charles Scott, was a very close friend of Nevius and was very familiar with his understanding of the 'three self' principle for mission work. That said, although he disagreed with aspects of Nevius' thinking on the issue of self-support, it would be inaccurate to assume that he did not make use of Nevius' overall emphasis on the 'three self' approach. Allen's attempt to 'fine tune' Nevius' formula only revealed the significant breakthrough missionaries had made for equipping indigenous Christians to empower their churches towards independence of foreign missions and their missionaries. David Bosch agrees and argues that the missionaries who practised the 'three self' formula (independence) over the 'pedagogical one'[5] (devolution) were advancing the indigenous people towards responsible leadership in the presence of hegemony.

> Even somebody as fiercely critical of the entire Western missionary enterprise as Hoekendijk had to admit that, in this respect, the Church really was ahead of the world. Around 1860 the autonomy of the young churches could be seen in large print on every sensible missionary programme, long before anybody in the West even dreamt about other kinds of autonomy for colonized countries. There certainly were more sensitivities in this respect in Western missionary circles than there were in the various colonial offices.[6]

---

1. Clark, *The Korean Church and the Nevius Method*, 29.
2. Allen, 'The "Nevius Method" in Korea', 13.
3. Ibid.
4. Ibid., 16.
5. Bosch, *Transforming Mission*, 450.
6. Johannes C. Hoekendijk in Bosch, *Transforming Mission*, 450; see Johannes C. Hoekendijk, *Kirche und Volk in der deutschen Missionswissenschaft*, (Munich: Chr. Kaiser Verlag, 1967).

Hubert Allen stated that it was during the time of his grandfather's ministry in China that 'his name was even put forward for consecration as bishop for the proposed new diocese of Shantung',[7] interestingly, the very region where Nevius had been a missionary church planter earlier (1880s).[8] When Nevius died in 1893, Mrs Nevius had asked [bishop] Charles Scott to read the English service at the gravesite in Chefoo (Yantai), and it was five years later that Allen's bishop had him do some ministry for one month in Chefoo, the very region where Nevius died.[9] His ministry presence there for one month begs the question whether Scott's missional plan for that area was possibly an extension of Nevius' previous work in that location. This is evidence of an ecumenical spirit of mission before Edinburgh 1910.

Voluntary Clergy: Allen's Theological Praxis for Expanding the Church

One overarching *apostolic principle* which captivated Allen's thinking during the 1920s and later was his advancement for the ordination of *voluntary* clergymen. While writing on this subject he was not articulating from an ivory tower posture as some sort of isolated missiological theorist setting out to publish his thoughts. Rather, after publishing *Voluntary Clergy* (1923),[10] *Voluntary Clergy Overseas* (1928)[11] and *The Case for Voluntary Clergy* (1930),[12] archival evidence discloses his letter correspondence (over 254 letters from 10 October 1921 – 10 March 1931)[13] where he engages with laymen, priests, archdeacons, canons, bishops, archbishops and academics, in discussing whether or not the practice of voluntary clergy is workable. These letters reveal not only his didactic perceptiveness, but also his personal side and pastoral nature.

---

7. Hubert Allen, *Roland Allen*, 32.

8. Roland Allen, 'The "Nevius Method" in Korea', 10.

9. Hubert Allen, *Roland Allen*, 31.

10. Roland Allen, *Voluntary Clergy*, London, SPCK (1923), USPG X622, Box 2, File J, Oxford, Bodleian Library.

11. Roland Allen, *Voluntary Clergy Overseas: An Answer to the Fifth World Call*, privately printed at Beaconsfield, (1928), USPG X622, Box 2, File J, Oxford, Bodleian Library.

12. Roland Allen, *The Case for Voluntary Clergy*, London: Eyre & Spottiswoode (1930), USPG, Rhodes House, Oxford, Box 2, File J.

13. Roland Allen archives, USPG X622, Box 6, Files K-M, Oxford, Bodleian Library.

Allen addressed another issue of 'a great dearth of candidates for Ordination' in England and overseas in *Voluntary Clergy* (1923).[1] He argued that the problem was not 'necessarily' a shortage of ministers but rather a 'dearth of a certain kind and type of religious minister' which the English Church was so 'accustomed' to possess.[2] He believed it was 'God's Providence'[3] for this problem to be disclosed because: (1) it instructed the Church to realize that 'this type is not the only type'[4] of minister within parish life; (2) that this vocation was 'singularly restricted to the very young' even though 'all native thought and practice protest against such a custom';[5] and (3) that there is a more expansive 'work and character of the Church' and that this problem was 'forcing us through the failure of our self-imposed limitations to learn the truth'[6] that the Church is a missionary society. He was convinced that the Anglican Church could learn from this shortage problem and solve the dilemma by ordaining voluntary clergy to assist incumbent parish priests both in England and overseas. How did the Anglican Church respond to his ideas?

Within the Anglican Communion, responses from the clergy and laity fluctuated between those, who, on one hand, believed Allen was 'out of touch' with the nature of missionary work, and yet, on the other hand, those who were convinced that his emphasis provided *solutions* to the growing problem of clergy shortage. Before comparing and contrasting the differing responses to his teaching it is necessary to clarify his view on stipendiary and non-stipendiary clergy.

> The apostolic qualifications are quite compatible with dependence for livelihood upon the offerings of the faithful, either in the form of endowments, or of subscriptions. The means by which the minister gains his living is not in the picture. He may earn it by a trade, or inherit wealth from his ancestors, or enjoy a salary, or receive dues as an official, or be supported by the Church. How he is supported is a mere external detail, which is not even mentioned. His call of God and his service do not depend upon such things as that. The Church unquestionably needs some men who give themselves wholly to prayer and the ministration of the Word and Sacraments, and such men must be supported by the faithful. . . . There are also many large

---

1. Allen, *Voluntary Clergy*, 1.
2. Ibid., 2.
3. Ibid., 1-2.
4. Ibid., 2.
5. Ibid.
6. Ibid., 12.

town parishes where the Church needs assistant priests of varied capacity, drawn from many classes of the people, who can speak, each to his own class, in the language familiar to it, understanding by experience the difficulties and temptations of that class. . . . The distinction between stipendiary and voluntary clergy is not a distinction between men who give their whole time to the service of God and His Church and men who give part of their time to that service, but a distinction between one form of service and another. Both stipendiary and voluntary clergy ought to be serving God and the Church all the time in all they do. . . . The voluntary cleric carries the priesthood into the market place and the office. It is his work not only to minister at the altar or to preach, but to show men how the common work of daily life can be done in the spirit of the priest.[7]

This distinction was furthermore clarified frequently due to misrepresentations. In fact, after Roland Allen's death it was an Anglican Canon – David Paton – whose persistent work on accumulating many of Allen's works, and, to whom missiologists are ever indebted, actually misrepresented Allen's view on this subject. Hubert Allen points out that

Canon David Paton failed to appreciate the intensity of Roland's feeling about this, and even allowed the phrase [part-time priests] to be used on the dust cover of the first edition of *The Ministry of the Spirit*; this so horrified Roland's son and daughter that they never thereafter felt able to cooperate with that scholar's further researches.[8]

Another interview that I conducted with Hubert Allen disclosed more details on the frustration his father and aunt had with Paton's reluctance to verify information before publication.[9] Hubert Allen said: 'Roland did not mean "part-time" or "half-time priests" – phrases which caused him to shudder . . . my father once commented that "He [Roland] had a great reverence for the priesthood, and he was a priest all the time, awake or asleep."'[10] Roland's concise comment establishes clarity here: 'A cleric can no more be a half-time cleric than a father can be a half-time father, or a baptized Christian a half-time Christian.'[11] One time when

---

7. Roland Allen, 'The Meaning and Place of Voluntary Clergy' from *The Case for Voluntary Clergy* (1930) as cited in Paton, *The Ministry of the Spirit*, 147-150.

8. Hubert Allen, *Roland Allen*, 122 (footnote 9).

9. Interview with Hubert Allen on 18 October 2010.

10. Hubert Allen, *Roland Allen*, 122.

11. Roland Allen, *The Case for Voluntary Clergy*, 89.

Hubert was visiting his grandparents in Nairobi (while discussing how much payment clergy should receive) he remembered his grandfather reply that the Church had a responsibility to properly pay its servants, and yet – 'being a priest is not a job. No one should be paid for being a priest. . . . It is a privilege and a vocation, not a job'.[1] This is the *spirit* of Roland Allen's thought! That said, he believed once a priest, always a priest. This issue of stipendiary and non-stipendiary clergy was not an issue with other denominations, but in the Church of England in Allen's day Anglican clergy were required by canon law to refrain from other livelihood.

On one hand, of the 254 letters (not counting the numerous newspaper articles) dealing with the *principle* of voluntary clergy practice it is helpful to consider some of the reactions which he encountered. In 1924 the diocesan bishop of Mombasa thought Allen's ideas to be unrealistic because Anglican churchmen would not accept the same practice as found among 'Wesleyan Methodists'.[2] Another reaction was from a clergyman in Western Canada (1925) whose concerns centred on possible jealousies which could occur if one 'country mission working hard to raise their clergyman's stipend' noticed how another mission received 'more services, free gratis, than they are'.[3] Still yet another argument against Allen's ideas came from an 'anonymous writer concerning *The Case of Voluntary Clergy*.[4] Within the book review the writer argues against the principle of voluntary clergy by asserting an example of the 'barbaric and completely indigenous African Church [that] has existed for centuries in Abyssinia' and that it still practised polygamy, therefore somehow proving her inability to consider the voluntary principle.[5] An argument ensued with a follow-up letter by Geoffrey Warwick defending Allen by stating: 'No analogy can be drawn from Abyssinia,' especially due to 'its adherence to Monophysitism, that Church remained in virtual isolation' for centuries from orthodox Christianity and not until the twentieth century did this church have

---

1. Hubert Allen, *Roland Allen*, 123.
2. Letter to the editor in *The Record*, 'The Bishop of Mombasa's Appeal' (7 February 1924): 89, USPG X622, Box 1, File A, Oxford, Bodleian Library.
3. A. Raymond Perkins, letter to the editor in the *Canadian Churchman*, 'Voluntary Clergy' (17 August 1925), USPG X622, Box 1, File A, Oxford, Bodleian Library.
4. A book review by an anonymous writer entitled 'A Voluntary Clergy' in the *Church Times* (4 April 1930), USPG X622, Box 1, File A, Oxford, Bodleian Library.
5. Ibid.

'its own native episcopate'.[6] Within the numerous letters mentioned earlier many of the arguments against Allen's ideas for the voluntary principle to function within his missionary ecclesiology generally pivot around institutional structures and philosophies of ministry which only supported the stipendiary methodology.[7]

On the other hand, many clergy and laity began to engage with this voluntary principle that Allen taught. Roger Beckwith (2003) agrees and said that 'Roland Allen's famous study of Paul's missionary work and of his practice of ordination in the course of it identifies six characteristics of the presbyters whom Paul ordained'.[8] Beckwith said:

> (i) They were ordained to work in their congregation of origin; (ii) they were not usually young; (iii) they were not highly trained for their work; (iv) they had the power of training and ordaining; (v) there was more than one of them to a congregation; (vi) they were self-supporting. It can hardly pass without mention that all but one of these six characteristics (the fourth) are to be found in the Non-Stipendiary Ministry recently introduced in the Church of England. This shows how easy it is for the Anglican ministry to return to its roots. In four of these characteristics, there was no change from the Jewish teaching elder, and in the other two (the first and third) the necessities of the situation would have been the cause.[9]

Beckwith's comment that Anglican ministry was able to return to its roots on this issue was confirmed earlier in Mark Hodge's *Non-Stipendiary Ministry in the Church of England* (1983) where he stated that the 'activities of a most important protagonist of non-stipendiary ministry, Roland Allen (1868-1947), were becoming significant'[10] and it was his *Voluntary Clergy* (1923) that contributed to the earlier

---

6. Ibid., Geoffrey Warwick's response to the above review in *Church Times* (April 1930): 449-50.

7. Roland Allen archives, USPG X622, Box 6, Files K-M, Oxford, Bodleian Library.

8. Roger Beckwith, *Elders in Every City: The Origin and Role of the Ordained Ministry* (Carlisle: Paternoster Press, 2003), 51.

9. Beckwith, *Elders in Every City*, 51.

10. Mark Hodge, Non-Stipendiary Ministry in the Church of England (London: The Central Board of Finance of the Church of England, 1983. Repr., London: the General Synod of the Church of England by CIO Publishing, 1984). David Paton, The Ministry of the Spirit, ix-xvi. See Allen, *Voluntary Clergy* (1923) and *The Case for Voluntary Clergy* (1930).

conversations.[1] Hodge points out that 'during the 1920s Allen untiringly pursued a one-man crusade to promote his radical solution' and that various bishops began to recognize that 'his case was "unanswerable"'[2] and began to accept his arguments which 'included Burrows of Chichester and Headlam of Gloucester. T.A. Lacey and Lowther Clarke of SPCK were also his allies'.[3] Later there were disappointments that Allen experienced after sending copies of *The Case for Voluntary Clergy* (1930) which he personally sent to every bishop who planned to attend the Lambeth Conference 1930. And yet, Hodge records that in 1963 the Church of England began to ordain non-stipendiary ministers.[4] The significant prophetic voice for the implementation of non-stipendiary priests (voluntary clergy) within the Church of England was Roland Allen.

Conclusion

The intention of this chapter was to explain the dynamics which helped shape Roland Allen's missionary ecclesiology. Allen's ability to systematically confront missionary methodologies of paternalism and devolution originated from his missiology which was rooted in his understanding of Pauline practice. His tenacious vision for missionaries to work in conjunction with responsible local bishops by applying substantive principles for the establishment of the Church through – Bible, Creed, Sacraments, Ministry – he believed could facilitate the new state of affairs in global Christianity. These factors are presented to provide an historical understanding of Roland Allen's missionary ecclesiology.

---

1. Mark Hodge, *Non-Stipendiary Ministry in the Church of England* (1984), 10-11.
2. Ibid., 11.
3. Ibid.
4. Ibid., 7. During the years 1963-1970 there were approximately 140 men ordained as non-stipendiary and from 1963-1982 there were 1,057 ordained as voluntary clergy.

8. Roland Allen's Apostolic Principles: An Analysis of his *The Ministry of Expansion: the Priesthood of the Laity*[1]

Preliminary Comments

Roland Allen confronted various aspects of Western missionary practices with its organizational colonial paradigm. He contrasted this model with his understanding of a Pauline paradigm of indigenous Church planting found in the New Testament. He argued that the Western missiological paradigm created and produced a dependency on its missionaries, due to various mission societies' need for control of the missions they established and maintained. With his organic approach to mission, he argued for a 'release of control' by the mission societies. His belief was that if the mission societies released control giving the works over to the indigenous converts, the latter could rely on the Holy Spirit's ability to govern, sustain and propagate the Church's growth apart from foreign influence. The centrality of his pneumatology was influenced by Paul's epistles and Luke's historical account of the Acts of the Apostles, which he called 'missionary history'.[2] Consider the following influence of Pauline practice upon his mission theology:

---

1. Roland Allen archives, 'The Ministry of Expansion: The Priesthood of the Laity' (unpublished 1930), USPG X622, Box 3, Number 27, Oxford, Bodleian Library. My first analysis of this work by Roland Allen was originally published as 'Roland Allen's Apostolic Principles: An Analysis of his "The Ministry of Expansion"' *Transformation*, July 2012, 29(3): 225-243. My second analysis of this work has been recently published as a chapter in *The Ministry of Expansion by Roland Allen: The Priesthood of the Laity*, J.D. Payne, editor, Published by William Carey Library (Pasadena), © 2017, and this chapter includes additional comments. This current chapter in this second volume includes sections from my previous publications and continues to unpack my ongoing research on the significance of Roland Allen's theology of the laity.

2. Paton, *The Ministry of the Spirit*, 15.

St Paul was a preacher of a Gospel, not of a law. . . . This is the most distinctive mark of Pauline Christianity. This is what separates his doctrine from all other systems of religion. . . . He did not establish a constitution, he inculcated principles. He did not introduce any practice to be received on his own or any human authority, he strove to make his converts realize and understand its relation to Christ. . . . He never sought to enforce their obedience by decree; he always strove to win their heartfelt approval and their intelligent cooperation. He never proceeded by command, but always by persuasion. He never did things for them; he always left them to do things for themselves. He set them an example according to the mind of Christ, and he was persuaded that the Spirit of Christ in them would teach them to approve that example and inspire them to follow it.[1]

In terms of Pauline theology, Allen believed that the Apostle's practice of church planting was permeated with a dependency on the Holy Spirit's ability to lead the Church into all truth, as revealed in John 16:13. That said, he believed that the Church's global expansion was based upon foundational *apostolic principles* organically energized through a realized pneumatology, empowered ecclesiology and an applied mission theology he believed stemmed from Pauline practice. For Allen, the apostolic principles are the centrality of his missionary ecclesiology. Arguably these key missionary principles are generated by the charismatic dynamic within Christianity which produces self-supporting, self-governing, self-propagating indigenous churches that find their rootedness in the Bible, a basic creed, trans-local and domestic ministers, and, an ongoing sacramental life.

What are some of the apostolic principles Allen emphasized?

The key *apostolic principles* Roland Allen emphasized are: (1) belief in the one, holy, catholic and apostolic Church – Scriptures, basic creed, orders, sacraments;[2] (2) apostolic evangelists called and sent to plant and equip indigenous churches;[3] (3) church planters organize, train and retire from young church plants as soon as possible;[4] (4) indigenous churches retain

---

1. Allen, *Missionary Methods*, 148-149.

2. Allen, *Missionary Methods*, 107; also Allen, *Spontaneous Expansion*, 147-49.

3. Allen, 'The Ministry of Expansion,' USPG X622, Box 3, Number 27, chapter 4: 5, Oxford, Bodleian Library.

4. Allen, *Missionary Methods*, 81-83, 95-107; Roland Allen (Chaplain to the Bishop of North China), 'The Work of the Missionary in Preparing the

self-support, self-government, self-propagation;[5] (5) self-supporting churches which produce home-grown leadership from the inception (non-devolution);[6] (6) ordination of indigenous voluntary clergy authorized to administer the sacraments frequently;[7] (7) the ministry of the Holy Spirit empowers the spontaneous expansion of the Church;[8] (8) all Christians are missionaries – the Church is a missionary body;[9] (9) the priesthood of the laity, by which he referred to the empowerment of the community;[10] and (10) an ordered ministry in apostolic succession through missionary ecclesiology.[11] Having identified these apostolic principles, I now want to unpack them in relation, primarily, to the context of the beginning chapters of Allen's 'The Ministry of Expansion: the Priesthood of the Laity' and, secondarily, to various comments within other significant works he wrote.

A cursory and selective study of Roland Allen's writings has caused some to misrepresent his missiology. One must come to terms with what he meant by words such as: *Church, Spirit, mission, apostolic, catholic, apostolic succession, indigenous, expansion, sacraments, orders* and *principles*.

Way for Independent Native Churches,' a paper read before the Federation of Junior Clergy Missionary Associations in connection with the SPG, Resume of Proceedings at the 19th Conference of Delegates, John Rylands Library, Manchester, 11-12 November 1903, USPG X622, Oxford, Bodleian Library.

5. Allen (1927: 147-59), a paper read at the *Church Missionary Society Conference of Missionaries*, High Leigh, 1927, Box 2, Number 23. Allen R, 'The Establishment of Indigenous Churches', typed manuscript refused by the *International Review of Missions*, 1927: 17, USPG X622, Box 3, Oxford, Bodleian Library.

6. Paton, *Ministry of the Spirit*, 112.

7. Allen, *Voluntary Clergy* (1923). Also, Allen, *The Case for Voluntary Clergy* (1930).

8. H.R. Boer, 'Roland Allen – Voice in the Wilderness', *World Dominion Press*, vol. xxxii, no. 4, July/August (1954: 224-31). Cf. Allen, *Missionary Methods*, 48.

9. Paton, *Ministry of the Spirit*, 40, 61, 67, 75, 77-80, 165. Also, Allen, 'The Work of the Missionary in Preparing the Way for Independent Native Churches', (1903), USPG X622, Oxford, Bodleian Library.

10. Allen, 'The Priesthood of the Church', *Church Quarterly Review*, art. IV (1933): 234-44, USPG X622, Oxford, Bodleian Library.

11. Allen, 'The Ministry of Expansion' Preface: 3-4. Cf. 'The doctrine of apostolic succession means that, according to the institution of Christ, a ministry ordained in due form by (Episcopal) succession from the Apostles . . . is an integral part of that visible Church . . . involves also the transmission of special gifts of grace . . . transmitted by those only who have themselves, in succession, received that grace, and the authority to transmit it, from its one original source' in Arthur W. Haddan, *Apostolical Succession in the Church of England* (London, Oxford, and Cambridge: Rivingtons, 1879), 1-2.

First of all, he defined these words from what he believed was Pauline missionary principles and practices. Second, as a High Churchman this presupposed a framework of belief that embraced historic Christianity – the faith once delivered to the saints (Jude 3) – that being, *apostolic* and *catholic*. And, when reading him carefully, one will find a 'catholic' understanding of the Christian faith, especially articulated through the first five centuries of the 'undivided' Church. That said, an understanding of his mission theology will contribute significantly to contemporary missiology.

What about Apostolic Succession?[1]

The ongoing conversation of 'apostolic succession' continues to remain an ecclesiastical topic within the context of the established Church today. Some contemporary evidence of this is shown through the writings of the Roman Catholic theologian from Belgium, Edward Schillebeeckx (1914–2009), wherein he indicated a radical break from a 'mechanical' belief in apostolic succession.[2] As a leading theological voice within Roman Catholicism since Vatican II, his challenge to the Church's position on apostolic succession reasserts the need for further discussion within the Church of Rome. The same can be said of the Anglican Church. Former differences of opinion within the Church of England during the nineteenth century manifested themselves through knee-jerk reactions among High, Low and Broad Churchmen, as well as between liberals and evangelicals. Albeit the nineteenth-century ecclesiastical emphasis to maintain the episcopal order of apostolic succession with a specialized priesthood, the Tractarian leaders of the Oxford Movement in the early 1830s[3] stood in contrast to certain Broad Churchmen, such as Samuel Coleridge and Thomas Arnold, who set out to emphasize the universal priesthood of the laity for the Church of England.[4]

---

1. Allen, 'The Ministry of Expansion', Ch. 2, 3, USPG X622, Oxford, Bodleian Library. Also, Haddan, *Apostolical Succession in the Church of England*, 1-2.

2. See Edward Schillebeeckx, *Ministry: A Case for Change* (London: SCM Press, 1984); and also, Schillebeeckx, *The Church with a Human Face: A New and Expanded Theology of Ministry* (London: SCM Press, 1985).

3. See, for example, John Henry Newman, "Tract One: Thoughts on the Ministerial Commission", in *Tracts for the Times* (London: J.G. & F. Rivington, 1838), vol. 1, 2; see also, R.W. Church, *The Oxford Movement: Twelve Years, 1833-1845*, Geoffrey Best (ed.) (Chicago: University of Chicago Press, 1970), 81-84.

4. cf. Allen C. Guelzo, *For the Union of Evangelical Christendom: The Irony of the Reformed Episcopalians* (University Park, Pennsylvania: The Pennsylvania State University Press, 1994), 117.

On one hand, these former discussions concerning the issue of apostolic succession and its validity or relevance within the Church posited one aspect concerning the historicity of the Church's institutional life. On the other hand, the Anglo-Catholic emphasis of the Oxford Movement articulated especially through the writings of Charles Gore and Robert Campbell Moberly argued for a more disciplined approach to Church order at home in England, and yet, apparently did not consider how this could be applied to 'pioneer' regions where the Anglican Church had been spreading within British colonies. This seemingly neglected application was confronted by Roland Allen from within the context of High Church missiology. He did *not* argue against the validity of apostolic succession, as presented by Gore and Moberly, rather he challenged their legal, formal, and strained theory[5] which he believed resulted in an exclusiveness that denied any 'lay expression' of sacramental grace, due to the absence of ordained clergy under apostolic succession within these remote regions.[6]

In terms of lay presidency at the Lord's Table, what did Allen believe? First, according to Hubert Allen, his ecumenical style of ministry never diminished his devotion to Anglican High Churchmanship.[7] Secondly, concerning Roland's tenacious persona, as he addressed various institutional deficiencies and unreasoned practices in the Church, making a distinction between two types of Anglican Churchmen, the 'conformist' and the 'radical', Hubert Allen notes that, while his brother Willoughby Charles Allen was a 'conformist', Roland himself was a 'radical'.[8] This makes sense, for, while, on one hand, as a High Church Anglican, he did believe in the appropriate administration of the Holy Communion by ordained priests and bishops (that was divine order), but on the other hand, his view for the Church's expansion to pioneer regions organically emerging within new territories – even if properly ordained clergy were not locally present[9] – still necessitated the continuance of the sacramental meal whenever Christians met together.[10] According to his sacramental emphasis, whenever the

---

5. Allen, 'The Ministry of Expansion: The Priesthood of the Laity', Preface, 3.

6. Ibid., Preface 3.

7. Hubert Allen articulated how his grandfather remained faithful to a High Anglican belief in the centrality of the Eucharistic sacrament; Interview with Hubert Allen on 18 October 2010.

8. Interview with Hubert Allen on 18 October 2010.

9. Allen, 'The Ministry of Expansion', Preface, 1.

10. Cf. Matthew 18:20; I Corinthians 11:17-34.

Church gathered together for worship, the Lord's Supper ought to be practised on a regular basis. Who, therefore, was qualified to administer the Holy Communion if ordained clergymen were absent? He came to the conclusion that *they must act for themselves* since, he believed, if Christ is spiritually present in the Holy Communion, 'it is Christ who consecrates the elements Himself, and that He will not desert them because they have no ordained priest at hand'.[1] He argued for its continual practice in these cases even if ordained clergy were not present to preside.[2] He believed there were sufficient grounds to justify such an action through apostolic practice as recorded in the New Testament among the young (first century) churches of Samaria, Lydda, Joppa, Phoenicia, Cyprus, Antioch, Galatia and Rome[3] and that which is recorded in the *Didachē*.'[4] He thought apostolic precedent provided a basis for such action.

Soteriology Trumps Ecclesiology

Allen's central understanding for the celebration of the sacrament of the Holy Communion within a trans-denominational or ecumenical format – a true expression of communion among Christians from different backgrounds – is indicative of how his 'catholic' faith trumped ecclesiastical differences. Evidence of his incipient ecumenism in the early part of the twentieth century is expressed within the following comments:

> If the Holy Ghost is given, those to whom He is given are certainly accepted in Christ by God. . . . Men may separate them, systems may part them from the enjoyment and strength of their unity; but, if they share the one Spirit, they are one. . . . Men who hold a theory of the Church which excludes from communion those whom they admit to have the Spirit of Christ simply proclaim that their theory is in flat contradiction to the spiritual fact.[5]

He attempted to deal with the apparent tension between a strict form of clericalism that denied sacramental celebration as a means of grace whenever professional clerics were absent[6] and a sacramental

---

1. Allen, 'The Ministry of Expansion', Chapter 1:1, 6, 7, 9.
2. Ibid., Ch. 1: 1, 9.
3. Ibid., Ch. 4, 2-4.
4. Ibid., 4.
5. Allen, *Pentecost and the World*, 85-6.
6. Allen, 'The Family Rite' (unpublished, 1943), USPG X622, Box 7, Oxford,

form which refused to withhold grace to those who gathered together as a community of faith and believed Christ was spiritually present to consecrate the elements.[7] He believed that to withhold the sacrament was a violation of apostolic principle. Allen's sacramental emphasis in 'The Ministry of Expansion: the Priesthood of the Laity' moved away from a theoretical treatise on the subject by personally identifying himself with the 'scattered sheep'.[8] His initial concern consisted of small congregations spread throughout remote areas of the world which conducted services without any 'ordained priests' to serve those communities sacramentally. With this context in view, he proceeded to challenge that which he believed was the 'teaching which strangles us' located within these two books, written by 'two great theologians . . . Gore . . . Moberly'.[9]

In 1889, Gore wrote an 'apology' concerning what he believed was 'the principle of the apostolic succession' in his book *The Ministry of the Christian Church*.[10] After the writing of Gore's book, in 1897, Moberly wrote *Ministerial Priesthood*, essentially as 'a study of the Anglican Ordinal'.[11] Allen believed these books did not specifically address the spontaneous growth of the Church, which was occurring within distant lands, where congregational life grew organically without the presence of episcopally ordained clergymen. In essence, he thought that Gore and Moberly were myopic, or, as we tend to say, 'out of touch' with the expansion of the Church outside the Western context. Consider Allen's comments:

> Those are the books which are most easily obtainable, and have now long been the standard works for many theological students. Therefore I have restricted myself almost entirely to them. In so doing I recognize sadly that I must appear to many careful readers, and to all careless ones, to be opposing those good and eminent men. That is most unfortunate . . . I would gladly have avoided it, but I am compelled to run that risk because of the widespread influence which they exercise, and the fact that appeal is so often

Bodleian Library.

7. Allen, 'The Ministry of Expansion', Ch. 1, 7.

8. Ibid., Preface, 1.

9. Ibid., Preface, 2.

10. Charles Gore, *The Ministry of the Christian Church*, London: Rivingtons, Preface v, (1889; new edition 1919) by C.H. Turner, as cited in *Dictionary of the Christian Church* (1997).

11. Robert Campbell Moberly, *Ministerial Priesthood*, London: John Murray, Preface v (1897; Oxford: Horace Hart, Printer to the university, 1898).

made to them by the men who teach what I maintain to be false. I am compelled to do it because if I had not mentioned them I should have seemed to be ignoring most powerful objections to the practice which I advocate.[1]

Allen attempted to contextualize some apostolic principles to what he observed were neglected regions which lacked episcopal response and this 'compelled' him to argue against their theory of apostolic succession.[2] Observe his words on apostolic practice:

> It is high time that we should definitely face the question whether we will not in the future return to the biblical apostolic practice and by establishing apostolic churches open the door for that expansion and make it the foundation of our missionary policy; for we are at a turning point in our missionary history, and what is to be the future course of that history will depend upon the attitude which we take up on this question.[3]

For Allen, apostolic succession exists not to sideline the ministry in some sort of ecclesiastical castle but from historic precedent to equip the ministry to proactively advance the apostolic faith and reproduce apostolic churches spontaneously.

Convictions about Holy Communion

In terms of *lay presidency* at the Lord's Table, what did Allen believe? First, according to Hubert Allen (grandson of Roland Allen), his ecumenical style of ministry never diminished his devotion to Anglican High Churchmanship.[4] Second, concerning Allen's tenacious persona when he addressed various institutional deficiencies and unreasoned practices in the Church, he took a *radical* position.[5] This makes sense, for, while, on one hand, Allen did believe in the appropriate administration of Holy Communion by ordained priests and bishops, on the other hand, in pioneer regions, where properly ordained clergy were *not* locally present,[6] he believed that Anglican order still necessitated

1. Allen, *The Ministry of Expansion*, Preface, 2.
2. Ibid., 3.
3. Allen, *Spontaneous Expansion*, 41–42.
4. Hubert Allen articulated how his grandfather remained faithful to a High Anglican belief in the centrality of the Eucharistic sacrament; Interview with Hubert Allen on 18 October 2010.
5. Interview with Hubert Allen on 18 October 2010.
6. Allen, *The Ministry of Expansion*, Preface, 1.

the continuance of the sacramental meal whenever Christians met together.[7] Who, therefore, was qualified to administer Holy Communion if ordained clergymen were absent? Allen came to the conclusion that the Church must act for themselves since, if Christ is spiritually present in the Holy Communion, 'it is Christ who consecrates the elements Himself, and that He will not desert them because they have no ordained priest at hand'.[8] He believed there were sufficient grounds to justify such an action, as recorded in the New Testament among the young churches of Samaria, Lydda, Joppa, Phoenicia, Cyprus, Antioch, Galatia and Rome.[9]

Summary of Preface

In the Preface to *The Ministry of Expansion*, Allen initiates the conversation by confronting a certain 'cruel bondage' which he believed kept churches hindered from receiving the sacramental grace due to non-existent ordained clergy within their context.[10] His passion comes through clearly on this matter within the opening paragraphs with phrases such as, 'I see Christians scattered as sheep having no shepherd . . . I feel compassion . . . and I write as one of them . . . I speak of our fears . . . our hesitations . . . our common condition'.[11] He then calls upon the bishops to solve the current deficiency.

First, Anglican order necessitates a basic assumption that Christ's sacraments are for all His children and that it is unnatural to deny sacramental grace to anyone.[12] Second, he argued that there is a proclivity in human nature to create customs and traditions which ultimately disallow basic principles. However, when the basic principles of sacramental grace are freely administered, whether clergy are present or not, this grace will generate life.[13] Third, the deficiency of any proactive approach from the bishops at the Lambeth Conference, as stated in their report (1930) to address with compassion and strategy the current crisis of 'hundreds of thousands'[14] of communicants without any resident priests to administer the sacraments, was considered unacceptable according to

---

7. See Matthew 18:20; I Corinthians 11:17-34.

8. Allen, *The Ministry of Expansion*, Ch. 1:1, 6, 7, 9.

9. Ibid., Ch. 4: 2-4.

10. Allen, *The Ministry of Expansion*, Preface: 1.

11. Allen, *The Ministry of Expansion*, Preface: 1.

12. Ibid., Ch. 1: Outline, The Fundamental Principles.

13. Ibid.

14. Ibid., Ch. 1: 5.

his analysis. Fourth, his assessment of the crisis did *not* suggest that he ruled out the necessity to maintain Anglican order through the significance of episcopal ordination. That said, Allen believed the bishops needed to demonstrate a pre-emptive approach to the crisis by offering to ordain[1] indigenous leadership wherever a community of Christians gather for worship. Fifth, the non-existent priests and bishops excludes nothing, therefore, he believed, this vacancy made room for Christians to sacramentally act for themselves.

Allen believed that the indigenous Church ought to be empowered – from the beginning – to administrate its own activities. This was foremost in his thought: 'I should like to see it accepted as a general principle that converts should be presented by members of the Church to the Church, and accepted by the Church and baptized on the authority of the whole local church acting as a church.'[2] The possibility to engage the laity to take ownership of its local activities stemmed from his apostolic missionary ecclesiology which sought to empower the members to act for themselves when necessary.

Fundamental Principles

An overview of Allen's first chapter discloses three significant points: (1) that Christ ordained His sacraments for *all* His children; (2) that Christ's command to observe the sacrament of the Lord's Table [regularly] applies to all; and, (3) that it is unnatural to deny this sacramental grace of Communion even when an ordained minister is not present to preside.[3] After many years of first-hand missionary experience, especially within countries where British colonialism had extended its borders, Allen observed how many colonialists (members of the Church of England) were living within regions without any Anglican priests, and, therefore, were deprived of the sacraments. Since the ecclesiological practice within the Church of England necessitates the frequent practice of the Lord's Table by duly ordained priests, Allen came to the conclusion that whenever Anglicans relocated to regions where priests were not present, he proposed the following: 'Faithful Christians must obey Christ as well as they can, assured that it is Christ who consecrates the elements Himself, and that He will not desert them because they have no ordained priest at hand.'[4] Allen argued that in this case Christ's

---

1. Ibid., Ch. 1: 7.
2. Allen, *Missionary Methods,* 99.
3. Allen, *The Ministry of Expansion,* Ch. 1: 1-9
4. Ibid., Ch. 1: 6, 7.

command trumps ecclesial custom, and, in order to reinforce this point quoted Jesus' words: 'Where two or three are gathered together in my name there am I in the midst of them' (Matthew 18:20).[5] This pastoral concern for the spiritual health of fellow Anglicans compelled Allen to address this deprivation of the Lord's Table as 'worse than unnatural'[6] for, in his opinion, it advanced 'a theory . . . a tradition . . . a custom' at the expense of the command 'to receive the grace which Christ offered'[7] in the Holy Communion.

It is important to point out *again* that Allen's position was not an argument against the Anglican order of apostolic succession but against the exclusiveness that denied any lay expression of sacramental grace,[8] and, which was previously pointed out, advocated a 'teaching which strangles us'.[9] On one hand, his pneumatology of 'Spirit *before* Order' was highlighted within the conclusion of this chapter as he proposed:

> I am certain that they [Anglicans without any resident priests] would find grace to help in time of need [Heb. 4:16]. 'O taste and see how gracious the Lord is' [Psalm 34:8]. . . . Christ gave us the sacraments. Taste and see. If a priest appears occasionally, receive him: but in his absence act for yourselves.[10]

On the other hand, his ecclesiology of 'Spirit *with* Order' within this chapter 'did not argue that episcopal ordination was of no importance'[11] but rather that it was a 'divine order [that] is for building up, not for destruction: it is to maintain the sacraments of Christ not to annul them: it is to establish the Church not to hinder its establishment'.[12] That said, Allen's ecclesiological argument affirmed the *normal* 'Order' of Anglican clergy (ordained by bishops) administering the Lord's Table. He also affirmed a *flexible* 'Order' for the laity to administer the Lord's Table in given situations in which clergy were not present upon the belief that 'it is Christ who consecrates the elements Himself'.[13]

---

5. Ibid., Ch. 1: 9.
6. Ibid., Ch. 1: 3.
7. Ibid., Ch. 1: 4.
8. Ibid., Preface: 2
9. Ibid.
10. Ibid., Ch. 1: 9.
11. Ibid., Ch. 1: 7.
12. Ibid., Ch. 1:9.
13. Ibid., Ch. 1: 7.

The Church is a Missionary Body

For sake of clarity, mission, according to Allen, always began with the establishment of the Church as a missionary community, which always was evidenced through its faithfulness to Holy Scripture, a basic creed, the ministry and the sacraments. For him, these were apostolic principles that were foundational to the establishment of the Church. He always recognized the necessity for leadership to 'lead' and 'empower' all members of the local Church (Ephesians 4:11-16). The missiologist Ake Talltorp points out that Allen's emphasis on the laity's calling as 'unofficial missionaries' was probably influenced through the missionary writings of his friend, Father H.H. Kelly, and also the Anglican Canon – W.H. Temple Gairdner.[1] In terms of Kelly, Talltorp said Allen shared the idea of every Christian as a missionary with Herbert Kelly, who, already in 1908, had written:

> 'It is really next to no use at all for a priest to teach, to preach, to instruct, if the laity are not themselves preaching, teaching, living the Church. . . . Lay Christianity and Lay Christians can only be rightly made by laymen. It is the priest's true business to guide, to feed, to inspire, to build; but the essential work of manifesting the Faith, of using it, of bringing men to it, must be done by its members.'[2]

According to these Anglican missionaries (i.e., Allen, Kelly, Temple Gairdner), the *apostolic principle* – all Christians are missionaries – highlighted how the Church is a missionary body[3] in the world. Mangisi Simorangkir cites Allen's understanding of Pauline missiology:

> The secret of success in St Paul's work 'lies in the beginning at the very beginning. It is the training of the first converts which sets the type for the future'.[4] In his conclusions he said that a sense of mutual responsibility of all Christians for each other should be carefully inculcated and practised. . . . [5] Christians are a ministering community rather than a community gathered around a minister or missionary.[6]

---

1. Talltorp, *Sacrament and Growth*, 60-1.
2. Ibid., 60. Talltorp quoted from Herbert H. Kelly, *An Idea in the Working* (London/Oxford, 1908), 54.
3. Paton, *The Ministry of the Spirit*, 40, 61, 67, 75, 77-80, 165. Also, Allen, 'The Work of the Missionary in Preparing the Way for Independent Native Churches' (1903), USPG X622, Oxford, Bodleian Library.
4. Allen, *Missionary Methods*, 105.
5. Ibid., 195.
6. Mangisi Simorangkir, 'Theological Foundation of Mission: An Asian

Allen's Missionary Ecclesiology

This concept of the indigenous Church which 'from the beginning' is empowered to administer its own activities was foremost in his thought. He did not accept the concept that the Church is indigenous only after its local leadership had somehow proved their ability to govern by the benchmark of foreign mission policy. The ministering community was called to function according to the *apostolic principle* of mutual responsibility as he said:

> I should like to see it accepted as a general principle that converts should be presented by members of the Church to the Church, and accepted by the Church and baptized on the authority of the whole local church acting as a church.[7]

However, could this approach work successfully among suppressed people groups? The answer is, yes. Allen's missionary ecclesiology extended to all people. In fact, his praxis enhanced the poor and the suppressed for he believed that the Gospel of Christ did not discriminate between anyone on the basis of race or social class. An example of his influence on the poor and lower castes of India is documented through the evidence recorded in letters between Bishop V.S. Azariah and Allen.[8] Susan Harper addresses how much influence he had on Azariah and the people of India, saying:

> Azariah continued to consult Allen during his tenure in Dornakal and invited him to address a conference of Dornakal's clergy in December 1927 concerning the barriers to church growth created by the existence of a stipendiary professional clergy and the advantages of ecclesiastical self-support.[9]

Allen wrote in his diary concerning his visit to Dornakal that his books were completely sold out and then discovered that he was being

---

Perspective', Regnum Edinburgh 2010 Series, Volume 4, *Mission Continues: Global Impulses for the 21st Century*, ed. Claudia Wahrisch-Oblau and Fidon Mwombeki (Oxford: Regnum, 2010), 23.

7. Allen, *Missionary Methods*, 99.

8. Cf. the bilateral communication between Bishop V.S. Azariah and Allen, e.g. Azariah's letter to Allen and his reply to Azariah, USPG X622, Box 6, Oxford, Bodleian Library.

9. Susan Billington Harper, *In the Shadow of the Mahatma: Bishop V.S. Azariah and the Travails of Christianity in British India* (Grand Rapids and Cambridge: Eerdmans, 2000) 211.

quoted 'in season and out of season'.[1] His missiological writings so affected Azariah's thinking that it also mobilized his church-planting methodology, especially with the later development of ecumenism, particularly evidenced in the formation of the Church of South India. Azariah is well known to be the main catalyst for Church expansion, which preceded the development of the Church of South India (CSI). This *catholic* expression of Christianity began to move forward after Azariah's address at the World Missionary Conference in Edinburgh, 1910,[2] and after reading many of Allen's writings.[3] The possibility to engage the laity to take ownership of its local activities stemmed from his missionary ecclesiology, which sought to empower the members to act for themselves when necessary. The next chapter takes a step back to analyze what happened within the Church of England when it developed some habits and traditions, both good and bad.

Habit and Tradition

This next chapter of Allen's work began with recognition of how unreasoned habits within the established Church of England quite often neglected to consider a place of ministry for the laity.[4] Fixed patterns of practice within the Church of England remained as habits and traditions not to be reformed.[5] Allen examined 'our hesitation to minister for ourselves' as that which stemmed from custom, not as that rooted through any reasoned conviction.[6] Then, he drew attention to Anglican mission expansion, wherein 'we went abroad and found ourselves where there was no priest at all'.[7] He systematically addressed how basic services of the Church were taken for granted in England, only to be in need of

---

1. Roland Allen, 'Diary of a Visit in South India', USPG X622, Box 7, File: N, Oxford, Bodleian Library.

2. Cf. Brian Stanley, *The World Missionary Conference, Edinburgh 1910*, Studies in the History of Christian Missions (Grand Rapids/Cambridge: Eerdmans, 2009).

3. In 1912 Azariah wrote 'I have been enjoying Mr Roland Allen's volume immensely . . . I wish someone would send a copy of this book [*Missionary Methods: St Paul's or Ours?*] to all South India's Church of England missionaries. . . .' V.S. Azariah's letter to Isabel Whitehead (Bishop White-head's wife; 17 April 1912), Sundkler Collection, cited from Harper's *In the Shadow of the Mahatma* (2000) 210.

4. Ibid., Ch. 2: Outline, Habit and Tradition.

5. Ibid.

6. Ibid., Ch. 2: 1.

7. Ibid.

any priests within a foreign land. His perception of minimal visionary thinking on the part of English bishops to address the problem was only indicative of a systemic failure.[8]

He argued that in past history, the English Church had learned to adapt to its growing challenges by appointing indigenous leadership whenever and wherever it was necessary. Consider his comments concerning the growth of the indigenous Church of England in the sixth century, when Pope Gregory the Great sent Augustine and his associates as missionaries to England:

Indigenous Bishops in England

In our own history, St Augustine was consecrated bishop, not of England, but of Canterbury. He was consecrated in AD 597; seven years later there were two other bishops, in Rochester and London. Forty years later (AD 644) a native was consecrated to Rochester, and he by himself consecrated the first native bishop of Canterbury in AD 654, and at that time all the bishops derived from Augustine were natives; that is within sixty years of St Augustine's landing. Of course, nearly all the clergy were natives.

If we examine Bishop William Stubbs' *Registrum Sacrum Anglicanum*, we find that the last of the Augustinian mission to be consecrated was Honorius (AD 627) to Canterbury. In that year Felix, a Burgundian, was consecrated to Dunwich. After that the only foreign bishops were Theodore of Tarsus (AD 668) to Canterbury, Agilbert (AD 650) to Dorchester, and Leutherius (AD 670) to Winchester. Both these last two were from Paris, which was much nearer in every respect to the south of England than Canton or Shanghai to Peking [Beijing]. Between the years AD 669 and AD 687 Theodore consecrated twenty bishops, of whom only one was not a native of this island.

If we look at the Sees established – Lichfield was founded in AD 656, and all the names of its bishops are native; Lindsey was founded in AD 678, and the names of all its bishops are native; at Dunwich, after Felix the Burgundian, all the names are native; at Elmham (AD 673 – AD 1055) they are all native; at Worcester (AD 680 – 1095) they are all native; at Hereford (AD 676 – 1079) they are all native. In fact, See after See was established, and See after See was established with a native bishop.[9]

---

8. Ibid.

9. Paton, *The Ministry of the Spirit*, 179, as cited from the chapter entitled 'Domination' in Allen's *The Case for Voluntary Clergy* (1930).

Allen's forthright appeal to the historic English Church's ability to adjust to current needs (from the seventh century to the eleventh century) is an example of how he reasoned when dealing with contemporary challenges. And yet, what was the Church of England to do after it had extended its influence through colonial control in distant lands without enough trained clergy to meet the immediate needs? The answer to this question is found in Chapter 3, which advances the apostolic principle of training home-grown leadership.

Charismatic Ministry

Allen began Chapter 3 by providing a set of declarations. First, he addressed his readers with the assumption that they already 'know this ministry' about which he is writing.[1] Second, he reminded them that this type of minister already appears within their missions overseas, for they are noted by the way they 'work spontaneously, unordained and undirected . . . cannot be classed' and tend to be out of place and 'not at home in the organization of a mission'.[2] Third, this type of ministry did not oppose Church order.[3] Fourth, 'the language of the New Testament suggests that it was familiar then', and yet, 'the language used by modern writers seems to exclude it'.[4] Fifth, there remained the position which must accept this type of 'language as used only within the limits of the organized Church'.[5] Sixth, since various charismatic ministers regularly celebrated the Lord's Supper, Allen thought it necessary to 'enquire whether this is not also outside the limits of any argument used by modern theologians who would appear to forbid it'.[6]

Some clarity and definition is in order in the attempt to understand Allen's use of the words *charismatic, charis* and *charisma.* Lesslie Newbigin properly identified that 'Allen was not a prototype of the contemporary evangelical charismatic – much as I think he would have welcomed the charismatic explosion'.[7] First, Newbigin's accurate analysis of Allen's

1. Allen, 'The Ministry of Expansion', Ch. 3: Outline.
2. Ibid.
3. Ibid.
4. Ibid.
5. Ibid.
6. Ibid.
7. See Bishop Lesslie Newbigin's analysis in the *Foreword* of Hubert Allen's *Roland Allen: Pioneer, Priest, and Prophet* (Grand Rapids: Eerdmans and Cincinnati: Forward Movement Publications, 1995) xiii-xv.

thinking is disclosed in the charismatic dynamic of the missionary Spirit emphasis that is rooted in his ecclesiology as 'the Pentecostal gift'.[8] However, this does not imply that he was a charismatic in the sense of the modern understanding of speaking in tongues; neither does it suggest that he was opposed to this grace (*charis*). Instead he emphasized it, in a primary sense, of *charismatic ministry* to equip the Church through 'that direct internal impulse of the Spirit',[9] and also, in a secondary sense, for the Church's empowerment from 'a spiritual illumination'[10] through the gifts of the Spirit (*charismata*).

Secondly, his use of the word *charismatic* ought to be understood as an extension of his belief in the abiding validity of apostles, prophets and teachers – 'wandering evangelists'[11] as he called them – who demonstrated significant trans-local ministry 'ascension' gifts (Ephesians 4:8). Allen recognized the significance of the Church's applied *charisma* – as a gift of grace – within the ordination rite. That said, the person called in ministry accepted both the *charisma* from the Church's rite (laying on of hands for ordination) and commission to officially serve, in addition to the individual *charisma* given by the Holy Spirit. Thus, Allen devoted himself to the clarity of thought concerning the transcendence of the Spirit's work in the life of the Church and states this in Chapter 3:

> By 'charismatic' ministry I mean here a ministry which is exercised by a man who is moved to perform it by an inward, internal, impulse of the Holy Spirit who desires and strives after the salvation of men in Christ. I do not deny that men receive a charisma, a gift of grace, for their ministry in ordination; but I use the word 'charismatic' to express the ministry which is exercised in virtue of that direct internal impulse of the Spirit, as distinguished from the ministry which is exercised by those who have been ecclesiastically ordained or commissioned.[12]

Allen's ecclesiology engaged the 'both-and' approach rather than the 'either-or' attitude of charismatic ministry within Christian mission. This means he recognized both the significance of the Church's applied 'charisma' – as a gift of grace – within the ordination rite,[13] as well as the

8. Roland Allen, *Pentecost and the World*, 11.

9. Allen, *The Ministry of Expansion*, Ch. 3: 1.

10. Allen, *Pentecost and the World*, 46.

11. Allen, *The Ministry of Expansion*, Ch. 3: 6 and 4: 5.

12. Allen, 'The Ministry of Expansion', Ch. 3: 1.

13. In the Anglican ordination service the Bishop leads the congregation in

transcendent empowerment, which he called the 'direct internal impulse of the Spirit'.[1] That said, he accepted both the 'charisma' of commission through the Church corporately, in addition to the individual 'charisma' expressed pneumatologically.

In terms of the *charisma* which was evident among those not ordained by the Church, he cited both Sadhu Sundar Singh of India and the 'Prophet Harris' of West Africa.[2] Singh and Harris were indicative of a plethora of ministers with *charisma* who functioned outside the context of the established Church. Allen stated that

> they are men whom missionary teachers would deem ill qualified for the work. . . . No man sends them out to do it . . . they work outside all ecclesiastical organization, independent of all ecclesiastical authority and supervision . . . with no recognition, no commission, no ordination . . . but are moved solely by an internal impulse . . . yet they certainly perform a ministry . . . in the eyes of those among whom they work.[3]

Allen recognized these unique expressions of *charisma* at work in what he would call the 'apostolic method'. He was not alone in thinking this way about Harris. Lamin Sanneh, almost 80 years after Harris' death (1929), speaks of Harris' ministry.[4] Harris encouraged thousands of Christian converts (French Government officials calculated about 100,000 converts)[5] to receive instruction within both Protestant and Roman Catholic communions.[6] Both Allen and Sanneh recognized that Harris had this type of *charisma*, even though he was not commissioned by any ecclesiastical body.

Various missiologists have recognized Allen's pneumatological contribution to the study of mission theology. The missiologist Harry R. Boer said:

---

the hymn *Veni, Creator Spiritus* before giving a proclamation of charisma – 'Receive the Holy Ghost for the office and work of a Priest in the Church of God. . . . Take thou authority to preach the Word of God and to minister the Holy Sacraments. . . .' *Book of Common Prayer* (1662).

1. Allen, 'The Ministry of Expansion', Ch. 3: 1.
2. Ibid., Ch. 3: 2. This evangelist's name is William Wade Harris.
3. Ibid., Ch. 3: 3-5.
4. Cf. Lamin Sanneh, *Disciples of All Nations: Pillars of World Christianity* (Oxford: Oxford University Press, 2008) 201.
5. Sanneh cites from William J. Platt, *From Fetish to Faith: The Growth of the Church in West Africa* (London: Cargate, 1935), 87.
6. Sanneh, *Disciples of All Nations*, 195.

No review of the place which the Spirit as power occupies in missionary literature may fail to mention the name of Roland Allen. He is pre-eminently the missionary thinker of the Spirit. Allen's conception of the missionary task finds in the doctrine of the Spirit its determinative factor, and from it he drew important conclusions for the practical execution of the work.[7]

Boer's assessment of Allen's doctrine of the Holy Spirit and how it relates to mission is only one example of his contribution to missiology today.

Apostolic Method

For those who are familiar with Allen's missiological writings would not find any hesitance with his use of the word 'apostolic' when addressing the planting of the Church and the training of its leadership. For example, he called for a return to the principles of 'apostolic method'[8] when developing local leadership by an appeal to Pauline practice in contrast to contemporary methods used in the early 1900s. For Allen, the 'apostolic method' derived from 'apostolic order'. Consider his definition of 'apostolic order' when applied to the primary focus of the missionary:

> If the missionary had no local Church to care for; if it was his business to go up and down the country striving to convert men to Christ and to bring them to realize that they could have the fullest Church life the moment that they were willing to receive it; if wherever they heard his message the Church was established, two things would inevitably follow: first, settlers who desired Church life, seeing that it was at hand, seeing that they could enjoy it if they would, and that there was nothing to hinder them if they would serve, would realize their power. There are many, very many, good Church people scattered about the world who would respond, and wherever they responded, there the Church would be. Secondly *the missionary, being no longer bound to minister to settled groups, would be able to proceed from place to place over a very wide area, and his success would consist not in finding a group which would restrain his further progress, but in establishing a Church from which he could make a further advance*

---

7. Harry R. Boer, *Pentecost and Missions* (London: The Lutterworth Press, 1961. Repr., Grand Rapids: Eerdmans, 1964), 61.

8. Allen, *Missionary Methods*, 85; Paton, *The Ministry of the Spirit*, 164.

[emphasis added]. If the members of any group over the widest
areas had not, in a very short time, a full Church life, it would
be entirely their own fault, because such a system would supply
the need of every group that wanted Church life. Working on
that apostolic order, every group in the world could have its full
Church life.[1]

Allen believed the Pauline emphasis on leadership gifting[2] provided
a contextual setting to argue for historic apostolic ministry once again,
as evidenced by those first 'wandering evangelists and prophets' – not
known by the established order of apostles – who had established
communities throughout Antioch, Lydda and Rome.[3] Within the context
of leadership gifting, he pointed out that these functions of prophets,
evangelists, pastors and teachers actually 'follow apostles in a list of
the gifts'.[4] When applying apostles to his early twentieth-century
context, what did he mean? Allen believed these apostles – 'wandering
evangelists'[5] – were the gifted missionaries who planted and equipped
the churches. They were the 'itinerant' missionaries who were known
to work outside the established order,[6] yet could function within the
established structure wherever and whenever resident elected leadership
(i.e., bishops, deacons)[7] accepted their vocation. For Allen, this was
apostolic order. Even Moberly recognized that 'Apostles no doubt would
be thought of as characteristically non-local'.[8] This apostolic work is an
extension of the apostolate, which is how Allen understood this itinerant
ministry.

In 1997, a group of British theological and sociological scholars
wrote *Charismatic Christianity: Sociological Perspectives* and specifically
addressed this emphasis on the apostolic ministries. In particular, Nigel
Wright explained the use of this word by saying:

> Of primary importance in the Restoration movement is the
> recovery of apostolic ministries understood as the concomitant
> of spiritual gifts. . . . Clearly, apostleship is not understood as the
> reconstituting of the original twelve, who were marked out as

---

1. Allen, *Voluntary Clergy Overseas*, 64–65.
2. Romans 12:6-8 is cited in Allen, *The Ministry of Expansion*, Ch. 3: 6.
3. Allen, *The Ministry of Expansion*, Ch. 3: 6.
4. Ibid.; See also, Ephesians 4:11; I Corinthians 12:28.
5. Allen, *The Ministry of Expansion*, Ch. 3: 6 and Ch. 4: 5.
6. Ibid., Ch. 3: 3.
7. Ibid., Ch. 4: 5.
8. Ibid., Ch. 3:9; Moberly, *Ministerial Priesthood*, 163-164.

being historically unique by the Resurrection appearances, but as the recovery of a spiritual function in the Church in line with the five-fold ministry referred to in Ephesians 4:11.[9]

Is Wright correct? My research proposes that Allen thought in the same way. Wright's comment that 'apostleship is not understood as the reconstituting of the original twelve . . . historically unique by the Resurrection appearances'[10] makes the distinction between the 'original' apostles from 'subsequent' apostles, i.e., those who do 'apostolic' work as an extension of the apostolate, which is how Allen understood this itinerant ministry served the Church.

Even later in life he continued to apply apostolic ministry in this sense to current situations. Consider his correspondence with a bishop of Central Tanganyika after an appeal was made in *The Times*:

> In a diocese like yours, surely you are in the position rather of an apostle than of a territorial bishop. You cannot do everything. . . . In the life of St Paul we see how it was done in the lives of many succeeding apostles. They knew that their *one* work [original emphasis] was to establish the Church, and to establish the Church they needed *nothing* [original emphasis] that was not before them on the spot. They needed Christian men: they were there in the persons of non-Christian men. They gathered together the souls whom God called, and they established them, ordaining elders among them to lead and to feed.[11]

This emphasis of apostolic principles and ministry was paramount in Allen's missionary ecclesiology. At the end of Chapter 3, he concludes with a brief story from Mildred Cable's book *Through Jade Gate*, 1927,[12] which tells of a missionary teacher, who was invited to the Chinese district of Kansu to instruct various people in the Bible. He stated that Cable was amazed to see many churches planted there already by one evangelist named Dr Kao, who, had 'not only baptized his converts

9. Edited by Stephen Hunt, Malcolm Hamilton and Tony Walter, *Charismatic Christianity: Sociological Perspectives* (Hampshire: Macmillan Press, 1997), 62.

10. Ibid.

11. Allen's letter to the Bishop of Central Tanganyika, USPG X622, Box 6, letter 137A, 10 June 1930, Oxford, Bodleian Library.

12. Allen, 'The Ministry of Expansion', Ch. 3, 11, where he made reference to Mildred Cable and Francesca French, *Through Jade Gate and Central Asia: An Account of Journeys in Kansu, Turkestan and the Gobi Desert* (London: Constable & Co., 1927).

but taught them all to observe the Lord's Supper'.[1] This spontaneous expansion of churches in areas where Christians were celebrating the sacrament without any resident clergy appeared to him to be a positive sign of 'charismatic' ministry at work by evangelists not necessarily commissioned by episcopal authorities. Was this something 'new' or has the Church endorsed this practice in its past history? This question is briefly answered in Chapter 4 – 'The Practice in the Early Church'.

The Practice in the Early Church

Allen began this chapter by first examining the New Testament, drawing attention to the churches of Samaria, Antioch, Cyprus, Lydda, Phoenicia, Joppa, Galatia and Rome.[2] Moving beyond the Scriptures, he then drew attention to the non-canonical *Didachē* in which there seemed to be no evidence that the Eucharistic officers were even 'ecclesiastically ordained'.[3] By appealing to the *Didachē*, he attempted to find evidence that Christians 'celebrated the Lord's Supper in the absence of a priest'.[4] He appealed to the evidence found in Tertullian and critiqued 'Bishop Gore's repudiation of that evidence examined'.[5] Allen was convinced that there was sufficient evidence in the early Church for what he was suggesting to be applied to his situation.[6]

From this chapter the reader gets a glimpse of Allen's commitment to the *primacy* of Scripture while defining apostolic ministry as well as his willingness to cite early Church *tradition* by appealing to the *Didachē*.[7] Allen made use of *reason* to argue from Scripture and tradition when applying his interpretation of these 'evangelists called apostles, prophets and teachers, who wander about, and Churches established by them whose local officers are called bishops and deacons and are elected'.[8] He clearly distinguished between itinerant apostolic order (i.e., apostles, prophets, teachers) and the resident local ministry (i.e., bishops, deacons) from what he believed was the *Didachē's* application of apostolic

---

1. Allen, 'The Ministry of Expansion', Ch. 3, 11.
2. Ibid., Ch. 4: Outline.
3. Ibid.
4. Ibid.
5. Ibid.
6. Ibid.
7. J.B. Lightfoot and J.R. Harmer, "The *Didachē* or The Teaching of the Twelve Apostles" in *The Apostolic Fathers*, 2nd edition, edited and revised by Michael W. Holmes (Grand Rapids: Baker Book House, 1989), 149-58.
8. Allen, *The Ministry of Expansion*, Ch. 4: 5.

instruction.[9] The *Didachē* referred to the Eucharistic meal (*Didachē* 14:1-3) as a common expression of the faith with the understanding that not all of these primitive churches had resident clergy, as also seen in the instruction to give 'the first fruits' (i.e., the tithe) to the poor 'if you have no prophet [settled in your community]' (13:3). This reference to a 'prophet' who might settle within a certain community implied their vocation to be itinerant in nature. This point is critical within Allen's understanding of the vocation of itinerant evangelists.[10]

We Cannot Go Back

In Chapter 5, Allen parsed some of Moberly's comments and 'abstractions' (*Ministerial Priesthood*, 109-10) that tended to disparage the newer churches (younger churches) that were 'springing up', many of which were *independent* of the 'organized' Church.[11] Allen argued that the newer churches within pioneer regions were experiencing challenges very similar to that which the early Christians experienced, such as being 'remote from the ecclesiastical authorities'.[12] Allen was not arguing 'against an ordained ministry' rather he defended the legitimacy of these newer 'churches [that] were springing up' outside the influence of the organized Church.[13] The fact that the laity were already managing these developing churches, he argued, seemed to be 'in open defiance of [the] authority [and of] the limits of the organized Church'.[14]

Allen went on to argue against what he thought was an improper use of the word 'Covenant' in the rationale that 'Bishop Gore and Dr Moberly' used when they – and their followers – promoted the 'legal, formal, strained' *interpretation* of apostolic succession, that being, the ecclesial custom that denied the laity any authorization to administer the sacraments.[15] His missiology argued for a return to an apostolic understanding: 'the promise is not without the Covenant, but within it'.[16]

---

9. Thomas O'Loughlin, *The Didachē: A Window on the Earliest Christians* (London: SPCK, 2010), 168-170.

10. Allen, *The Ministry of Expansion*, Ch. 4: 5.

11. Ibid., Ch. 5: 5. Allen's original edition of *The Ministry of Expansion* referred to these newer churches as 'infantine'. Thus, for the sake of clarity, these churches will be referred to as 'newer' churches.

12. Ibid., Ch. 5: 1.

13. Ibid., Ch. 5: 5.

14. Ibid., Ch. 5: 7.

15. Ibid., Preface: 3.

16. Ibid., Ch. 5: 10.

And, that any 'custom [and] habit', which denies the laity to administer the sacraments when clergy are not physically present, is a misapplication of what 'the covenant of promise' means under the definition of 'the Gospel' (Galatians 3:1-9).[1] Those who disagreed with Allen's return to the early Church's practice of lay presidency (in given circumstances) argued that such a return was not progress but reverting backwards.[2] Allen insisted that it was 'not backward for us' to return to *apostolic precedent* because 'we are back in their day [with the same] spiritual needs'.[3]

The Priesthood of the Laity

Allen wrote 'that the ministers'[4] who celebrate the Eucharist are doing this 'not vicariously for the congregation, but representatively, and that it is the whole body which offers' the sacrifices of praise and thanksgiving.[5] His analysis of Gore and Moberly's 'logical conclusion' was, in his opinion, false, as it would 'make the sacraments entirely depend upon the will of a bishop'.[6] The belief that this 'doctrine as set out by these theologians [asserted that] none of us are empowered to act [implies that] Christ's sacraments are annulled for us', and this, he believed, was against the apostolic teaching concerning 'the universal common priesthood of Christians'.[7] He then cited Bishop Lightfoot who argued:

> It may be a general rule [but] an emergency may arise when the spirit and not the letter must decide . . . [that] the higher ordinance of the universal priesthood will over-rule all special limitations . . . [and the] layman will assume functions which are otherwise restricted to the ordained minister.[8]

Bishop Lightfoot's recognition that 'an emergency may arise' for sacramental administration *by the laity*, is contrasted with Moberly's and Gore's interpretation.[9] This clearly demonstrated how Allen advanced

1. Ibid., Ch. 5: 8-9.
2. Ibid., Ch. 5: 1.
3. Ibid., Ch. 6: 1.
4. Ibid.
5. Ibid.
6. Ibid., Ch. 6: 3-4.
7. Ibid., Ch. 6: 4, 7.
8. Ibid., Ch. 6: 8. See J.B. Lightfoot, *Commentary on Philippians: The Christian Ministry* (London, 1868), 268.
9. Allen, *The Ministry of Expansion*, Preface, 3.

the apostolic faith's Trinitarian understanding of the Church's 'one and the many' – individual (Christian) and group (Church) – in which '[the] Christian, is a member of a priestly body and shares all the powers of the body, the universal being in the particular because the Spirit is one in the universal and in the particular'.[10]

The law of the universal priesthood of the Church, Allen believed, could not be understood as a separate law of episcopal ordination. Both are united together, he argued, and 'are not two laws, but one [that is] a gospel law', which, according to Bishop Lightfoot, 'opens to us the door of grace'.[11] This understanding related to the legitimacy of lay presidency for administering sacraments in 'emergency' situations, as Lightfoot also argued.[12] Allen concluded this chapter by empathizing with the 'men who are beyond the reach of ordination or whose ordination may be hindered by a tradition not less legal and cruel than this'.[13]

Presumption

Allen begins his final chapter with making a distinction between 'settled churches and [those] outside them' and then unpacks the significance of 'that ministry of expansion' which has its stimulus from 'the charismatic ministry'.[14] Here, he specifically states the centrality of his missiology – the Holy Spirit's sovereignty over Church expansion.[15] Some 'felt that it would be *an act of presumption to dare* to hold a service of any kind' without the presence of regularly ordained ministers.[16] Allen disagreed on the grounds that whenever the Holy Spirit empowers the laity 'to observe His Last Supper' it is *not* a presumptuous act, and therefore, is 'it not then greater presumption to disobey Him than to obey Him?'[17] Next, he argues for the early Church practice whereby 'dioceses were small, and the bishop was the representative of a Christian community which knew him, and which he knew personally'.[18] A restoration of this practice, he believed, would solve the problem.

---

10. Ibid., Ch. 6: 9-12.

11. Ibid., Ch. 6: 10.

12. Ibid., Ch. 6: 10-12.

13. Ibid., Ch. 6: 13.

14. Ibid., Ch. 7: 6-7.

15. Ibid., Ch. 7: 8.

16. Ibid., Ch. 7: 9. Emphasis in the original.

17. Ibid., Ch. 7: 10.

18. Ibid., Ch. 7: 11.

Allen argued that, within Anglican missionary methods, a new problem had developed whereby 'vast dioceses leave large numbers of groups without any ordained priests' and subsequently, in order to solve this problem, imposed a European model of theological education upon indigenous candidates seeking ordination.[1] This, he argued, placed too much credence on 'the act of an individual [priest]' rather than 'the act of a Church which meets to perform its own proper rite'.[2] This shift, he argued, looked 'not at the group but at individuals' and presented 'a great gulf between the priest and the Church'.[3] This gets at the heart of Allen's ecclesiology, which argued for candidates to be trained locally and *not* to be sent to a theological seminary elsewhere. He believed the diocesan bishop exemplified true apostolic order as he (and duly appointed diocesan teachers) trained candidates for ordination within the bishop's own diocesan context.

Consequently, Allen reiterated the purpose for his *apologia* by re-emphasizing that 'this book ['The Ministry of Expansion: the Priesthood of the Laity'] ought properly to be addressed', *not* for those within the existing and settled churches, but rather for those who are 'geographically beyond the reach of any bishop [and] outside the boundary of the organized Church'.[4] Allen recognized that among those denominations 'who utterly reject the doctrine of apostolic succession',[5] still tend to restrict lay presidency, as soon as they become highly organized and practise the system of 'ordained stipendiary ministry'.[6] He concluded this 'little book' by reaffirming reverence to the Anglican order of episcopacy and 'the relationship which should exist between the ministry of expansion and the settled ministry'.[7] His *apologia* for *the ministry of expansion* was rooted in the charismatic dynamic that works within and extends from the *priesthood of the laity*. Hence, in many respects, Allen can be considered a pioneer in modern missiology.

Conclusion

This research concluded that Allen's argument for apostolic mission – as disclosed in *The Ministry of Expansion* – stemmed from an integrated

---

1. Ibid., Ch. 7: 13.
2. Ibid., Ch. 7: 12-13.
3. Ibid.
4. Ibid., Ch. 7: 13-14.
5. Ibid., Ch. 7: 15.
6. Ibid., Ch. 7: 16-18.
7. Ibid., Ch. 7: 18-20.

pneumatology (Spirit) and ecclesiology (Order) that was shaped by the Apostle Paul's missionary principles, methods and practices. Although Allen conventionally maintained his belief in apostolic succession and High Church episcopacy for the planting of indigenous churches, it became evident that his understanding of the Holy Spirit's empowerment of the laity actually proposed the prioritization of 'Spirit *before* Order'. This produced, on one hand, the inevitability for the existence of independent churches and, on the other hand, in his attempt to preserve what he believed were principles which undergirded apostolic order, was compelled to challenge bishops to proactively advance the apostolic order by ordaining the laity who were already serving these younger churches. We saw that Allen's observations of this charismatic dynamic of the Church's expansion within the non-Western world compelled him to argue on behalf of these 'younger' or 'newer' churches. He defended the legitimacy of these newer churches that were emerging outside the influence of the organized Church – Spirit *before* Order – whereby the priesthood of the laity faithfully served these communities of faith. As a missionary analyst, he interpreted his context as similar to the early stages of the younger churches of Samaria, Lydda, Joppa, Phoenicia, Cyprus, Antioch, Galatia and Rome. Throughout Allen's missionary journeys and itinerant ministry he affirmed the sovereign acts of the Holy Spirit that were at work within these younger churches. And, it is this pastoral concern that provided the impetus for him to write *The Ministry of Expansion*.

Allen's emphasis on a return to the early Church's practice of lay presidency (in given circumstances), he believed, was a return to *apostolic precedent*. His defence for sacramental ministry in the newly formed churches actually created a context for a *well-ordered* ecclesiology to eventually emerge, that being, 'Spirit *with* Order'. We saw that as an Anglican clergyman and missionary Allen had reverence for divine order. Disclosed within the context of this previously unpublished work, he clearly distinguished between itinerant apostolic order (i.e., apostles, prophets, teachers) and the resident local ministry (i.e., bishops, deacons) from what he believed was primarily inspired within the Bible, and, secondarily, outlined within the early Church's application of apostolic instruction as revealed in the *Didachē*. In the final analysis of *The Ministry of Expansion*, it is important to disclose that Roland Allen's missiology actually proposes a 'Spirit-*inspired* ecclesiology', that being, a 'Spirit-*empowered* Order, designed to accommodate the *charismatic* dynamic in order to equip, commission, send and expand the Church throughout the world.

9. The Church as 'The Family Rite'

'The Family Rite' (1943)[1]

From amongst the various works of Roland Allen, there emerges a sage-like reflective piece of ecclesiastical writing referred to as 'The Family Rite'.[2] Within the archives exists a document notebook containing Allen's handwritten thesis which basically contrasts a 'Family Rite' from a 'Temple Rite'. David Paton's *Reform of the Ministry* printed its contents (including footnotes) in 1968 and subsequently he, and Charles Long, included it in 'A Roland Allen Reader' entitled *The Compulsion of the Spirit* (1983), which does *not* include all of the original footnotes.[3] 'The Family Rite' sheds light on Allen's understanding of the father's priestly role within the family structure and provides a basis for the advancement of house churches. During Allen's latter years of life in Africa, he did argue for a 'family rite' sacramental practice as a model for missionary ecclesiology. Today, Bible scholars and missiologists are indebted to Canon David Paton for his arrangement of previously unpublished works by Roland Allen and the time spent on getting certain works published, especially 'The Family Rite'. That said, I must digress temporarily in order to address some items of importance.

After analysis of Roland Allen's original document and extensive comparison with Paton's initial publication (1968) the evidence discloses normal editorial adjustments (e.g., paragraph divisions)[4] but also

---

1. Earlier unpublished work by Roland Allen 'The Family Rite' (1943/44), USPG X622, Box 7, Oxford, Bodleian Library.

2. No title is listed in the original manuscript. The current title 'The Family Rite' was used by David Paton due to the continued use of the phrase throughout the document and then published in David Paton's *Reform of the Ministry* (London: The Lutterworth Press, 1968), 189-219.

3. Ibid.; David Paton & Charles H. Long, (eds.), *The Compulsion of the Spirit*, A Roland Allen Reader (Grand Rapids: Eerdmans and Cincinnati: Forward Movement Publications, 1983), 137-47.

4. Paton made over thirty different paragraph divisions for editing purposes from Allen's original text.

includes *unnecessary* words and the deletion of *important* words, which at times changes the meaning of the text.[5] For example, Paton's publication misplaced *footnote 10* ('It is noteworthy that Christ never seems to have expected that his denunciations would convert Scribes & Pharisees') and placed it one and a half pages later, thus, affecting the context of the argument. And, Paton inserts the word 'always'[6] at a point at which it is not located in the original, he also left out 'religious'[7] where Allen chose to use this word these are a few examples of Paton's 'occasional' careless editing. In fact, a significant change falls within the context of Allen's comments disclosing how under Christendom there was unavoidable tension between Church courts and State courts.[8] As he begins to compare this with how family law is different, Allen wrote: 'In the family there is law.'[9] However, Paton translates this as: 'In the family there is no law.'[10] The addition of 'no' to this sentence clearly changes the meaning. Assuming that this was an unintentional misprint does not rectify the other careless errors in Paton's publication. That said, Paton inserted or deleted words in thirty-two places in his publication.[11]

The thesis of this work is an *apologia* for 'The Family Rite' as the core foundation for the local church and he believed that this meant the head of the household was to lead his family in worship. Roman Catholic theologians also use this familial understanding as seen in Francis Anekwe Oborji's phrase 'the universal church-family'.[12] In order to understand Allen's thesis, it is helpful to also read the letter (paper) Roland's son, Iohn [John], wrote to him the year before, which provides the backdrop for 'The Family Rite'.[13] However, before highlighting some points of the earlier letter, it is important to juxtapose the following paragraph (approximately a third of the way through this manuscript) which discloses Roland's thinking:

5. Special appreciation is given to my research assistant (my wife, Susannah) who carefully examined this handwritten work and compared it with Paton's publication.

6. Paton, *Reform of the Ministry*, 191.

7. Cf. Paton, 192 with Allen's use of the word 'religious' in footnote 6, 'The Family Rite', USPG X622, Box 7, Oxford, Bodleian Library.

8. Allen, 'The Family Rite', 14.

9. Ibid.

10. Paton, 211.

11. Paton, *Reform of the Ministry*, 191, 192, 193 (2), 196 (2), 197, 198 (3), 199 (4), 203, 205, 206 (2), 208, 211, 213 (2), 215 (4), 217 (2), 218 (4).

12. Oborji, *Concepts of Mission*, 97.

13. Iohn Allen's letter to his father which Roland entitled as 'The Family v. The Temple Rite' (23 May 1942), USPG X622, Box 7, Oxford, Bodleian Library.

Take, for instance, the use of Sacraments. So far as I know I am the
only priest of the C. of. E [Church of England] who has practised
the celebration of H.C. [Holy Communion] as a family institution
deliberately and advisedly. My experience then has taught me much
of which I was before ignorant. I had always been convinced that,
in the beginning, Christians observed the Rite in their houses, as
the Passover had been observed, as a family rite [Exodus 12], but
that very soon, on the basis of the conviction that all Christians
were brethren & [and] that there was one family in Christ, those
who could, in any one place, met together as one family to observe
it. So it was/became the Rite of a group, a local church, and for
that church elders, or priests, were ordained & [and] appointed
who in the Service took the place of the Father in the family.
Then as the numbers & [and] wealth of the Christian community
increased, inevitably the Rite took on the form of a Temple Rite, its
ornaments elaborated, its form stereotyped down to the minutest
detail, till we reach the artificial rubrics of some of the Greek
Rites. By this way the Elders or Bishops of the early days became a
Body of Professional Clergy over against the laymen. They alone
knew the Temple secrets. . . .[1]

He wrote this in his mid-seventies and on the surface it looks as though
he might have experienced some type of paradigm shift away from
institutional Christianity towards a 'home church' model. His reference
to how the 'Passover had been observed, as a family rite'[2] conveys his
interpretation of this feast's practice according to Exodus 12:

The LORD said to Moses and Aaron in the land of Egypt. . . . Tell
all the congregation of Israel that on the tenth day of this month
every man shall take a lamb according to their fathers' houses,
a lamb for a household. And if the household is too small for a
lamb, then he and his nearest neighbour shall take according to
the number of persons; according to what each can eat you shall
make your count for the lamb (Exodus 12:1-4).

Allen's *apologia* for restoring 'The Family Rite' as the core foundation
for the local church (in light of the Old Testament pattern disclosed
in the Passover) appears to stem from his biblical understanding that
the head of the household was responsible to lead his family in worship,
especially with the father's priestly role to administer the Passover meal.

---

1. Allen, 'The Family Rite', 6-7.
2. Ibid.

This suggests that Allen's sacramental practice to administer the Holy Communion within his household finds its covenantal basis in the Passover meal. In retrospect, Iohn's previous letter unpacks Roland's thinking. This letter summarizes various questions that both father and son engaged in for some time. Firstly, the concept of the 'family observance' took precedence in Roland's 'small church' or 'cell group' model, but not at the expense of eliminating 'a meeting house' anywhere.[3] Roland engaged with Iohn's concern about the need for 'mass expression' and said: 'There is no suggestion of the family observance destroying at once the present temple order, for celebration of H.C. [Holy Communion,] still less for the sort of national service in which men express their common social religion led by the King. . . . '[4] When Iohn thought that his father's idea suggested that church buildings were not necessary, Roland countered his concern by saying he was 'jumping into the unknown'.[5] Iohn's question was not speculative, however, because his father was a minimalist when it came to church buildings and rituals.

Secondly, Roland clarified that any establishment of 'a public Altar over against the Bishop's Altar' ought not to be practised if the intention is to cause a schism, but rather he believed that the re-emergence of the family rite 'would tend to their spiritual health' in an edifying way.[6] At the centre of his thought was the idea that the implementation of voluntary clergy was 'the first step' but that it 'must come slowly and by degrees'.[7] Thirdly, the discussion between them dealt with the tension between the extremes of legalism and anarchy. Roland admitted that the Judaizers' argument against Paul for 'freeing the Gentiles from the Law' was easily interpreted as an emphasis whereby 'freedom would be anarchy'.[8] He speculates that this type of freedom, in this case, 'the Family Rite', as being against the 'professional stipendiary system', is a perceived form of anarchy. This begs the question concerning the right to justifiably rebel against the institutional Church for that matter.[9] His answer was: 'I believe in Sacraments and therefore believe that they are incapable of being destroyed by any such error.'[10] For Allen, the sacraments trump institutional customs.

3. Iohn Allen's letter, 'The Family v. The Temple Rite' (23 May 1942), 1.
4. Ibid.
5. Ibid., 2.
6. Ibid., 2.
7. Ibid., 2.
8. Ibid., 3.
9. Ibid., 4.
10. Ibid., 4.

The Need for Reform

His missionary ecclesiology accepted the 'need of reform' by placing the Eucharistic practice within the context of 'the Family Rite' and not just in 'the Temple Rite'.[1] He argued for 'liberty of thought and action based essentially on goodwill' in order to produce small churches that could easily reproduce themselves. This argument for separate expressions of the Christian community he believed was healthy and tended towards a sign of maturity. He emphasized how this was the mature expression among the European countries, which were 'not based on quarrels, it is rather designed to preserve unity'.[2] That said, when arguing for the right to freely establish 'Family Rite' churches, that being, what he also called the 'organization of a little church on the apostolic model',[3] then the experience of celebrating the Eucharist enhances catholicity – *e pluribus unum*.

When observing the Church's customs over time, he wondered whether or not she had any capacity for 'universality'.[4] His disappointments with the Church's 'system' stemmed from a wider observation of 'Christianity', which he says 'as known to us, as something temporary, a stage in the history of religion, and local'.[5] This agonizing comment caused him to analyze the infallible utterances of the Roman Catholic Church and he described those decrees as 'a form of ecclesiastical Nazism'.[6] For Allen, this describes a form of 'the Temple Rite' that he thought was detrimental to 'the priesthood' of the Church, as previously argued.[7] He believed the difference was between the 'internal compulsion' (Family Rite) and the 'external commandment' (Temple Rite).[8] 'The Christian law is an internal compulsion or impulse towards an ideal: Legalism is an attempt to put an external commandment in its place, [and] must accept external obedience as its fulfilment.'[9]

---

1. Ibid., 4.
2. Ibid., 4.
3. Allen, *Spontaneous Expansion*, 156.
4. Allen, 'The Family Rite', 4.
5. Ibid.
6. Ibid., 4. See Maurice, *The Kingdom of Christ*, 'The Romish System', vol. 1, 282-288.
7. Allen, 'The Ministry of Expansion: the Priesthood of the Laity,' USPG X622, Oxford, Bodleian Library. Also, Talltorp, *Sacrament and Growth*, 60-61 and H.H. Kelly, *An Idea in the Working* (London-Oxford, 1908), 54.
8. Allen, 'The Family Rite', 14.
9. Ibid., 14.

His ecclesiological *apologia* promoted this 'Family Rite' not only in theory but also in practice. He and Beatrice observed the Eucharist at home[10] and practised it daily before breakfast.[11] The more he celebrated the Holy Communion at home, he found himself less stringent on use of the lectionary and basically set aside certain rubrics. 'When I began to celebrate the Holy Communion at home with my wife as a regular thing, I began by thinking of the act as a performance of the Temple Rite as it might be in the private chapel.'[12] But the more he practised this rite within his home he said that 'I liked it, and approved it. I still used the form prescribed in the Prayer Book [the Anglican *Book of Common Prayer*], because I was sure that I could not better it, but I did not follow it slavishly.'[13] This level of liturgical flexibility from a High Anglican in the 1940s demonstrates his spiritual journey to contextualize his ecclesiology within the missionary context while living in Africa. Similar reasoning continued in South America within the Province of the Southern Cone years after Allen's death (1947). Alan Hargrave argues in favour of 'lay presidency' and bases this practice upon Allen's theory and practice as disclosed in how 'the Family Rite' in actuality 'points to its relationship to the Passover, which is essentially a "family rite" rather than a "temple rite" '.[14] Hargrave engages with Allen's practice: 'Rather than destroy the universality of the event, he [Allen] feels it upholds it, since it creates a model which provides a richer vision for the universal. Note his emphasis on ecclesiology. His primary focus is the community of believers, not the minister.'[15]

Arguably, later in life Allen still maintained the kingdom signs[16] of the one, holy, catholic and apostolic Church: Bible, creeds, ministry and

---

10. Ibid., 7.

11. Allen argues for an early celebration based on his interpretation of Acts 20:7-12; Iohn Allen's letter, 'The Family v. The Temple Rite' (23 May 1942), 4-5.

12. Allen, 'The Family Rite', 7.

13. Ibid.

14. Alan Hargrave, *But Who Will Preside? A review of Issues concerning 'Lay Presidency' in parts of South America and in the Anglican Communion at Large*, Grove Worship Series no. 113 (Bramcote, Nottingham: Grove Books, 1990), 14; cf. Paton, *Reform of the Ministry*, 201f. See also, John Woodhouse, 'Lay Administration of the Lord's Supper: A change to stay the same' in Melvin Tinker (ed.), *The Anglican Evangelical Crisis: A radical agenda for a Bible based church* (Geanies House, Fearn, Ross-shire, Scotland: Christian Focus Publications, 1995), 144-55.

15. Hargrave, *But Who Will Preside?* 14.

16. Maurice, *The Kingdom of Christ*, vol. 2, Chapter 4, 17-185.

sacraments, to be essential for the establishment of the Church. He did not waver from this position. At the end of 'The Family Rite' he did challenge what he believed to be an inconsistency within Anglican practice.

> Baptism is as much a Sacrament according to the Prayer Book as Eucharist. Then why this anomaly? Convenience and Habit. The thing has become familiar, [and] no one questions it. . . . If a deacon can baptize (and it is generally acknowledged that a layman can), why cannot he, (and by the same rule, a layman), celebrate? A deacon is not at his ordination given authority to minister any sacraments. It is said that no celebration of H.C. [Holy Communion] is valid unless it is ministered by a priest, then why is a Baptism valid when the minister is not a priest? . . . It is said that necessity compels deacons [and] laymen to baptize in the absence of a priest. If that is true, why does not the same necessity apply to the celebration of H.C. [Holy Communion]? Is there some subtle distinction between the two Sacraments which the Prayer Book does not recognize?[1]

Allen's *apologia* declared that 'Christian law is an internal compulsion or impulse towards an ideal',[2] that is, where 'truth' produces freedom. And, it is this freedom which he believed is a byproduct of the truth which is in 'Christ, from whom the whole family in heaven and earth is named' (Eph. 3:14-15). His missionary ecclesiology stemmed from a belief in a Trinitarian – *missio Dei* – who then empowers and sends the one, holy, catholic and apostolic Church as fully equipped missionaries into all the world.

In the latter years of his life, his ecclesiology was still influenced by an Anglican order (as a good form), but for him – faith trumped form. A year after writing 'The Family Rite' he engaged with the idea of 'religious toleration'.[3] In continuation with his earlier emphasis on the 'internal compulsion' of Christian law, he argued that 'Christian law is internal'[4] in order to promote religious toleration. Allen believed that 'the practice of religious toleration' rests upon two fundamental points: (1) 'The conviction that truth is indestructible [and] can meet every conceivable

---

1. Allen, 'The Family Rite', 17.
2. Ibid., 14.
3. Unpublished (1944) work by Roland Allen 'Religious Toleration', USPG X622, Box 7, Oxford, Bodleian Library.
4. Ibid., 18.

attack, certain to conquer'[5] and (2) 'Religious faith is essentially internal; it cannot be enforced by any external compulsion'.[6] The principle that he based this upon was from the words of the first bishop of Jerusalem – St James – whom Roland Allen quoted at the conclusion of his paper for this defence of toleration: 'The wrath of man worketh not the righteousness of God' (James 1:20).

Conclusion

According to Allen's sacramental emphasis, whenever the Church gathered together for worship, the Eucharist ought to be practised on a regular basis. This chapter has analyzed his sacramental theology and how it was interwoven within his missionary ecclesiology. Over his lifetime he encountered many newer churches, which had emerged within the majority world (specifically in Asia and Africa) and observed how they were already functioning without ordained ministers. Who, therefore, he asked, was qualified to administer the Holy Communion if ordained clergymen were absent? He came to the conclusion that they must act for themselves. Thus he argued for the continual practice of Communion in these cases even when ordained clergy were not present to preside. How could he, as an Anglican clergyman, one who was fostered and mentored at the feet of some of Oxford's principal Anglo-Catholic defenders of apostolic succession, defend such a break from seemingly normal churchmanship? He believed there were sufficient grounds to justify such an action and he thought apostolic precedent provided a basis for such action. Allen's central understanding for the celebration of the Holy Communion within a trans-denominational format – a true expression of communion among Christians from different backgrounds – is indicative of how his catholic faith trumped ecclesiastical differences. The quintessence of his sacramental practice is examined further as the focus is placed on his last main works entitled 'The Family Rite' (1943) and 'Religious Toleration' (1944). These works provide a final summation of the significance that his sacramental theology played into his belief for the spontaneous expansion of the Church. This analysis discloses how, in Allen's latter years, he argued for a 'family rite' sacramental practice as a model for missionary ecclesiology.

---

5. Ibid.
6. Ibid., 19.

10. Epilogue: Roland Allen
A Missionary Life and *A Theology of Mission*

I have aimed to analyze the context and development of Roland Allen's missiology within these two books, thus providing, overall, an *intellectual biography* of his work, and, in particular, a focus on his theology of indigenization. A thorough examination of his missionary ecclesiology disclosed that he integrated pneumatology and ecclesiology – Spirit and Order – within the framework of a missionary theology of Church growth. This was enhanced, not by strategic methodologies, but through a belief in the ministry of the Holy Spirit and the application of apostolic principles. This research has unpacked his conviction that Pauline missiology is *timeless* and capable of producing indigenous self-governing, self-supporting and self-extending churches without foreign control. While such debates and discussions are now relatively commonplace within Christian missiology, a century ago this was not the case. Indeed, in many respects my research has shown that Allen can be considered a pioneer.

A Reflective Summary

This research concludes that Allen's argument for an apostolic missionary ecclesiology stemmed from his belief that Pauline missionary methods provided the best prototype for 'missional Christianity'. After examining his writings, especially his unpublished works in which he references the *Didachē*, it is obvious that this early document also shaped his ecclesiological thinking. That said, this research has shown how he wrestled with aspects of Western missions' institutional and task-oriented methodologies, in contrast to his understanding of Pauline pneumatology, which he believed was the major stimulus for the empowerment and expansion of the Church's witness. Although Allen conventionally maintained his belief in High Church episcopacy for the planting of indigenous churches, it became evident that his pneumatological emphasis actually proposed the prioritization of 'Spirit *before* Order'. This produced, on one hand, the inevitability for the existence of independent churches and, on the other hand, in his attempt to preserve what he believed were principles that undergirded apostolic order, a commitment to the ordination of indigenous leaders. This, we have seen, empowered a sacramental ministry to exist within the newly formed churches, which, in turn, created a context for 'Spirit *with* Order'. In the final analysis, Allen's missionary ecclesiology actually proposes a 'Spirit-*inspired* ecclesiology', that is, a 'Spirit-*empowered* Order' designed to accommodate the charismatic dynamic whereby the 'direct internal impulse of the Spirit'[1] sovereignly acts – quite often before any actual apostolic confirmation transpires (cf. Acts 8:14-17).

The archival research indicates that, later in life, Allen continued to advance a sacramental emphasis within the 'little church' model he had previously advocated. His decision to refer to it as the 'Family Rite' was based upon the Passover observance (Exodus 12).[2] The research discloses that Allen's model suggested that churches – smaller and flexible – within close proximity and relating to each other in a diocesan context had the capability to better reproduce themselves spontaneously. In contrast, he believed the Church's later decision to develop a more centralized approach – the 'Temple Rite' – misinterpreted the apostolic order and, instead, introduced a form of clergy professionalism 'over against the laymen'.[3] These two books have examined the ways in which 'the admission of selected individuals to membership in a professional order',[4] thereby hindered the contributions of both indigenous leadership and local laity from advancing Church expansion. The evidence also discloses his opposition to aspects of the 'external commandment' generally associated with institutional ecclesiastical structures, since he believed it dishonoured the 'internal compulsion' of the pneumatological principle within the life of these smaller churches.[5] The analysis of Allen's missionary ecclesiology presented above concludes that he believed the mission of the Church was *not* intended to be task-orientated, but rather an organic emanation of the Church's *being*. In addition, at the core of his indigenous *apologia* was this principled missionary theology – mission *not* maintenance. In other words, he developed an intentional approach for short-term apostolic mission *instead of* long-term foreign maintenance. It was this understanding of the Church's mission, combined with the

---

1. Allen, 'The Ministry of Expansion: the Priesthood of the Laity', 3:1.
2. Allen, 'The Family Rite', 6-7.
3. Ibid.
4. Allen, 'Voluntary Clergy and the Lambeth Conference', *The Church Overseas* (1931) 153.
5. Allen, 'The Family Rite', 14.

backdrop of Allen's charismatic missiology, which compelled him to trust in the transcendent 'missionary Spirit'[1] to empower the indigenous Church for its holistic development without foreign hegemony. Therefore, these two volumes disclose how his missiology was shaped, primarily, by Pauline missionary methods, and secondarily, by examples of the missiological situation as articulated within the non-canonical *Didachē* which stems from the context of the early Church.

Overview of the Research

The main part of this historical analysis reveals the influences upon Allen's thought of his family, fellow churchmen and theologians and the missionary circumstances in which he found himself. *Roland Allen: A Missionary Life* examines the ecclesiological and missiological *milieu* that pervaded his earlier theological development. Firstly, my numerous interviews with Hubert Allen, on one hand, disclose how his grandfather's evangelical faith was influenced by his mother, while, on the other hand, his Oxford education had shaped his high churchmanship. Secondly, my archival research reveals how his missionary experience in China occasioned his methodological critique of the 'mission station system' and various paternalistic missionary practices. Initial evidence is proposed in this chapter (and unpacked in subsequent chapters) for Allen's emerging missiology of indigenization, which slowly developed while serving in China due to the direct influence by Charles Scott and the indirect influence of John Nevius. My findings suggests that Allen's incipient formation for indigenous church-planting stems from the direct influence that the Presbyterian missionary, John Nevius, had on his friend, Charles Scott (Allen's bishop), and how this filtered down to Allen from Scott during his missionary service in North China. Scott's implementation of Nevius' missionary methods of indigenous self-support, self-government and self-propagation within his diocese were clearly embraced and practised by Allen within the context of this diocese. My analysis argues that Nevius' comments on the 'injurious effects of the paid-agent system'[2] clearly influenced Allen's thought to eventually develop his own apologia against the mission station system and predict its eventual demise.[3] That said, it is clear from my research that, although Nevius' missionary methods had an earlier impact on his thought, Roland Allen was not uncritical of his ideas. Notably, some thirty years later, he published an article in which, after

---

1. Allen, *Pentecost and the World*, 11-21.
2. Nevius, The Planting and Development of Missionary Churches, 27.
3. Allen, 'Devolution', 5-31.

much reflection and further missionary experiences, he disagreed with a certain aspect of Nevius' 'three self' principle for mission work. Although Allen agreed with Nevius in principle that self-support was to originate at the beginning stages of planting indigenous churches, he disagreed with Nevius' interpretation that self-support referred to money. Allen emphatically stated that it is here that Nevius' system broke down because he did not recognize 'self-support' in its broader application of 'spiritual as well as material'[4] in reference to the Church's ability to supply its own local leadership. My analysis discloses how Allen clearly believed that Nevius – though well intentioned – failed to implement the 'three self' approach properly at the inception of missionary church-planting and, therefore, inadvertently created a system of devolution. I argue that Allen's version actually disseminates a non-hegemonic methodology that systematically supports a more mature version due to the integration of the 'three self' principles immediately when indigenous churches are planted.

The next section examines the ways in which Allen's missionary experience in China motivated him to evaluate the missiological situation of his day and documents how his contribution to the study of indigenous church-planting provided continuing relevance for theories of Church growth in the majority world during the early stages of a dismantling colonialism. My analysis of his *magnum opus, Missionary Methods: St Paul's or Ours?* (1912), and his co-authored book *Missionary Survey as an Aid to Intelligent Cooperation in Foreign Missions* (1920) reveals his desire to articulate carefully a missionary ecclesiology founded upon a philosophy of ministry, which acquired its impetus from theological and missiological reflection within the problematic environment of mission station practices. The initial chapters explain how Allen's missiology within a colonial context was motivated to articulate and practise a missiology of indigenization which empowered Chinese Christians to manage their own churches.

The core historical analysis within these two books discloses how Allen's thinking about Paul's missionary methods was enhanced through his engagement with the works of William Ramsay and Adolf von Harnack. It was Harnack's emphasis on an ecclesiology governed by a charismatic faith that empowers Church expansion, rather than a highly organized system, that informed Allen's charismatic missiology. We have also seen the evidence reveal that his opposition to foreign hegemony, exercised through mission stations, did not develop into a personal disassociation from colonial institutions. This was largely as a result of his acceptance of Ramsay and Harnack's theses regarding early Christianity's

4. Allen, 'The "Nevius Method" in Korea', 11-13.

success under Roman authority. However, Allen also recognized, that while British colonial infrastructure constituted an imposition upon certain indigenous people, nevertheless, it provided a necessary orderliness and quite often promoted peace within multi-ethnic cultures. Hence, as is now widely recognized, one cannot simply disengage from embedded colonial structures without significant violence being done to indigenous societies. The engagement with this hegemonic tension and his critique of the 'imperialistic spirit' is not dissimilar to later concerns articulated by contemporary postcolonial theorists such as Robert Young (2001) who have argued that the globalization of powers from above have led to the imposition of injustices upon the people they colonized. While Allen was not a direct influence on Young, it is clear that his work is prescient in this respect, sharing a commonality with certain ideas that have emerged from postcolonial analysis. Allen's concern that the misplaced effort put into the desacralization of certain indigenous customs amongst the colonized, provides a critique that is not dissimilar from Young's arguments against Western imperialism. Having said that, to claim that Allen's cross-cultural missiology sought to dismantle colonialism would be an *inaccurate* portrayal of the historical and archival evidence. Indeed, while Allen's thinking was prescient, to claim much more than this would be anachronistic. His contribution rests with the principles of indigenization, which helped to found churches led by local leaders who were 'fully equipped' to manage their own affairs without foreign control. The facts disclose that Allen's missionary ecclesiology is designed *to empower* and *not to control*.

In this volume, *Roland Allen: A Theology of Mission*, the archival evidence discloses the backdrop of how apostolic principles formed the basis for his missionary theology. This section of analysis unpacks the ways in which his Pauline hermeneutic exposed the missional deficiencies within the dominant missionary methodologies of the West, especially the mission station system that he categorically stated 'is *not* the Church'. Arguably, his apostolic principles (which he believed were timeless) were examined and shown to stem from his high ecclesiology in which the Church is understood as one, holy, catholic and apostolic. Firstly, the foundations of his missional *apologia* for the indigenous Church are:

(1) to embrace the Bible;
(2) to develop a basic creed properly understood by all members;
(3) to ordain local ministers; and
(4) to make the sacraments always available.

Secondly, my research explains how apostolic evangelists were sent as 'temporary' trans-local ministers to plant churches and then to immediately equip local leadership for the development of these churches. Thirdly, we see how indigenous churches were to immediately maintain self-government, self-support and self-propagation. Fourthly, archival evidence reveals his ongoing conviction that these churches were not to engage in a process of devolution, but rather they should place their trust in the 'charismatic dynamic' to support the maintenance of administration and sacramental practice in order to enhance spontaneous church expansion. Fifthly, by examining his unpublished works, the research concludes that his 'theology of the laity' promoted the (now popular) belief that 'all Christians are missionaries'. Sixthly, archival evidence reveals the centrality of his belief in apostolic succession and that this necessitated active episcopal involvement by bishops to promote the expansion of churches to pioneer regions. It is because of Allen's tendency to confront bishops who were hesitant to ordain indigenous leaders and/or refrain from extending the Church's life beyond their 'comfort zone' that his tenacious commitment to apostolic order compelled him to remind them of their responsibilities within the episcopal office.

The problem presented by Western missionary paternalism and institutional devolution is exposed in Allen's diagnosis of the missionary situation and the proposed ways to restore apostolic order. The conclusions in this chapter are drawn from his discussions of the failures in missions due to their imposed systems – laws and customs – instead of their empowerment of the indigenous churches to apply the principles of self-government and self-support. The research discloses how Allen drew upon Maria Montessori's educational methods, particularly her analyses of studying, observation and experimentation. Encorporating her ideas into his thinking, he developed an approach to education in general that could be used to address the contemporary paternalistic tendencies within the missionary situation. He concluded that missionaries would be more effective if they focused on understanding how the converts solved local problems and exercised leadership without foreign interference. This level of indigenous independence has been disclosed throughout these two volumes as three particular apostolic principles:

(1) by teaching converts from the beginning to identify their responsibilities to govern their own churches;
(2) by limiting any use of foreign elements; and
(3) for missionaries to implement an exit strategy of retirement from the very churches they had planted.

Allen's major contribution in terms of a charismatic missiology, as developed most fully in arguably his finest work, *Pentecost and the*

World (1917), is analyzed and reveals how an integrated pneumatology and ecclesiology formed the basis for his church-planting missionary theology, thus encompassing an historic apostolicity and catholicity. The infrastructure for his missionary ecclesiology of 'Spirit and Order' was enhanced by the integration of the sacraments for Church growth. In particular, Allen emphasized how the pneumatological dynamic works in harmony with the sacraments to nurture an emerging Church, in which 'the missionary Spirit' organically empowers all members for missionary action. Pulling several of the above strands together, the final chapters analyzed and explained Allen's sacramental theology and how this was interwoven within his missionary ecclesiology.

Allen's Impact and Contemporary Relevance

It is rather ironic that Allen's influence today encompasses an ecclesiastical sphere far beyond the Anglican Communion. From one side, my analysis has identified his significant contribution to Anglican missiology in India through his friendship with and influence of Bishop Azariah's ministry within the Dornakal churches and their expansive missionary undertakings outside their diocesan borders. The archival research disclosed two letters (1912) from Bishop Henry Whitehead[1] (Madras) thanking Allen for supporting Azariah's consecration as the first indigenous bishop in India. Allen's advocacy of Azariah was refreshing to Whitehead, since most of what he heard were negative comments and that it 'is a great pity that *"The Guardian,"* [*sic*] [and] other papers in England' had decided to demonstrate 'un-Christian motives, caste feeling, party spirit, [and] envy'.[2] Ongoing correspondence between Azariah and Allen discloses how Azariah not only thanked him for writing *Voluntary Clergy* (1923) but also diffused Allen's worry that this teaching might be cause 'for a martyr's crown in India'.[3] Azariah assured him that the episcopacy was 'in favour of an order of permanent Deacons and Voluntary Permanent Deacons'.[4]

From the other side, although it is a little odd bearing in mind his significance, that he is not discussed more in academic missiology within

---

1. Letters from Whitehead to Allen (7 June 1912 and 11 June 1912), USPG X622, Box 1, File A, Oxford, Bodleian Library.
2. Ibid., 7 June 1912.
3. Letter from Azariah to Allen (29 December 1923), USPG X622, Box 1, File A: 12, Oxford, Bodleian Library.
4. Ibid.

the Church of England today,[5] his influence is conspicuously apparent among not only the independent branches of the Western and non-Western Church, but also among the established Protestant and Roman Catholic communions. But it is necessary to understand that his influence – though rather controversial in his day – actually developed steadily after his death. This definitely echoed true with the prescient comment by Allen that his works would not be understood, as he told his grandson, until he had 'been dead ten years'.[6] For after his death in 1947, it was the Barthian thinker and missiologist, Hendrik Kraemer, in his *A Theology of the Laity* (1958) who cited from Roland Allen's *The Spontaneous Expansion of the Church, and the Causes which Hinder It*,[7] in order to disclose how the significant growth of the Church during the first centuries was accomplished through the laity's witness. Allen's contribution to Kraemer's missiology is the first example whereby he had an influence on a major ecumenical theologian a decade after his death. Shortly after Kraemer's book was published, two other noteworthy missiologists – Sir Kenneth Grubb and Lesslie Newbigin – men who already had been reading Allen's works, each contributed to writing the *Foreword* in 1962 for both republished books: *Missionary Methods: St Paul's or Ours?* (1912) and *The Spontaneous Expansion of the Church* (1927). Grubb comments in the 1962 publication of *Missionary Methods* that after 'many previous editions, it is still only the few who have heeded his teaching'.[8] In actuality, a Reformed missionary in Nigeria, Harry Boer, in 1948 wrote an article for *World Dominion* in appreciation of Allen's work. And, in his *Pentecost and Missions* (1961) he engaged with Allen's missiology throughout the book.[9] Unlike many later missiologists, who generally quote only from Allen's two most published books,[10] Boer purposefully quoted from some

---

5. There are exceptions, however, with Timothy Yates' *Christian Mission in the Twentieth Century* (Cambridge: Cambridge University Press, 1994), 59-63, 65, 67, 70, and 74, where, for example, he correctly discloses Allen's criticism of Rufus Anderson and Henry Venn's emphasis that the 'three self' model was a 'goal to be aimed at' instead of Allen's view that it should start 'from the beginning' (62); and also, Dan O'Connor's *Three Centuries of Mission: The United Society for the Propagation of the Gospel 1701-2000* (London: Continuum, 2000), 99-102, 106 and 134, where he correctly highlights Allen's implementation of 'his new ideas' of indigenous principles with the young congregation in Yung Ch'ing' (101).

6. Hubert Allen, *Roland Allen*, vii.

7. Kraemer, *Theology of the Laity*, 20; cf. Allen, *Spontaneous Expansion*, 143-146.

8. Kenneth G. Grubb (Publisher's Foreword) in *Missionary Methods*, vi.

9. Boer, *Pentecost and Missions*, 48, 61, 63-64, 99, 136, 163 and 210ff.

10. *Missionary Methods* (1912) and *Spontaneous Expansion* (1927).

of his articles[1] and other books[2] that later missiologists tend to neglect. Hubert Allen pointed out to me that it was Boer who best understood his grandfather's thinking on how the Holy Spirit's power effects mission expansion.[3]

Between Grubb's honest analysis and Boer's advocacy of Allen's works, these publications incited a substantial interest in Allen's works. Grubb's influence with World Dominion Press to republish these works, including *The Ministry of the Spirit: Selected Writings of Roland Allen*, edited by David Paton (1960), caused the missiological thought of Allen to spread. It was the Anglican canon, David Paton, who then carried Allen's missiological baton within ecumenism after the dismantling of colonialism. Paton's contribution to Allen's legacy is commendable, but it is worth mentioning that he did misrepresent some of Allen's teachings on the principle of voluntary clergy and upset the Allen family.[4] The main voice within Christianity who advocated Allen's works, as my research discloses, was Lesslie Newbigin. According to Bishop Newbigin, he believed 'that Allen was right'[5] and that it was his emphasis on an apostolic ministry which relied upon the pneumatological dynamic and also placed the sacraments as central to the community's life, thereby contributing much to mission studies.[6] In

1. Allen, 'The Revelation of the Holy Spirit in the Acts of the Apostles', *International Review of Missions*, vol. VII (April, 1918): 162; Allen, *Mission Activities Considered in Relation to the Manifestation of the Spirit*, 2nd edition, 33-page pamphlet (London: World Dominion Press, 1930): 32.

2. Allen, *Pentecost and the World*, 39-41, 42-43, 85, 87; Allen, *Educational Principles and Missionary Methods*, 41-42; and, Roland Allen and Sydney James Wells Clark, *A Vision of Foreign Missions* (London, 1937), 132.

3. Interview with Hubert Allen on 4 February 2011. Hubert told me that his father (John Allen) thought Harry Boer understood Roland's thinking better than any other missionary author.

4. Interview with Hubert Allen 18 October 2010. Hubert said his father and aunt were so upset with Paton's claim that Roland's teaching on 'voluntary clergy' advocated a theory of 'part-time priests', that they denied Paton any further access to Roland's archives. His actual belief was: 'A cleric can no more be a half-time cleric than a father can be a half-time father, or a baptized Christian a half-time Christian' argues Roland in *The Case for Voluntary Clergy*, 89; cf. Paton in R.A. Denniston (ed.) *Part-Time Priests* (Skeffington & Sons, 1960), 117; and Hubert Allen, *Roland Allen*, 122.

5. Newbigin, *The Gospel in a Pluralist Society*, 146-47.

6. Ibid., 147.

1962, Newbigin argued that Allen's impact had affected the 'assumptions of churches and missions, and slowly but steadily the number of those who found themselves compelled to listen has increased'.[7] Among those who listened was the Church Missionary Society's John V. Taylor who in 1963 called Allen 'that great prophet of missionary method'[8] mainly because he approached 'the African world view with humility and respect'.[9]

In 2006, the contemporary missiologist Brian Stanley argued that Allen's missional pneumatology can be summarized as: 'if the Holy Spirit is given, a missionary Spirit is given'.[10] Stanley went on to say that 'Allen thus foreshadows also the prominence which (in marked contrast to his own day) is now given to the Holy Spirit in Christian theology and in the churches of the majority world, so many of which are Pentecostal in emphasis'.[11] In terms of the Pentecostal emphasis within the majority world, the Gambian-born Lamin Sanneh, in his *Disciples of All Nations*, devoted almost twenty pages to Allen's missiology[12] in which Sanneh also engaged with his pneumatology: 'For Allen, mission was the work of the [S]pirit, not just in the flaky sense of bustling excitement and disorderly enthusiasm but in the sense of openness to the mind of Christ and to the witness of the apostles, especially to that of Paul.'[13] Kwame Bediako (Ghana) said that 'Roland Allen argued convincingly . . . that the outlook of the Western missionary enterprise was hindering the freedom of the emergent Christian communities of Africa and Asia . . . to trust converts sufficiently to the Holy Spirit'.[14] It was Francis Anekwe Oborji, the Nigerian-born Roman Catholic professor of missiology (Pontifical Urban University, Rome), when highlighting the 'success' of Pauline mission said that 'Allen suggests [that it] was due to the fact that he trusted both the Lord and the people to whom he had gone'.[15]

---

7. Newbigin in Roland Allen's *Missionary Methods, Foreword*, i.

8. Taylor, *The Primal Vision*, 33.

9. Ibid.

10. Stanley in Roland Allen's *Missionary Principles* (Bungay, Suffolk: Richard Clay & Sons, 1910. Repr. Cambridge: The Lutterworth Press, 2006), Foreword, VI.

11. Ibid.

12. Sanneh, *Disciples of All Nations*, 205, 218-34, 242 and 248.

13. Ibid., 219.

14. Kwame Bediako, 'Biblical Christologies in the Context of African Traditional Religions', Vinay Samuel & Chris Sugden (eds.), Sharing Jesus In the Two Thirds World (Oxford: Regnum Books International, 1983), 88-89.

15. Oborji, *Concepts of Mission*, 92.

Oborji agreed that 'Allen alerted his readers [*Missionary Methods*] to the glaring difference between Paul's missionary methods and those of contemporary mission agencies'.[1] Another Roman Catholic priest and missionary to the Tanzanian Maasai people, Fr Vincent Donovan, was influenced by his writings and said 'Roland Allen's insights and questions challenged most of the missionary theories I had ever heard [causing] me to proceed cautiously from real practice and experience towards a new and different theory of mission'.[2] The African missiologist, Jehu Hanciles, when addressing the critics of Henry Venn's 'three self' model interestingly argued that 'Roland Allen' had an approach that was actually 'in a manner evocative of Venn's thinking' and that 'Allen's central thesis . . . in actuality captures superbly the predicament that gave birth to Venn's strategy in the first place'.[3] Hanciles identified more of a kinship between Venn's and Allen's ideas than Allen was ever willing to admit.

The aforementioned African missiologists and missionaries who engaged with Allen's works are indicative of the approach of various leaders from within the 2008 Global Anglican Future Conference (GAFCON) who were influenced by him: Bishop Michael Nazir-Ali, Roger Beckwith, Vinay Samuel and Chris Sugden. GAFCON's confessional statement – *The Jerusalem Declaration* – basically echoes Allen's Anglican apologia in terms of a clear 'Gospel' emphasis, primacy of Scripture, creedal fidelity (1-5); clerical orders and sacramental practice (6-8); and missional ecclesiology that is dependent on the pneumatological dynamic (9-14).[4] As my research discloses, two archbishops – Nicholas Okoh (Nigeria) and Eliud Wabukala (Kenya) – argued that the current crisis in Anglicanism is due to the fact that 'the Church of England [ought to] go back to the basic principles and develop new structures while remaining firmly within the Anglican Communion' and further that 'its leadership should be focused not on one person or one Church, however hallowed its history, but on the one historic faith we confess'.[5] These statements from the younger churches of Anglicanism articulate Allen's principles of missionary ecclesiology today.

---

1. Ibid.
2. Vincent J. Donovan, *Christianity Rediscovered* (London: SCM Press, 2009), 27.
3. Hanciles, *Euthanasia of a Mission*, 254.
4. Nicholas Okoh, Vinay Samuel and Chris Sugden (eds.), *Being Faithful: The Shape of Historic Anglicanism Today*, a Commentary on the Jerusalem Declaration (London: The Latimer Trust, 2009), 6-7.
5. E. Thornton, 'We should elect our chair, say Primates', *Church Times* (April 2012): 5.

Jin Huat Tan (Malaysia) identifies that the interdenominational Borneo Evangelical Mission (BEM) 'adopted the teachings of Roland Allen . . . especially his distinctive Catholic pneumatology . . . and his Pauline pattern of church planting . . . and Roland Allen's writings became the textbook of the BEM'.[6] Tan stated that the first promotion of Allen's works at the BEM was in 1953 specifically through the influence of the principal of Australia's Melbourne Bible Institute (MBI) – C.H. Nash – an Anglican, who 'was teaching Roland Allen's ideas in MBI'.[7] Here are signs of the significant influence of his work which began to spread throughout the South Pacific and Southeast Asia shortly after Allen's death in 1947.

Other missiologists who have been influenced by Allen's works are J.H. Bavinck (Reformed) who agreed with his emphasis that Pauline methods did not advocate any need for having paid agents to expand the Church's mission;[8] R. Bruce Carlton (Southern Baptist) said that 'Allen knew that more missionaries was not the answer to global evangelization'[9] but rather that it was through the indigenous Church's ability to expand; Ake Talltorp (Church of Sweden) understood how Allen's sacramental theology was central 'for the growth and expansion of the Church in Mission';[10] Dean Gilliland (Charismatic) agreed with Allen's reliance on the pneumatological dynamic for the development and appointment of indigenous leaders saying that 'Christians are not only what they are by nature [but] are a Spirit-bearing body [and that] St Paul looked at his converts as they were by grace';[11] David Bosch (Dutch Reformed) recognized the significant contribution Allen's *Missionary Methods* has made and said it 'occupies pride of place in this regard and has had a profound influence particularly in English-speaking missionary circles';[12] and also, Michael Goheen (Christian Reformed) – Newbigin scholar and missiologist – stated that 'Allen's work has had a formative influence on Newbigin's critique of the relationship between Western missions organizations and the younger churches [and] has developed much fruitful reflection on the missionary church'.[13] My research has examined

6. Tan, *Planting an Indigenous Church*, 276.

7. Ibid., 101.

8. Bavinck, *Science of Missions*, 212-13.

9. R. Bruce Carlton, *Strategy Coordinator: Changing the Course of Southern Baptist Missions* (Oxford: Regnum, 2010), 177.

10. Talltorp, *Sacrament and Growth*, 67.

11. Gilliland, *Pauline Theology*, 150; cf. Allen, *Missionary Methods*, 125.

12. Bosch, *Transforming Mission*, 123.

13. Goheen, *"As the Father Has Sent Me"*, 10-11.

the effects of his missionary theology upon subsequent missionaries and missiologists. On one hand, in Eckhard Schnabel's *Paul the Missionary* (2008), he clearly disagreed with Allen's assumption that Paul's missionary focus was 'on provinces rather than on cities'.[1] On the other hand, this criticism only reveals Schnabel's engagement with various works of Allen. He went on to affirm the significant contribution that Allen's missiology conveyed to the contemporary reader as he stated that these are 'by no means outdated' and that his *Missionary Methods* (1912) 'deserves to be read in the twenty-first century,'[2] as disclosed within the pages of his *Preface* and Introduction.[3]

Real work remains to be done on Roland Allen's missiological thought. Firstly, the importance he placed upon apostolic ministry implied a belief in modern day 'apostles'. His defence for this contemporary ministry was assumed to be valid and there is no evidence that he engaged with those of a theological cessationist opinion. Because Allen did not articulate a theology of the apostolate – other than an *apologia* from the biblical text and the *Didachē* – it remains unclear how this office is to function in comparison to the early apostles. Missiologists such as Stuart Murray have advanced similar ideas, but much work on Allen's ideas need to be pinned down as to why he thought this way. Secondly, the archives contain many unpublished papers on Jesus' parables. Only one of the parables – *The Good Samaritan*[4] – has been broadly published and, until now, there has not been any scholarly analysis of these perceptive papers. Thirdly, although his most popular books stem from an understanding of the New Testament, some might conclude that he was disinterested in the Old Testament. My analysis of his sermons discloses the opposite. That is why I devoted one chapter in *Roland Allen: A Missionary Life* to advance some clarity concerning his loyalty to the authority of the Old Testament text, especially his teachings on the abiding validity of the Ten Commandments. Further work is needed though to unpack his theology of covenantal continuity. Arguably there is room for a new application of Allen's missionary ecclesiology concerning the priesthood of the laity. His vision for the expansion of the indigenous Church combined through *Spirit and Order* in a changing Christendom *milieu* could significantly influence a renewed application of his primary apostolic principles to the *newer* structures within World Christianity today.

---

1. Schnabel, *Paul the Missionary*, 286.
2. Ibid., 13.
3. Ibid., 11-14, 21.
4. Paton, *Reform of the Ministry*, 179-188.

Bibliography

Primary Sources

Roland Allen's Books and Pamphlets

Allen, Roland & Alexander McLeish, *Devolution and its Real Significance* (London: World Dominion Press, 1927)

Allen, Roland, *Discussion on Mission Education* (London: World Dominion Press, 1931)

Allen, Roland, *Education in the Native Church* (London: World Dominion Press, 1926. Repr., 1928)

Allen, Roland, *Educational Principles and Missionary Methods: The Application of Educational Principles to Missionary Evangelism* (London: Robert Scott, 1919)

Allen, Roland, *Foundation Principles of Foreign Missions* (May 1910), Box 2, File J. (Repr., entitled *Essential Missionary Principles*, Cambridge: The Lutterworth Press, 1913. Repr. entitled *Missionary Principles – and Practice*, Grand Rapids: Eerdmans, 1964; *Missionary Principles – and Practice*, London: World Dominion Press, 1964); *Missionary Principles – and Practice* (Cambridge: The Lutterworth Press, 2006)

Allen, Roland, *Gerbert, Pope Silvester II* (London: Spottiswoode & Co, 1892).

Allen, Roland, *Jerusalem: A Critical Review of 'The World Mission of Christianity'* (London: World Dominion Press, 1928)

Allen, Roland, *Le Zoute: A Critical Review of 'The Christian Mission in Africa'* (London: World Dominion Press, 1927)

Allen, Roland, *Mission Activities: Considered in Relation to the Manifestation of the Spirit* (London: World Dominion Press, 2nd edition, 33-page pamphlet, 1930)

Allen, Roland, *Missionary Methods: St Paul's or Ours? A Study of the Church in the Four Provinces* (London: Robert Scott, February 1912; in the Library of Historic Theology. Repr., October 1913. Revised edition published by World Dominion Press, 2nd edition August 1927. Repr.s 1930, 1949, 1956. Reset – with memoir by Alexander McLeish – Grand Rapids: Eerdmans, 1962. Repr., 1993. Repr., Cambridge: The Lutterworth Press, 2006), *New Foreword*: Bishop Michael Nazir-Ali, III-IV

Allen, Roland, *Missionary Principles – and Practice*, (1st edition [Roland's handwritten marked copy] entitled *Foundation Principles of Foreign Missions*, Bungay, Suffolk: Richard Clay & Sons, May 1910. Repr., Cambridge: The Lutterworth Press, 1913, entitled *Essential Missionary Principles*; Grand Rapids, Michigan: Wm. B. Eerdmans, 1964; London: World Dominion Press, 1964, Cambridge: The Lutterworth Press, 2006)

Allen, Roland and Thomas Cochrane, *Missionary Survey as an Aid to Intelligent Co-operation in Foreign Missions* (London: Longmans, Green, 1920. Repr., BiblioBazaar, 2008)

Allen, Roland, *Non-Professional Missionaries,* privately printed at Beaconsfield (1929)

Allen, Roland, *Pentecost and the World: The Revelation of the Holy Spirit in 'The Acts of the Apostles'* (London: Oxford University Press, 1917)

Allen, Roland, *Sidney James Wells Clark: A Vision of Foreign Missions* (London: World Dominion Press, 1937)

Allen, Roland, *The Case for Voluntary Clergy* (London: Eyre & Spottiswoode, 1930)

Allen, Roland, *The Establishment of the Church in the Mission Field: A Critical Dialogue* (London: World Dominion Press, 1927)

Allen, Roland, *The 'Nevius Method' in Korea* (London: World Dominion Press, 1930), Box 4

Allen, Roland, *The Place of Faith in Missionary Evangelism* (London: World Dominion Press 8, 1930): 234–41

Allen, Roland, *The Siege of the Peking Legations* (London: Smith, Elder, 1901)

Allen, Roland, *The Spontaneous Expansion of the Church* (London: World Dominion Press, 1927. Repr., 2nd edn. 1960, reissued, Grand Rapids: Wm. B. Eerdmans Publishing Co., 1962. Repr., Cambridge: The Lutterworth Press, 2006)

Allen, Roland, *Voluntary Clergy*, (London: SPCK, 1923), Box 2, File J

Allen, Roland, *Voluntary Clergy Overseas: An Answer to the Fifth World Call*, (privately printed at Beaconsfield, England, 1928), Bodleian Library Box 2, File J

Allen's Translations From Swahili Writings

'The Story of Mbega' (part 1) by Abdullah bin Hemedi lAjjemy, *Tanganyika Notes & Records* (1936–37)

'Inkishafi – A Translation from the Swahili', *African Studies* (December 1946), Box 4

'Utenzi wa Kiyama (Siku ya Hukumu)', an appendage to *Tanganyika Notes & Records* (c. 1946), Box 4

'Utenzi wa Kutawafu Naby', (author unknown), an appendage to *Journal of the East African Swahili Committee*, (June 1956; re-edited as 'Utendi wa Kutawafu Nabii', Edwin Mellen Press, 1991)

'Utenzi wa Abdirrahmani na Sufiyani' by Hemed Abdalla el Buhry, *Johari za Kiswahili*, no. 2, (1961)

Roland Allen's Articles and Unpublished Works

1900

'Of Some of the Causes Which Led to the Preservation of the Foreign Legations in Peking', *The Cornhill Magazine* (27 September) 754–776, Box 2, File J: 1, the Church of England Mission

'Of Some of the Causes Which Led to the Siege of the Foreign Legations in Peking', *The Cornhill Magazine* (November) no. 53/491, 669-680, Box 2, File J: 1, the Church of England Mission

'Of Some of the Causes which Led to the Preservation of the Foreign Legations in Peking', *The Cornhill Magazine* (December) 754-76, no. 54; no. 492, Box 2, File J

1901

'The Development of Independent Native Churches and their federation in union with the Church of England', paper read to a clerical Society in East London, Box 3: 1

'Of some of the Conclusions which may be drawn from the Siege of the Foreign Legations in Peking', *The Cornhill Magazine* (February) 202-12, no. 56 & no. 494

'Church in Japan', *Church Missionary Intelligencer* (April) Box 2, File J: 2

1902

'A Church Policy for North China – I', LIEN, *The Guardian*: 879, Box 1, File B

'The Churches of the Future', *The Guardian* (18 June)

'The Churches of the Future', *The Guardian* (25 June)

'A Church Policy for North China – II', *The Guardian* (July) Box 1, File B

'The Unceasing Appeal for Men for Foreign Missions', *The Guardian* (23 July)

1903

'The Anglican Mission at Yung Ch'ing, North China', (20 February) Box 2, File J: 3

'The Chinese Character and Missionary Methods', *The East and The West* (July) 317-329, Box 2, File J: 35

'The Work of the Missionary in Preparing the Way for Independent Native Churches', (11-12 November) Box 2, File J: 4

1904

'Independent Native Churches', *The Guardian* (24 August) no. 3064/1389, Box 1, File B & File C

1907

'Letter to the Parishioners of Chalfont St Peter', (25 November) Repr. in Hubert Allen's *Roland Allen: Pioneer, Priest, and Prophet* (1995): 183-88

1908

'Canada Immigration', *The Times* (4 April) Box 1, File A

'Opium Suppression in China', *Church Times* (1 May), Box 1, File B

'The Supply and Training of Candidates for Holy Orders', *The Times* (11 June), Box 1, File J

'The Progress of Education in China', *Cornhill* (November) 655-65, Box 2, File J: 5A & 5B (1-11)

1909

Paper presented *SPG: Laymen's Missionary Association: The Day of Intercession* (January) 37-40, Box 2: 6

'A Grave Indictment', *Church Times* (August), Box 1, File A
'A Grave Indictment', *Church Times* (17 September), Box 1, File A
'A Grave Indictment', *Church Times* (1 October), Box 1, File A
'Missionary Policy in China', *Church Times* (19 November), Box 1, File B
'Spiritual Means for Spiritual Work', *SPG Laymen's Missionary Association* (January & 30 November) Box 2, File J: 6
'The Message of the Christian Church to Confucianists', *The East and The West* (October) 437-452, Box 2, File J: 7

1910
'Foundation Principles of Foreign Missions', (May) Box 2, File J

1911
'An Indian Church Society: A New Movement among Native Christians', *Church Times* (21 July) Box 1, File B
'A Native Church in the Making', *Church Times* (8 September) Box 1, File B
'The "Will to Convert in Mission Schools"', *The East and The West* (October) 408-417, Box 2, File J: 8
'A Native Church in the Making: A Contrast', *Church Times* (10 November) Box 1, File B

1912
'The Influence of "Mission Stations" upon the Establishment of Indigenous Churches', *English Church Review* (November) 500-08, vol. III, no. 35, Box 2, File J: 9

1913
'The Influence of Foreign Missions on the Church at Home', *The Commonwealth*, XVIII (August) 242-246, Box 1, File B
'Educational Principles and Missionary Methods', *The English Review*, vol. IV, no. 37 (January) 14-25, Box 2, File J: 10

1915
'The Influence of Western Education upon Religion in Non-Christian Lands – I', *The Challenge* (30 April) Box 1, File B
'The Influence of Western Education upon Religion in Non-Christian Lands – II', *The Challenge* (7 May) Box 1, File B
'The Right to Ordination', *Challenge* (30 July) Box 1, File B

1918
'The Christian Education of Native Churches', *Church Missionary Review* (December) 398-405, Box 2, File J: 12

1919
Book review, *Church Quarterly Review*, art. 1. – 'Concerning some Hindrances to the Extension of the Church', no. CLXXVII (October) Box 2, File J: 13a-b
Church Times (14 November) Box 1, File A

1920

'Islam and Christianity in the Sudan', *The International Review of Missions* (October) 531-43, XIX/36, Box 2, File J: 14

'The Whole and the Parts in Foreign Missionary Administration', *Church Missionary Review* (December) Box 2, File J: 15

'The Relation Between Medical, Educational and Evangelistic Work in Foreign Missions', *Church Missionary Review*: 54-62

'The Whole and the Parts in Foreign Missionary Administration', *Church Missionary* Review: 329-37

'Missionary Survey as an Aid to Intelligent Cooperation in Foreign Missions', *World Dominion Press*

1921

'The Mission in Corea: Another Call for Men', *Church Times* (21 October) Box 1, File A

'A Tyrannous Tradition', *The Challenge* (18 November) Box 1, File B

1922

'A Conscience Clause in India', *The Record* (19 January) Box 1, File B

'Colonial and Continental Church Society', *The Record* (4 May) Box 1, File A

'SPG Anniversary', *Church Times* (5 May) Box 1, File A

'Materialism and Atheism: Dangers of South America', *The Guardian* (5 May)

'The Future of a Great Work: Colonial and Continental Church Society', *The Guardian* (5 May) Box 1, File A

'Mission Colleges and Schools: The Worth-while Line', *The Challenge* (26 May) Box 1, File B

'Mission Colleges and Schools: The Meaning of Christian Education', *The Challenge* (2 June) Box 1, File B

'Mission Colleges and Schools: A Strategic Position', *The Challenge* (9 June) Box 1, File B

'Mission Colleges and Schools: The True Strategic Position', *The Challenge* (16 June) Box 1, File B

'Western Education and Village Evangelisation: A Criticism of the Report of the C.M.S. Delegation to India', *The Record* (22 June) Box 1, File C

'The Case for Voluntary Clergy: An Anglican Problem', *The Interpreter* (July) Box 2, File J: 16

'Church People Abroad', *Daily Telegraph* (12 July) Box 1, File A

'Mission Colleges in India', *The Record* (9 November) Box 1, File A

'The Serious Dearth of Clergy', *The Guardian* (8 December) Box 1, File A

1923

'Supply of Clergy', *Church Times* (5 January) Box 1, File A

'Brotherhood: A Contrast between Moslem Practice and Christian Ideas', London: *World Dominion* 1: 92-94

'Christian Education in China', *Theology* (March) 129-134, Box 2, File J: 17

'The Algoma Association: Help for the Church in Canada', *Church Times* (23 March) Box 1, File A

'The Church in South Africa: Admission of Sub-Deacons in Johannesburg', *The Guardian* (18 April) Box 1, File A

'The Church Overseas: South Africa, Diocese of Johannesburg, Admission Of Sub-Deacons', *Church Times* (20 April) Box 1, File A

'Colonial and Continental Church Society: Mr Gladstone's Speech', *The Record* (3 May) Box 1, File A

'Materialism and Atheism: Dangers of South America', *The Guardian* (5 May), Box 1, File A

'Universities' Mission to Central Africa: The Bishop of Zanzibar's Letter', *Church Times* (25 May) Box 1, File A

Archbishop's address, Synod (June) Box 1, File A

Letter to the editor, *Church Times* (7 September) Box 1, File A

'The "Colonial and Continental" Centenary Autumn Meeting: Message from H.R.H. the Prince of Wales', *The Record* (15 November) Box 1, File A

'The Church Overseas: Dr Haynes' Work at Bloemfontein – Basuto Movement for Independent Church. A Trek Through Zululand', *The Guardian* (14 December) Box 1, File A

1924

'The Bishop of Mombasa's Appeal', *The Record* (7 February) Box 1, File A

'News and Notes: 230 Miles for a Service', *The Guardian* (8 February) Box 1, File A

'Voluntary Clergy', *The Record* (6 March) Box 1, File B

'The Church Overseas', *The Guardian* (21 March) Box 1, File A

'Voluntary Clergy', *The Record* (29 May) Box 1, File A

A response from Allen (23 May) to 'Fr Wilfrid Shelley's letter', *Church Times* (30 May) Box 1, File A

'Church Revenues Report', *The Guardian* (30 May) Box 1, File A

'Catholics and a Missionary Policy', *Church Times* (16 May) Box 1, File A

'Catholics and a Missionary Policy', *Church Times* (23 May) Box 1, File A

'Catholics and a Missionary Policy', Allen's response (23 May) to Fr Wilfrid Shelley's previous article, *Church Times* (30 May) Box 1, File A

Letter to editor, *The Living Church* (1 November) Box 1, File A

'The Church in Western Canada: Need of Voluntary Priests', *Church Times* (5 December) Box 1, File A

1925

'The Church in Western Canada: Need of Voluntary Priests', *Church Times* (16 January)

'A Constitution for the Indian Church', *World Dominion* 3 (March) 64–68, Box 2, File J: 18

'Leadership – Train Leaders', an article rejected by the *Church Missionary Review* (July), Box 3: 3

'The Essentials of an Indigenous Church', *Chinese Recorder* 56: 491-96

'The Essentials of an Indigenous Church', *World Dominion* 3: 110-117

'The Native Church and Mission Education', *World Dominion* 3: 153-60

'Education in the Native Church', *World Dominion* 4: 37-44

1926

'Money: The Foundation of the Church', *The Pilgrim*, 6/4 (July) 417-428, Box 2, File J: 20

'The Maintenance of the Ministry in the Early Ages of the Church', *World Dominion* 4: 218-24

'The Rectory of Fairstead', *Truth* (22 September) Box 1, File E

Address delivered to the Diocesan Synod of Pretoria (26 October) Box 3, File G: 30

1927

'Diary of a Visit in South India', Box 7, File N (1927-28): 1-85, USPG Archives, Rhodes House, Oxford

'The Establishment of Indigenous Churches', *International Review of Missions* 17, X Series, Box 3

'Itinerant Clergy and the Church', *The East and The West*, 1927, Box 3, File G: 30

'The Use of the Term "Indigenous"', *International Review of Missions* 16 (April) 262-70, Box 2, File J: 22

'The Church and an Itinerant Ministry', *The East and The West* 25/9 (April) 123-133, Box 2, File J: 2

'Indigenous Churches: The Way of St Paul', *The Church Missionary Review* (June) 147-159, Box 2, File J: 23

'Voluntary Service in the Mission Field', *World Dominion* 5: 135-43

'Devolution – The Question of the Hour', *World Dominion* 5: 274-87

'The Establishment of Indigenous Churches', refused by the *International Review of Missions*, Box 3: 5

1928

'Voluntary Clergy', article refused by *St. Martin's Review* (14 May) Box 3: 6

Reviews by Allen of 'Industrialism in Japan' (Walter F. France) and 'Buddhism and Buddhists in Japan' (Robert C. Armstrong), *Church Quarterly Review* (October) Box 2, File J: 24

'The Findings of the Jerusalem Conference', *Theology* (November) 296-301, Box 2, File J: 25

'General Smuts on Missions in Africa', *Times Report* (18 November) Box 3: 7

Review of an article by K.S. Latourette 'What is happening to Missions?' *Yale Review* (December) Box 3: 8

'The Need for Non-Professional Missionaries', *World Dominion* 6: 195-201

'The Work for Non-Professional Missionaries', *World Dominion* 6: 298-304

'Business Man and Missionary Statesman: Sidney James Wells Clark: An Appreciation', *World Dominion* (December) 3-9

1929

Letter to the editor, *The Guardian* (4 January) Box 1, File C

'The Imperialism of Missions', *The Living Church* (26 January) Box 1, File B: 14

Review by Allen of 'Our Church's Youngest Daughter', (Eyre Chatterton, Bishop of Nagpur), *Church Quarterly Review*, Box 2, File J: 26

Reviews by Allen of 'Japan and Christ' by M.S. Murao, and 'A Transvaal Jubilee'
   by J.A.I. Agar Hamilton, *Church Quarterly Review*, Box 2, File J: 27
Review by Allen of 'Essays Catholic and Missionary', *Church Quarterly Review*
   (April) Box 2, File J: 28
'New Testament Missionary Methods', *The Missionary Review of the World* 52:
   21-24, Box 1, File B
'The Methodists and the Prophet Harris', *World Dominion* (April) Box 2, File J: 29
Review by Allen of 'Indirect Effects of Christian Missions in India' by R.S.
   Wilson, *Church Quarterly Review* (April) Box 2, File J: 30a-b
'Missionary Methods', *The Congregational Quarterly* (April) 165-169, Box 2, File
   J: 31
'Business Man and Missionary Statesman: Sidney James Wells Clark: An
   Appreciation', *World Dominion* 7: 16-22
'The Provision of Services for Church People Overseas', *Theology* 19: 23-30

1930

'The Ministry of Expansion: the Priesthood of the Laity', (unpublished), Box
   3, File G: 27
'The Place of "Faith" in Missionary Evangelism', *World Dominion Press*
Review by Allen of 'A History of Christian Missions in China' by K.S. Latourette
   (January) *Church Quarterly Review*, Box 2, File J: 32
'The Church and the Ministry in the Mission Field', (5 January) Box 3: 9
'The Case for Voluntary Clergy', *St. Martin's Review*, no. 471 (May) 241, Box 1, File D
Letter to the editor, *The Guardian* (9 May) Box 1, File D
'The Case for Voluntary Clergy', London: Eyre and Spottiswoode (July) 333-
   340, Box 1, File E
Letter to the editor, 'Railway Church', *The Record* (August) Box 3, File G: 10
'The Place of Medical Missions', *World Dominion* 8: 34-42
'Lambeth Conference on Voluntary Clergy', *Witness and Canadian Homestead* (22
   October) Box 1, File B

1931

'Voluntary Clergy and the Lambeth Conference', *The Church Overseas: An
   Anglican Review of Missionary Thought and Work*, vol. IV, no. 14 (April) 145-
   53, Box 2, File J: 33
'The Chinese Government and Mission Schools', *World Dominion* 9: 25-30
'The "Nevius Method" in Korea', *World Dominion* 9: 252-58

1932

'Is the Church Out of Touch with People?' *The East African Standard* (14 May)
   Box 8: 3
'A Cathedral Sermon', *The East African Standard* (21 May) Box 8: 4
Letter to the editor, 'The Church in Kenya', *The East African Standard* (24 June)
   Box 7: 3, 37
Letter to the editor, 'The Church in Kenya', *The East African Standard* (24 May)
   Box 8: 7, 8

'A Cathedral Sermon', *The East African Standard'* (28 May) Box 8: 4

'A Survey of the Condition of the Anglican Church in Kenya', *The Times of East Africa* (28 May) Box 8: 1, 2

Allen's response to the *Churchman* (three questions), *The East African Standard* (4 June) Box 8: 5

'Auxiliary Clergy for Church in Kenya?' *The East African Standard* (4 June) Box 8: 9

'The Church in Kenya', *The East African Standard* (16 June) Box 8: 10

Letter from Allen 'Voluntary Clergy', *Kenya Church Review* (September) no. 14, 4

'Voluntary Clergy', *E.A. Standard* (September) no. 14: 4–5

1933

'The Priesthood of the Church', *Church Quarterly Review* 116 (January) 234–44, Box 2, File J: 34

'The Application of Pauline Principles to Modern Missions', *World Dominion* 11: 352–57

'Missionary Finance', (28 December) Box 1, File D

'Men for the Ministry', (28 December) Box 1, File E

1934

'The Cathedral', *The East African Standard* (5 February) Box 8: 11

'The Cathedral Appeal', *The East African Standard* (16 February) Box 8: 12

'The Work of the Church in Kenya', *The East African Standard* (11 April) Box 8: 13

Letter to the editor, 'Church Attendance', *The East African Standard* (7 July) Box 8: 39

'Kenya Sunday', *The East African Standard* (29 September) Box 8: 14

1935

Letter to the editor, 'Conference on Christian Co-operation', *The East African Standard* (23 July) Box 8: 21

Letter to the editor, 'Conference on Christian Co-operation', *The East African Standard* (30 July) Box 8: 21

Letter to the editor, 'Conference on Christian Co-operation', *The East African Standard* (31 July) Box 8: 22

Letter to the editor, 'Conference on Christian Co-operation', *The East African Standard* (2 August) Box 8: 22

Letter to the editor, *The East African Standard* (22 October) Box 8: 15

Letter to the editor, 'Prophecy', *The East African Standard* (29 October) Box 8: 15

Letter to the editor, 'Religious Teaching', *The East African Standard* (11 November) Box 8: 16

Letter to the editor, 'Prophecy', *The East African Standard* (20 November) Box 8: 17

Letter to the editor, 'Prophecy', *The East African Standard* (29 November) Box 8: 17

Letter to the editor, *The East African Standard* (29 November) Box 8: 18

1936

Letter to the editor, 'The British Empire: Nucleus of World Unity', *The East African Standard* (20 March) Box 7, File N: 40

Letter to the editor, 'The Church in Kenya', *The East African Standard* (7 April) Box 8: 24

Letter to the editor, 'A Vacant Bishopric', *The East African Standard* (17 April) Box 7: 41

Letter to the editor, 'The Church in Kenya: A Vacant Bishopric', *The East African Standard* (21 April) Box 8: 24

Letter to the editor, 'Kenya Contrasts: The Missions and Polygamy', *The East African Standard* (1 May) Box 8: 25

'A Week-end Sermon: Regrets I', *The East African Standard* (1 May) Box 8: 26

'A Week-end Sermon: Regrets II', *The East African Standard* (8 May) Box 8: 27

Letter to the editor, 'Kenyan Contrasts: The Christian Missions', *The East African Standard*, (11 May) Box 7: 42

Letter to the editor, 'Christian Missions', *The East African Standard* (13 May) Box 8: 28

Letter to the editor, 'The Work of Missions', *The East African Standard* (16 May) Box 8: 28

Letter to the editor, 'Kenya Contrasts: Polygamy and Mission Teaching', (27 May) Box 8: 29

'A Week-end Sermon: God and Man', *The East African Standard* (5 June) Box 8: 29

Letter to the editor, 'Voluntary Clergy', *The East African Standard* (23 June) Box 8: 63

Letter to the editor, 'On Being Rude – Bumble in Nairobi', *The East African Standard* (29 June) Box 7: 43

Letter to the editor, 'On Being Rude – Bumble in Nairobi', *The East African Standard* (30 June) Box 8: 63

Letter to the editor, 'African Girlhood: A Mission Problem', *The East African Standard* (24 July) Box 8: 30

Letter to the editor, 'African Girlhood', *The East African Standard* (7 August) Box 8: 66

Letter to the editor, 'African Girlhood: Mission Problem', *The East African Standard* (11 August) Box 8: 31

Letter to the editor, 'African Girlhood', *The East African Standard* (22 August) Box 8: 32

Letter to the editor, 'A Mission Problem', *The East African Standard* (25 August) Box 8: 33

Letter to the editor, 'A Mission Problem', *The East African Standard* (28 August) Box 8: 33

Letter to the editor, 'Native Customs: The Position of Missions', *The East African Standard* (14 September) Box 7: 44

Letter to the editor, 'Native Customs: The Position of Missions', *The East African Standard* (16 September) Box 8: 34

Letter to the editor, 'African Customs: A Kavirondo Case', *The East African Standard* (2 October) Box 8: 35

Letter to the editor, 'The League of Nations', *The East African Standard* (27 November) Box 8: 36

Letter to the editor, 'Security: The League of Nations', *The East African Standard* (4 December) Box 8: 37

1937 (File E)

Letter to the editor, 'Christianity in Britain', *The East African Standard* (2 April), Box 8: 39

Letter to the editor, *The East African Standard*, (16 April) Box 7: 45

Letter to the editor, 'Christianity in Kenya', *The Spectator* (18 June) Box 1, File E

Letter to the editor, 'Christianity in Kenya', *The Spectator* (July) Box 1, File E

Letter to the editor, 'Clergy in Kenya', *The Spectator* (30 July) Box 1, File E

Letter to the editor, 'Clergy in Kenya', *The Spectator* (30 July)

Letter to the editor, 'The Church and Paid Clergy', *East Africa and Rhodesia* (19 August) Box 8: 38

Letter to the editor, 'The Church in East Africa – The Provincial Problem', *The East African Standard* (17 January) Box 8: 40

Letter to the editor, 'The Church in East Africa – The Provincial Problem', *The East African Standard*, (21 January) Box 8: 41

'Church Province Plan Checked – Nairobi Conference of Dioceses will not now take Place' *The East African Standard* (21 January) Box 8: 61

'The Church in East Africa – An Invitation and the Sequel', *The East African Standard* (13 January) Box 8: 62

Letter to the editor, 'The Bible and Prophecy', letter to the editor, *The East African Standard*, (30 April) Box 7: 46

Letter to the editor, 'Divine Planning', *The East African Standard* (14 June) Box 8: 40

Letter to the editor, 'Divine Planning', *The East African Standard* (17 June) Box 8: 40

Letter to the editor, 'A New Chaplain', *The East African Standard* (16 August) Box 8: 42

Letter to the editor, 'The Work of a Chaplain', *The East African Standard* (6 September) Box 8: 42

1939

Letter to the editor, 'The Church of England in Kenya', *The East African Standard* (22 May) Box 8: 43

Letter to the editor, 'The Church of England in Kenya', *The East African Standard* (26 May) Box 8: 44

Letter to the editor, 'Refugees', *The East African Standard* (2 June) Box 8: 44

Letter to the editor, 'The Church in Kenya', *The East African Standard* (24 July) Box 8: 43

Letter to the editor, 'The Church in Kenya', *The East African Standard* (28 July) Box 8: 44

Letter to the editor, 'To the Communicants at St. Mark's Church', (26 November) Box 8: 71, 72

1940

Letter to the editor, 'A Limuru Church', *The East African Standard* (23 January) Box 8: 46

Letter to the editor, 'A Limuru Church (1)', *The East African Standard* (26 January) Box 8: 46

Letter to the editor, 'A Limuru Church', *The East African Standard* (31 January) Box 8: 46

Letter to the editor, 'A Limuru Church (2)', *The East African Standard* (2 February) Box 8: 46

Letter to the editor, 'The Church of England in Kenya', *The Sunday Post* (7 March) Box 8: 47

Letter to the editor, 'An Appeal to Laymen – The Church of England in Kenya', *The Sunday Post* (17 March) Box 8: 48

1941

Letter to the editor, 'War Aims', *The East African Standard* (6 May) Box 8: 49

Letter to the editor, 'Refugees', *The East African Standard* (9 May) Box 8: 49

Letter to the editor, 'Refugees', *The East African Standard* (19 May) Box 8: 50

Letter to the editor, 'Refugees', *The East African Standard* (1 June) Box 8: 50

Letter to the editor, 'Refugees', *The East African Standard* (14 June) Box 8: 73

Letter to the editor, 'Refugees', *The East African Standard* (19 June) Box 8: 74

Letter to the editor, 'Refugees', *The East African Standard* (24 June) Box 8: 74

1942

Letter to the editor, 'The Bible', *The East African Standard* (19 May) Box 7: 47

Letter to the editor, 'The Bible', *The East African Standard* (9 June) Box 7: 47

Letter to the editor, *The East African Standard* (June) Box 7: 48

Letter to the editor, *Hibbert Journal*, 'Theological Colleges' (September) Box 3, File G: 12

Letter to the editor, 'Peace and Goodwill,' *The East African Standard* (26 December) Box 7: 50

1943

'The Family Rite v. The Temple Rite', (unpublished) Box 1, USPG Archives, Rhodes House, Oxford.

Letter to the editor, 'Peace and Goodwill', *The East African Standard* (5 January) Box 8: 51

Letter to the editor, 'Peace and Goodwill', *The East African Standard* (8 January) Box 8: 52

Letter to the editor, 'Peace and Goodwill', *The East African Standard* (15 January) Box 8: 52

Letter to the editor, 'Church Reform', *The East African Standard* (27 January) Box 8: 53

Letter to the editor, 'Church Reform', *The East African Standard* (3 February) Box 7: 51

Letter to the editor, 'The Price of Maize', *The East African Standard* (26 May) Box 8: 53

Letter to the editor, *Church Times*, 'The Supply of Clergy after the War', (June) Box 3, File G: 11

Letter to the editor, 'East Africa Church Province', *The East African Standard* (24 September) Box 8: 53

Letter to the editor, *The East African Standard* (11 August) Box 8: 54

Letter to the editor, 'African Representation', *The East African Standard* (20 August) Box 8: 54

Letter to the editor, 'The Good Earth', *The East African Standard* (13 December) Box 8: 54

Letter to the editor, 'The Good Earth', *The East African Standard* (27 December) Box 8: 55

Letter to the editor, 'Church Reform', *The East African Standard* (8 February) Box 8: 55

1944

'Religious Toleration', (unpublished, 1944), USPG, Box 7

Letter to the editor, 'The Clergy', *The East African Standard* (February) Box 8: 57

Letter to the editor, 'A Church Statement', *The East African Standard* (10 April) Box 8: 57

Letter to the editor, 'Swing it, Padre!', *The East African Standard* (29 April) Box 8: 58

Letter to the editor, 'Bestial Doctrine', *The Sunday Post* (7 May) Box 8: 58

Letter to the editor, 'Kenya's Immorality', *Kenya Weekly News* (12 May) Box 8: 59

1946

Letter to the editor, 'The White Man's Burden', *The East African Standard* (8 October) Box 8: 59

1947

Letter to the editor, *The Sunday Post* (4 February) Box 8: 60

Letter to the editor, *The East African Standard* (4 February) Box 8: 60

Undated and/or Unpublished Manuscripts

'The doctrine of the Holy Spirit: Analysis', Box 3, File G: 13

'Dr Paul Monroe on the Imperialism of Missions in China', Box 3, File G: 14

'A Survey of the Condition of the Church in Kenya', Box 3, File G: 15

Letter to the editor, *The Guardian*, 'The Place of Voluntary Clergy in the Church', Box 3, File G: 16

'The Report of the Archbishop's Committee on the Supply of Candidates for Holy Orders is Now Before Us', Box 3, File G: 17

'Realization', Box 3, File G: 18

'The Transformation of an Indigenous Christian Movement into a Mission', Box 3, File G: 19, 20

'Medical Missions', Box 3, File G: 21

'The Lesson of the Archbishop's Western Canada Fund', Box 3, File G: 22

'The Medical Missionary', Box 3, File G: 23

'The Church and an Itinerant Ministry', Box 3, File G: 24

'Denationalization'; 'The Elements in Holy Communion'; 'Reading a Qualification for Holy Baptism: extracts from a report of a committee on Discipline submitted to the Bishop in 1926', Box 3, File G: 25

'Missionary Dialogues: The Devil', Box 3, File G: 26

'Acts: Analysis', Box 3, File G: 29

'Resume', Box 1, File A

'The Advancing Church – Assembly's Concern: Problems of Vacant Posts Overseas', *Home News*, Box 1, File E

'Priesthood of the Church', Box 7, File N

'The Influence of Western Education upon Religion in Non-Christian Lands', Box 7, File N

'The Teacher's First Consideration', Box 7, File N

'Provision of Services for Church People Overseas', Box 7, File N

'Influence of Foreign Missions on the Church at Home', Box 7, File N

Notebook: Mission Ke Nauker, Box 7, File N

Teaching Notes on the New Testament (Box 3)

'Acts' (1906-1907)

'I Corinthians'

'I Corinthians 3:2-13 'The Dispensation of Grace'

'II Corinthians 1-4, Appeal for Unity'

'Galatians'

'Ephesians'

'Ephesians 1:3-14'

'Philippians'

'Philippians: Final Exhortations'

'Gospel of St Paul to Thessalonians'

'II Thessalonians'

'II Thessalonians: Final Exhortations'

'Hebrews'

'Revelation: The Epistles to the 7 Churches'

Box 4, File H

Preface (Nairobi) MSS 'New Wine: New Patch'

1. The Sower; The Tares

2. The Net; The Seed growing secretly: the mustard seed: the leaven; The Hidden Treasure: the Pearls; The Unmerciful Servant; The Labourers; The Good Samaritan

3. The Importunate Friend; The Rich Fool; The Barren Fig Tree; The Great Supper

4. The Lost Sheep; The Lost Piece of Money; The Prodigal Son; The Unjust Steward; Dives and Lazarus; The Unjust Judge

5. The Pharisee and the Publican; The Ten Virgins; The Talents; The Two Sons; The Wicked Husbandmen

6. The Unjust Steward; The Pharisee and the Publican; The Rich Man and Lazarus; The Good Samaritan; The Prodigal Son; The Sower; The Unmerciful Servant

Letters

Allen's letter to the Bishop of Central Tanganyika, Box 6, letter 137A (10 June 1930); bilateral communication between Bishop V.S. Azariah and Allen, Box 6, USPG Archives, Rhodes House, Oxford. Deposited papers: Roland Allen

File K

10 Oct. 1921	Draft letter regarding the Bishop of Bloemfontein
25 Jan. 1922	Letter from the Bishop of Eastern Oregon
10 Aug. 1922	Letter from the Bishop of Bloemfontein
3 Aug. 1923	Letter from Canon Farrel
3 Aug. 1923	Letter from Rev Van Tassel Sutphen
9 Oct. 1923	Draft letter to the Bishop of Kootenay
2 Nov. 1923	Draft letter to W.C. Mayne, Cheshire
2 Nov. 1923	Draft of letter to the Bishop of Kampala
30 Nov. 1923	Letter from the Bishop of Saskatchewan
11 Dec. 1923	Letter from the Bishop of Kootenay
21 Dec. 1923	Draft letter regarding the Bishop of Mombasa's appeal
29 Dec. 1923	Letter from the Bishop of Dornakal
3 Jan. 1924	Draft letter to the Bishop of Saskatchewan
3 Jan. 1924	Draft letter to the Bishop of Kootenay
30 Jan. 1924	Draft letter to Bishop Azariah
10 May 1924	Draft letter to the Bishop of Lagos
13 May 1924	17 Draft letter to Mr Clark
13 May 1924	17 Draft letter to Mr Clark
24 May 1924	Letter from the Bishop of Algoma
22 June 1924	Reply from the Bishop of Lagos
17 July 1924	Letter from Leigh T. Tarleton
29 Oct. 1924	Letter from A.B. Varley, Saskatchewan
13 Nov. 1924	Draft of letter to the Bishop of Brandon
18 Nov. 1924	Letter from Natural Resources Intelligence Service, Ottawa
23 Nov. 1924	Letter from Davidson, Toronto
26 Nov. 1924	Draft letter, Varley, Regina
5 Dec. 1924	Draft letter, Davidson
9 Dec. 1924	Letter from Archdeacon of Calgary
11 Dec. 1924	Letter from Archdeacon Ingles, Toronto
23 Dec. 1924	2 Letters: Tilsley, Elizabethville, Congo & Allen
3 Feb. 1925	Letter from Varley, Regina
13 Feb. 1925	F. Junkinson's letter regarding the Bishop of Qu'Appelle's criticism of Allen's view of Voluntary Clergy
20 Feb. 1925	Letter from Luttman-Johnson, Saskatchewan

30 May 1925	Draft letter to Troth Williams
30 May 1925	Draft letter to H. Tilt, Kornal
12 June 1925	Draft letter to P.N. Waggett
15 June 1925	Reply from Waggett
16 June 1925	Draft letter to Waggett
24 June 1925	Draft letter to the Bishop of Melanesia
10 July 1925	Draft letter to Mr McIntyre, Toronto
10 July 1925	Draft letter to *The Record*
15 July 1925	Letters from Geoffrey Warwick and Thornton, of British Honduras
21 July 1925	Draft letter to Bishop Motoda, Tokyo
27 July 1925	Letter from Troth Williams
11 Aug. 1925	Draft letter to Lacey
12 Aug. 1925	Letter from Lacey
25 Aug. 1925	Correspondence between the Bishop of Saskatchewan and Junkinson
25 Aug. 1925	Letter from E.A. McIntyre, Toronto
9 Sept. 1925	Letter to Ralfe Davies
29 Oct. 1925	Draft letter to Lloyd
7 Jan. 1926	Letter from C.W.S. Williams, Oxford University Press
6 March 1926	Letter from the Bishop of Gloucester
12 March 1926	Letter from the Bishop of Gloucester
20 March 1926	Note from the Bishop of Chichester
22 March 1926	Draft letter to the Bishop of Chichester
13 Aug. 1926	Letter from Charles Williams, OUP
28 Aug. 1926	Letter from Waldeth, on behalf Mr Lancaster
2 Sept. 1926	Draft letter to the Bishop of Pretoria
2 Sept. 1926	Draft letter to the Bishop of Bloemfontein
4-11 Sept. 1926	Letter from the Bishop of Johannesburg
9 Sept. 1926	Letter from the Bishop of Bloemfontein
17 Sept. 1926	Draft headed "Aide Memoire" for Bishop of Pretoria
18 Sept. 1926	Letter from the Bishop of St. John's
30 Sept. 1926	Letter from C.E. Baber, Pretoria
29 Oct. 1926	Letter from Theodore Stibson, Kimberley
7 Oct. 1926	Letter from Troth Williams from Delhi
10 Nov. 1926	Letter from J. Agar Hamilton, Pretoria
28 Apr. 1927	Letter from Dr Leys
6 May 1927	Draft letter to Dr Leys
12 May 1927	Draft letter to Cochrane
15 July 1927	Draft letter to Spencer, Kumamoto, Japan
21 July 1927	Copy of letter to the Bishop of Bombay
4 Aug. 1927	Draft letter to the editor, *Church Times*
12 Aug. 1927	Draft letter to the Bishop of Chichester
6 Sept. 1927	Letter from Charles Williams, OUP
19 Sept. 1927	Letter from Spencer, Kumamoto, Japan

7 Oct. 1927   Draft letter to Spencer
24 Oct. 1927   Draft letter to the Bishop of Kampala
10 May 1928   Letter from Clarke, SPCK
16 May 1928   Letter from Clarke, SPCK
19 May 1928   Drafts of three letters to Cochrane
17 June 1928   Letter from Streeten, Bloemfontein
27 June 1928   Letter from the Bishop of Khartoum, Cairo
2 July 1928   Letter from the Bishop of Grahamstown
12 July 1928   Letter from Archdeacon Rix, Prince Rupert, B.C.
17 July 1928   Letter from John Popkin, Brandon, Manitoba
19 July 1928   Letter from Theodore Stibson (Bishop of Kimberley)
? Aug. 1928   Letter from Mary Scharlieb
6 Aug. 1928   Letter from Archbishop of York's secretary
7 Aug. 1928   Letter from Davidson, the Archbishop of Canterbury
7 Aug. 1928   Letter from the Bishop of Oxford
8 Aug. 1928   Letter from Geoffrey Warwick
9 Aug. 1928   Draft letter to the Bishop of Oxford
9 Aug. 1928   Letter from the Bishop of Grahamstown
10 Aug. 1928   Draft letter to the Bishop of Grahamstown
10 Aug. 1928   Letter from the Bishop of Kilmore, Cavan
11 Aug. 1928   Letter from the Bishop of Oxford
13 Aug. 1928   Letter from the Bishop of Southampton
13 Aug. 1928   Receipt from British Museum for copy of *Voluntary Clergy
                   verseas*
15 Aug. 1928   Letter from the Bishop of Lichfield
16 Aug. 1928   Letter from Geoffrey Warwick
17 Aug. 1928   Letter from the Bishop of Ontario
18 Aug. 1928   Postcard from the Bishop of Grahamstown
21 Aug. 1928   Letter from Henry Whitehead, Madras
22 Aug. 1928   Letter from Lancelot Cooke, Jerusalem
24 Aug. 1928   Letter from Bishop William White, Toronto
27 Aug. 1928   Postcard from the Bishop of Grahamstown
28 Aug. 1928   Letter from Adam, Diocese of Calgary
3 Sept. 1928   Letter from Bishop F. Norris, Peking, China
4 Sept. 1928   Letter from R.L.W. Lennan, Assam, India
5 Sept. 1928   Letter from Geoffrey Parratt, SPCK
5 Sept. 1928   Letter from Revd. J.M. Comyn-Ching, Edmonton, Alberta
11 Sept. 1928   Letter from Bishop Quinlan, Natal
16 Sept. 1928   Letter from Gerald Herring, Transvaal
24 Sept. 1928   Letter from the Bishop of Wellington, New Zealand
28 Sept. 1928   Letter from Henry L. Morley, Kamloops, B.C.
5 Oct. 1928   Copy of notice on the Church Congress by Geoffrey Warwick
8 Oct. 1928   Letter from the Bishop of Bradford
8 Oct. 1928   Letter from the Bishop of Middleton
9 Oct. 1928   Draft letter to Quinlan, Natal

17 Oct. 1928	Letter from Streeter, Bloemfontein
21 Oct. 1928	Letter from Bell, Salisbury, South Rhodesia
29 Oct. 1928	Letter from William C. Nelson, Bishop of Nelson, New Zealand
1 Nov. 1928	Letter from the Bishop of Fredericton, New Brunswick
7 Nov. 1928	Letter from Bishop Edward L. Parsons, San Francisco
12 Nov. 1928	Draft letter to the Bishop of Fredericton, New Brunswick
22 Nov. 1928	Letter from J.C. Davidson, Archdeacon of Toronto
30 Nov. 1928	Letter from G. Hibbert-Ware, Durban
31 Jan. 1929	Letter from R.A. Streeten
8 March 1929	Letter from the Bishop of San Joaquin, California
3 May 1929	Letter from W.K. Lowther Clark, SPCK
20 May 1929	Letter from the Bishop of Nyasaland
1 July 1929	Draft letter in reply to the Bishop of Nyasaland
14 Sept. 1929	Letter from the Bishop of Nyasaland
1 Nov. 1929	Draft letter in reply to the Bishop of Nyasaland
12 April 1930	Draft letter to the Bishop of Central Tanganyika
10 June 1930	Draft letter of the Bishop of Central Tanganyika
Not dated	Draft letter to the Bishop of Pretoria
Not dated	Visiting card Walter Anderson, Stovel Company Limited, Winnipeg

Correspondence Regarding Voluntary Clergy

File L

3 Dec. 1924	Draft letter to R.W. Allin
13 June 1925	Letter from George Hubback, Bishop of Assam
15 June 1925	Letter to the Bishop of Assam
18 June 1925	Letter from the Bishop of Assam
22 June 1925	Draft of letter to *The Guardian*
23 June 1925	Letter from the Bishop of Assam
25 June 1925	Letter to the Bishop of Assam
11 Aug. 1925	Draft letter to the Bishop of Assam
14 Aug. 1925	Reply from the Bishop of Assam
14 Aug. 1925	Draft letter to the Bishop of Assam
28 Aug. 1925	Letter from the Bishop of Assam
31 Aug. 1925	Letter to the Bishop of Assam
2 Sept. 1925	Letter from the Bishop of Assam
4 Sept. 1925	Letter to the Bishop of Assam
31 May 1926	Letter from the Bishop of Assam
4 Sept. 1926	Letter to the Bishop of Assam
13 Oct. 1926	Draft letter to the Bishop of Assam
21 Nov. 1926	Letter from the Bishop Assam
23 Dec. 1926	Draft letter to the Bishop of Assam
24 Jan. 1927	Letter from the Bishop of Assam

27 Feb. 1927	Draft letter to the Bishop of Assam
24 March 1927	Letter from the Bishop of Barking
17 April 1927	Letter from the Bishop of Assam
21 May 1927	Draft letter to the *Church Times*
14 June 1927	Letter from R.A. Bennett, *Truth*
16 June 1927	Draft letter to the editor of *Truth*
18 July 1927	Letter from the Bishop of Assam
10 Aug. 1927	Draft reply to the Bishop of Assam
18 Oct. 1927	Letter from R.A. Bennett, *Truth*
4 Dec. 1927	Letter from James Pederson, New York
12 Dec. 1927	Letter from R.A. Bennett, *Truth*
20 Jan. 1928	Letter from R.A. Bennett, *Truth*
26 Jan. 1928	Letter from F. Deaville Walker, *The Foreign Field*
1 March 1928	Letter from Sir John Murray
1 March 1928	Draft letter to the Bishop of Assam
7 March 1928	Letter from the Bishop of Assam
29 March 1928	Letter from C.E. Turner
31 March 1928	Draft letter to the Bishop of Egypt and Sudan (Llewellyn A. Gwynne)
31 March 1928	Draft letter to C.E. Turner
3 Apr. 1928	Draft letter to C.E. Turner
5 Apr. 1928	Draft letter to the editor, *The Record*
9 Apr. 1928	Letter from H.A. Kennedy, Edgbaston
26 Apr. 1928	Letter from the Bishop of Egypt and the Sudan
1 May 1928	Letter from C.E. Turner
1 May 1928	Draft letter to the Bishop of Assam
1 May 1928	Letter from Sir John Murray
21 May 1928	Letter from the Bishop of Egypt and the Sudan
27 May 1928	Letter from the Bishop of Assam
29 May 1928	Letter from *St. Martin's Review*
3 June 1928	Draft letter to the Bishop of Egypt and the Sudan
19 June 1928	Draft of letter to the editor, *The Times*
19 June 1928	Draft letter to the Bishop of Assam
11 July 1928	Letter from H. Maynard Smith
12 July 1928	Letter from the Bishop of Assam
13 July 1928	Letter marked from Cecil Bunbury
9 Aug. 1928	Draft of letter to the Bishop of Assam
20 Sept. 1928	Letter from the Bishop of Assam
27 Sept. 1928	Letter from the Coadjutor Bishop of Cape Town, South Africa
15 Oct. 1928	Draft reply to the Bishop of Cape Town
2 Nov. 1928	Draft of letter to the editor, *N.C.C. Review*
29 Nov. 1928	Letter from the Bishop of Assam
20 Apr. 1929	Letter from the Bishop of Southampton
22 Apr. 1929	Draft reply to the Bishop of Southampton
25 Apr. 1929	Reply from the Bishop of Southampton

26 Apr. 1929	Letter from the Bishop of Southampton
26 Apr. 1929	Draft of letter to Maynard Smith
27 Apr. 1929	Draft letter to the Bishop of Southampton
4 May 1929	Letter from the Bishop of Southampton
6 May 1929	Draft letter from the Bishop of Southampton
17 May 1929	Note from the Bishop of Southampton
11 June 1929	Draft of letter to Cochrane
24 June 1929	Letter from Douglas Jerrold, Eyre & Spottiswoode regarding *he Case for Voluntary Clergy*
2 July 1929	Copy of letter to Douglas Jerrold
26 Aug. 1929	Letter from R. M., Eyre & Spottiswoode
1 Nov. 1929	Draft of letter to the Bishop of Nyasaland
21 March 1930	Letter from Ruth Rouse, Wimbledon
24 March 1930	Letter from Ruth Rouse, C.A. Missionary Council, enclosing alterations to Memorandum on *Voluntary Clergy*
24 March 1930	Draft of letter to Ruth Rouse.
11 Apr. 1930	Letter from Douglas Jerrold, Eyre & Spottiswoode
12 Apr. 1930	Draft of reply from Douglas Jerrold
14 Apr. 1930	Letter from Douglas Jerrold
11 June 1930	Letter from the Bishop of Assam
25 Aug. 1930	Letter from Bishop Sanford
26 Aug. 1930	Draft of reply to Bishop Sanford
28 Aug. 1930	Letter from the Bishop of Grahamstown
29 Aug. 1930	Draft of reply to the Bishop of Grahamstown
2 Sept. 1930	Letter from the Bishop of Grahamstown
3 Sept. 1930	Draft of reply to the Bishop of Grahamstown
8 Sept. 1930	Letter from the Bishop of Grahamstown
10 Sept. 1930	Letter from the Bishop of Buckingham
12 Sept. 1930	Letter from the Bishop of Manchester
13 Sept. 1930	Draft reply to the Bishop of Manchester
15 Sept. 1930	Draft letter to the editor, *The Times*
17 Sept. 1930	Draft of letter to the Bishop of Grahamstown
22 Sept. 1930	Letter from the Bishop of Manchester
25 Sept. 1930	Draft of reply to the Bishop of Manchester
18 Feb. 1931	Letter from the Bishop of Cape Town
10 Mar. 1931	Draft reply to the Bishop of Cape Town

File M: These letters are itemized by number and designated as 'Reviews of Voluntary Clergy' (1922-23)
100.   Roland Allen (handwritten)
101.   The Bishop of Pretoria
102.   L. Ingham Baker
103.   Canon J.M. Wilson
104.   The Bishop of Southampton
105.   The Bishop of Gibraltar

106. The Bishop of Gibraltar
107. Translation of a letter from von der Goltz in *Theologische Literaturzeitung*
108. P.O. Smith
109. Eugene Stock
110. Bishop Henry Whitehead (Madras)
111. Typed review from the *Yorkshire Post*, 25 July 1923
112. C. Hopton
113. Eugene Stock
114. The Revd. H.O.S. Whittingstall

Allen's Sermons: Itemized numerically as 1-553

Secondary Sources

Adams, John, *The Evolution of Education* and *The Herbartian Psychology Applied to Education* (London: Ishister and Company, 1897)

Adeyemo, Tokunboh, *Africa Bible Commentary* (Nairobi: WordAlive Publishers, 2006)

Aikman, D., *The Beijing Factor: How Christianity is Transforming China and Changing the Global Balance of Power* (Oxford/Grand Rapids, 2003)

Allchin, A.M., *The Spirit and the Word* (Faith Publications, 1963)

Allen, Hubert J.B., *Roland Allen: Pioneer, Priest, and Prophet* (Cincinnati: Forward Movement Publications and Grand Rapids: Eerdmans, 1995)

Allen, Hubert J.B., 'The Parables of Christ are Timeless: An example of Roland Allen's originality introduced by his grandson' in *Transformation: An International Journal of Holistic Mission Studies*, vol. 29, no. 3 (July 2012) (London: SAGE Publications)

Allen, Hubert J.B., 'Would Roland Allen still have anything to say to us today?' *Transformation*, 29(3) (July 2012): 179-85

Allen, J.W.T., *Tendi: Six examples of a Swahili classical verse form with translations & notes*, (Nairobi: Heinemann, 1971. Repr., Bungay, Suffolk: Richard Clay, [The Chaucer Press], 1971), Rhodes House, University of Oxford, Special Collections & Western MSS, Bodleian Library of Commonwealth and African Studies, Rhodes House, Oxford University Library Service

Allen, Priscilla, 'Roland Allen – a Prophet for this Age', *The Living Church*, 192/16 (20 April, 1986)

Anderson, Gerald H., Robert T. Coote, Norman A. Horner and James M. Phillips, *Mission Legacies: Biographical Studies of Leaders of the Modern Missionary Movement* (Maryknoll: Orbis Books, 1994)

Anderson, Ray S., *The Soul of Ministry: Forming Leaders for God's People* (Louisville: Westminster John Knox Press, 1997)

Antonio, Edward P., (ed.), *Inculturation and Postcolonial Discourse in African Theology* (New York: Peter Lang Publishing, 2006)

Atherstone, Andrew, *Lay Presidency: An Anglican Option?* (Cambridge: Grove Books Limited, 2011)

Balia Daryl and Kirsteen Kim, (eds.), *Edinburgh 2010: Witnessing to Christ Today*, Volume II (Oxford: Regnum Books International, 2010)

Balthasar, Hans Urs von, *Paul Struggles with His Congregation: The Pastoral Message of the Letters to the Corinthians* (San Francisco: Ignatius Press, Translated by Brigitte L. Bojarska, 1992 [1st edition in German *Paulus ringt mit seiner Gemeinde* 1988])

Bate, H.N., 'Frank Edward Brightman 1856-1932', Proceedings of the British Academy, volume 19 (London: Humphrey Milford, Oxford University Press, no date)

Bavinck, John Herman, *An Introduction to the Science of Missions* (Grand Rapids: Baker Book House, 1961)

Beckwith, Roger, *Elders in Every City: The Origin and Role of the Ordained Ministry* (Carlisle: Paternoster Press, 2003)

Bediako, Kwame, *Theology & Identity: The Impact of Culture upon Christian Thought in the Second Century and in Modern Africa*, Regnum Studies in Mission (Oxford: Regnum Books, 1992)

Binns, L.E. Elliott, *Religion in the Victorian Era* (Cambridge: James Clarke & Co., 1936)

Bittlinger, Arnold, *Gifts and Graces: A Commentary on I Corinthians 12-14* (Grand Rapids: Eerdmans, 1974)

Blanch, Stuart, *Future Patterns of Episcopacy: Reflections in Retirement*, Latimer Studies 37, (Oxford: Latimer House, 1991)

Blyden, Edward Wilmot, *Christianity, Islam and the Negro Race* (London: W.B. Whittingham & Co., 1887)

Blyden, Edward Wilmot, 'The Call of Providence to the Descendants of Africa in America', (New York, 1862)

Blyden, Nemata, *West Indians in West Africa 1808-1880, The African Diaspora in Reverse*, (Rochester: University of Rochester Press, 2000)

Boer, Harry R., *Pentecost and Missions* (Grand Rapids: Eerdmans and London: The Lutterworth Press, 1961)

Boer, Harry R., 'Roland Allen – Voice in the Wilderness', *World Dominion Press*, vol. xxxii, no. 4 (July/August 1954), Box 8: 1, Rhodes House, Oxford. Deposited papers: Roland Allen

Bosch, David J., *Believing in the Future: Toward a Missiology of Western Culture* (Valley Forge: Trinity Press International, 1995)

Bosch, David J., *Transforming Mission: Paradigm Shifts in Theology of Mission* (Maryknoll: Orbis Books, 2002)

Boyd, William, *From Locke to Montessori: A Critical Account of the Montessori Point of View* (London: George G. Harrap & Company, 1914)

Brammer, John E., 'Roland Allen: Pioneer in a Spirit-Centered Theology of Mission', *Missiology*, V/2 (April 1977)

Branner, John K., *Roland Allen, Donald McGavran and Church Growth*, Master of Arts in Missiology Thesis for Fuller Theological Seminary (1975)

Bray, Gerald L., *Sacraments & Ministry in Ecumenical Perspective*, Latimer Studies 18 (1984)

Brown, David, *Legacy of a Dutch Catholic Radical.*

Brown, J.M., and R.E. Frykenberg, (eds.), *Christians, Cultural Interactions, and India's Religious Traditions* (Grand Rapids: Eerdmans, 2002)

Brown, Peter, *The Rise of Western Christendom*, second edition (Oxford: Blackwell Publishing, 2003)

Bruce, F.F., *Apostle of the Heart Set Free* (Grand Rapids: Eerdmans, 1995)

Bühlmann, Walbert, *God's Chosen Peoples* (Maryknoll: Orbis Books, 1982)

Burrows, William R., Mark R. Gornik, and Janice A. McLean, (eds.) *Understanding World Christianity: The Vision and Work of Andrew F. Walls* (Maryknoll: Orbis Books, 2011)

Cable, Mildred, and Francesca French, *Through Jade Gate and Central Asia: An Account of Journeys in Kansu, Turkestan and the Gobi Desert* (London: Constable & Co. Ltd., 1927)

Carey, Hilary M., (ed.), *Empires of Religion* (Basingstoke, Hampshire: Palgrave Macmillan, 2008); reference to David Livingstone in Esther Breitenbach, 'Religious Literature and Discourses of Empire: The Scottish Presbyterian Foreign Mission Movement,' in Hilary M. Carey (ed.), *Empires of Religion* (Basingstoke, Hampshire: Palgrave Macmillan, 2008)

Carson, D.A., *Collected Writings on Scripture* (Nottingham: Apollos [IVP], 2010)

Chamberlain, M.E., *The Scramble for Africa* (London and New York: Longman, 1999). An account of David Livingstone's missionary exploration in Africa is concisely recorded in Part Four: Documents, 'The Victorian Image of Africa', Document 1: David Livingstone: Humanitarian

Cheng, Andrew Chih-yi, *Hsuntzu's Theory of Human Nature and its Influence on Chinese Thought*, (Peking: Yenching University, 1928)

Church, R. W., *The Oxford Movement: Twelve Years, 1833-1845*, (ed.), Geoffrey Best (Chicago: University of Chicago Press, 1970)

Clark, Charles Allen, *The Korean Church and the Nevius Method* (Fleming H. Revell, 1930)

Clark, Sidney J.W., *The First Stage in the Christian Occupation of Rural China* (London: World Dominion Press, no date)

Cochrane, Thomas, *Roland Allen*, (London: World Dominion, 1948)

Congar, Yves M.J., *Lay People in the Church: A Study for a Theology of Laity* (London: Geoffrey Chapman, 1985)

Conn, H.M., and others, Manuel Ortiz and Susan S. Baker, (eds.), *The Urban Face of Mission: Ministering the Gospel in a Diverse and Changing World* (Phillipsburg: P&R Publishing, 2002)

Cook, Matthew, Rob Haskell, Ruth Julian, and Natee Tanchanpongs, *Local Theology for the Global Church: Principles for an Evangelical Approach to Contextualization*, Globalization of Mission Series (Pasadena: William Carey Library, 2010)

Cox, Harvey, *Fire From Heaven: The Rise of Pentecostal Spirituality and the Reshaping of Religion in the Twenty-First Century* (Cambridge: DaCapo Press, 1995)

Crehan, Joseph H., 'Priesthood, Kingship, and Prophecy', *Theological Studies* 42 (1981): 216-31

Cross, F.L. and Livingstone, E.A., (eds.), *Dictionary of the Christian Church*, Peabody: Hendrickson Publishers and Oxford: Oxford University Press, 1997)

Culverwell, E.P., *The Montessori Principles and Practice: A Book for Parents and Teachers* (London: G. Bell & Sons, 1918)

Daniel, Patrick, 'The Overseer as a Witness for the Gospel', a paper submitted to Dr Andrew Pitts at Phoenix Seminary for BL595 – Judeo/Greco-Roman Backgrounds to the New Testament, 2015

Dann, Robert Bernard, *Father of Faith Missions: The Life and Times of Anthony Norris Groves* (Milton Keynes: Authentic Media, 2004)

Dann, Robert Bernard, *The Primitivist Missiology of Anthony Norris Groves: a radical influence on nineteenth-century Protestant mission,* (Chester: Tamarisk Books/Oxford: Trafford Publishing, 2007)

Davies, Horton, *Worship and Theology in England: The Ecumenical Century, 1900 to the Present,* (Grand Rapids: Eerdmans, 1996)

Davis, Gerald Charles, Eric Chong and H. Boone Porter, *Setting Free the Ministry of the People of God* (Cincinnati: Forward Movement, 1984)

de Groot, J.J.M., *The Religious System of China: Its Ancient Forms, Evolution, History and Present Aspect, Manners, Customs and Social Institutions Connected Therewith,* six volumes (Taipei: Ch'eng Wen Publishing, 1892. Repr., 1976)

Donovan, Vincent J., *Christianity Rediscovered* (London: Canterbury Press, 2009)

Edgerton, Robert B., *Mau Mau: An African Crucible* (London: I.B. Tauris, 1990)

Ekstrom, Ragnar, *The Theology of Charles Gore* (Lund, 1994)

Elliot, Elisabeth (ed.), *The Journals of Jim Elliot* (Grand Rapids: Fleming H. Revell, 1978. Repr., 2008)

Etherington, Norman, (ed.), *Missions and Empire,* The Oxford History of the British Empire (Oxford: Oxford University Press, 2005)

Evans, G.R. & J.R. Wright, *The Anglican Tradition: a handbook of sources,* London: SPCK, 1991; Gregory the Great, Bishop of Rome (590-604), *Letter to Abbot Mellitus,* Doctrinal Documents, 1102

Fanon, Frantz, *The Wretched of the Earth* (1st edition [1961], France. Repr., London: Penguin Books, 2001)

Fee, Gordon D., *God's Empowering Presence: The Holy Spirit in the Letters of Paul* (Peabody: Hendrickson Publishers, 1999)

Ferguson, Everett, *Backgrounds of Early Christianity* (Grand Rapids: Eerdmans Publishing Company, 1993)

Ferguson, Niall, *Empire: The Rise and Demise of the British World Order and the Lessons for Global Power* (New York: Basic Books, 2004)

Ferguson, Niall, *Civilization: The Six Killer Apps of Western Power* (London: Penguin Books, 2011)

Finch, Sarah (ed.), *The Way, the Truth and the Life: Theological Resources for a Pilgrimage to a Global Anglican Future,* Theological Resource Team of GAFCON (Vancouver: Regent College Publishing and London: The Latimer Trust, 2008)

Forde, Gerhard O., *On Being a Theologian of the Cross: Reflections on Luther's Heidelberg Disputation, 1518* (Grand Rapids: Eerdmans, 1997)

France, R.T., *Women in the Church's Ministry: A Test Case for Biblical Interpretation* (Grand Rapids: Eerdmans, 1995)

French, Francesca, *Thomas Cochrane: Pioneer & Missionary Statesman* (London: Hodder & Stoughton, 1956)

Froebel, Friedrich W.A., *Chief Writings on Education*, translated by Fletcher and Welton

Gairdner, W.H. Temple, *Brotherhood – Islam's and Christ's* (Edinburgh: Edinburgh House Press, 1923)

Gairdner, W.H. Temple, *W.II.T.G. to His Friends* (London: Society for Promoting Christian Knowledge, 1930)

Gandhi, Mahatma K., *The Collected Works of Mahatma Gandhi*, 90 vols., (Delhi: Publications Division, Ministry of Information and Broadcasting, Govt. of India, 1958-84), 28: 47

Giles, Herbert A., *Religions of Ancient China* (London: Archibald Constable, 1905)

Gilliland, Dean S., *Pauline Theology & Mission Practice* (Eugene: Wipf and Stock Publishers, 1983)

Goheen, Michael W., *"As the Father Has Sent Me, I Am Sending You": J.E. Lesslie Newbigin's Missionary Ecclesiology* (Utrecht: Uitgeverij Boekencentrum, 2000)

Gonzalez, Justo L., *The Story of Christianity* (Peabody: Prince Press, 2004)

Gore, Charles, *Dissertations: on Subjects Connected With the Incarnation* (London: John Murray, 1895)

Gore, Charles, *Lux Mundi: A Series of Studies in the Religion of the Incarnation* (London: John Murray, 1890)

Gore, Charles, *Orders and Unity* (London: John Murray, 1909)

Gore, Charles, *The Ministry of the Christian Church* (London: Rivingtons, 1889. Repr., 1919), Preface v. by C.H. Turner

Grdzelidze, Tamara, Ed., *One, Holy, Catholic and Apostolic: Ecumenical Reflections on the Church*, Faith and Order Paper no. 197 (Geneva: WCC Publications, 2004)

Green, Michael, *Evangelism in the Early Church* (London, Hodder & Stoughton, 1970, 1985)

Guder, Darrell L., (ed.), *Missional Church: A Vision for the Sending of the Church in North America* (Grand Rapids: Eerdmans, 1998)

Guelzo, Allen C., *For the Union of Evangelical Christendom: The Irony of the Reformed Episcopalians* (University Park: The Pennsylvania State University Press, 1994)

Gutierrez, Gustavo, *The God of Life* (London: SCM Press, 1991)

Haddan, Arthur W., *Apostolical Succession in the Church of England* (London, Oxford and Cambridge: Rivingtons, 1879)

Hahn, Ferdinand, *Mission in the New Testament* (London: SCM Press Ltd, 1965)

Hanciles, Jehu, *Euthanasia of a Mission: African Church Autonomy in a Colonial Context* (Westport: Praeger, 2002)

Hargrave, Alan, *But Who Will Preside? A review of Issues concerning 'Lay Presidency' in parts of South America and in the Anglican Communion at large*, Grove Worship Series no. 113, (Bramcote, Nottingham: Grove Books, 1990)

Harnack, Adolf von, *The Mission and Expansion of Christianity in the First Three Centuries* (Gloucester: Peter Smith, 1972)

Harper, Susan Billington, *In the Shadow of the Mahatma: Bishop V.S. Azariah and the Travails of Christianity in British India*, Studies in the History of Christian Missions, (Grand Rapids: Eerdmans, 2000)

Harper, Susan, 'The Dornakal Church on the Cultural Frontier', (Chapter 9), in *Christians, Cultural Interactions, and India's Religious Traditions*, J.M. Brown and R.E. Frykenberg, (eds.), (Grand Rapids: Eerdmans, 2002), 185

Hastings, Adrian, *A History of African Christianity, 1950-1975* (Cambridge: Cambridge University Press, 1979)

Hawthorne, Gerald F., Ralph P. Martin, Daniel G. Reid, *Dictionary of Paul and His Letters* (Downers Grove: InterVarsity Press, 1993)

Herbart, Johann Friedrich, *The Science of Education*, translated by H.M. and E. Felkin (1892)

Hick, John, *God Has Many Names: Britain's New Religious Pluralism* (London/Basingstoke: The MacMillan Press, 1980)

Hill, Mark, *Ecclesiastical Law* (Oxford: Oxford University Press, 2001)

Hocking, William Ernest, *Re-Thinking Missions: A Laymen's Inquiry After One Hundred Years* (New York and London: Harper & Brothers Publishers, 1932)

Hodge, Mark, *Non-Stipendiary Ministry in the Church of England* (London: The Central Board of Finance of the Church of England, 1983. Repr., London: The General Synod of the Church of England by CIO Publishing, 1984)

Hoekendijk, Johannes C., *Kirche und Volk in der deutschen Missionswissenschaft*, (Munich: Chr. Kaiser Verlag, 1967)

Hoekendijk, Johannes Christiaan, *The Church Inside Out* (Philadelphia: Westminster, 1966)

Hopkins, C. Howard, *John R. Mott: 1865-1955, A Biography* (Grand Rapids: Eerdmans, 1979)

Howse, Ernest Marshall, *Saints in Politics: The 'Clapham Sect' and the Growth of Freedom* (London: George Allen & Unwin, 1973)

Hunsberger, George R., *Bearing the Witness of the Spirit: Lesslie Newbigin's Theology of Cultural Plurality* (Grand Rapids/Cambridge: Eerdmans, 1998)

Hunt, Stephen, Malcolm Hamilton and Tony Walter (eds.), *Charismatic Christianity: Sociological Perspectives*, (Hampshire: Macmillan Press Ltd, 1997)

Hutton, William Holden, *S. John Baptist College*, Oxford University College Histories (London: F.E. Robinson, 1898)

Jenkins, Philip, *The Next Christendom – The Coming of Global Christianity* (New York: Oxford University Press, 2002)

Jensen, Peter, *The Revelation of God: Contours of Christian Theology* (Downers Grove: InterVarsity Press, 2002)

Johnson, David, *Uppsala to Nairobi*, Report of the Central Committee to the Fifth Assembly of the World Council of Churches 1968-1975 (London: SPCK, 1975)

Keller, Catherine, Michael Nausner and Mayra Rivera (eds.), *Postcolonial Theologies: Divinity and Empire* (St. Louis: Chalice Press, 2004)

Kelly, Herbert, *An Idea in the Working* (London-Oxford, 1908)

Kim, Kirsteen, *Mission in the Spirit: The Holy Spirit in Indian Christian Theologies* (Delhi: ISPCK, 2003)

Kindopp, Jason and Carol Lee Hamrin (eds.), *God and Caesar in China: Policy Implications of Church-State Tensions* (Washington, DC: 2004)

Kirk, J. Andrew, *Liberation Theology: An evangelical view from the Third World* (Basingstoke: Marshall Morgan & Scott, 1985)

Kirk, J. Andrew, *What is Mission? – Theological Explorations* (London: Darton, Longman and Todd Ltd, 2002)

Koshy, T.E. *Brother Bakht Singh of India: An Account of 20th Century Apostolic Revival* (Secunderabad, Andhra Pradesh, India: OM Books, 2003)

Kraemer, Hendrik, *A Theology of the Laity* (London: The Lutterworth Press, 1958)

Kraemer, Hendrik, *The Christian Message in a Non-Christian World* (London: The Edinburgh House Press, 1969)

Kraft, Charles H., *Christianity in Culture: A Study in Dynamic Biblical Theologizing in Cross-Cultural Perspective* (Maryknoll: Orbis Books, 1980)

Latourette, Kenneth Scott, *A History of Christian Missions in China*, SPCK (New York: MacMillan, 1929)

Latourette, K.S., *A History of the Expansion of Christianity: Advance Through Storm 1914 and After*, Volume VII (London: Eyre & Spottiswoode, 1947)

Lawrence, Evelyn, *Friedrich Froebel and English Education* (The University of London Press, 1952. Repr., London: Routledge & Kegan Paul, 1969)

Legge, James, *The Four Books* (Hong Kong: Wei Tung Book Co., 1885)

Legge, James, *The Sacred Books of China: The Texts of Confucianism*, (1st edition [1879]. Repr., Delhi: Shri Jainendra Press, 1966)

Leithart, Peter J., *Between Babel and Beast: America and Empires in Biblical Perspective*, Theopolitical Visions 14 (Eugene: Cascade Books, 2012)

Livingstone, David and Charles, *Narrative of an Expedition to the Zambesi . . . 1858-64* (London: John Murray, 1865), 6, 8, 67, 596, as cited in M.E. Chamberlain, *The Scramble for Africa* (London and New York: Longman, 1999), 94

Lloyd, Trevor, *Lay Presidency at the Eucharist?* (Bramcote, Nottingham: Grove Books, 1977)

Lugard, Frederick John D., *The Dual Mandate in British Tropical Africa* (Edinburgh: Blackwood, 1922)

Lynch, Hollis R., *Edward Wilmot Blyden: Pan-Negro 1832-1912* (London: Oxford University Press, Ely House 1967)

Mason, Alistair, *History of the Society of the Sacred Mission* (Bury St Edmunds: St Edmundsbury Press Limited, 1994)

Maurice, Frederick Denison, *The Kingdom of Christ: or Hints to a Quaker Respecting the Principles, Constitution, & Ordinances of the Catholic Church*, Volumes 1 & 2 (London: 1838. Repr., London: SCM, 1958)

Mavromataki, Maria, *Paul: The Apostle of the Gentiles* (Athens: Haitalis, 2003)

McGavran, Donald Anderson, (ed.), *Church Growth and Christian Mission* (New York: Harper and Row, 1965)

McGavran, Donald Anderson, *Understanding Church Growth*, revised edition. (Grand Rapids: Eerdmans, 1983)

Meinardus, Otto F.A., *St Paul in Greece* (Athens: Lycabettus Press, 2006)

Metz, Johann-Baptist, *Theology of the World* (New York: Herder & Herder, 1969)

Metzner, Hans Wolfgang, *Roland Allen: Sein Leben und Werk: Kritischer Beitrag zum Verstandnis von Mission und Kirche* (Gutersloh, Gerd Mohn, Gutersloher Verlagshaus, 1970)

Michaelis, Wilhelm, 'Geist Gottes und Mission nach dem Neuen Testament', *Evangelisches Missions Magazin* (1932)

Mitchell, Roger Haydon, *Church, Gospel, & Empire: How the Politics of Sovereignty Impregnated the West* (Eugene: Wipf & Stock, 2011)

Moberly, Robert Campbell, *Ministerial Priesthood* (London: J. Murray, 1897)

Montessori, Maria, *The Absorbent Mind* (Madras: Kalakshetra Publications, 1969 [1949])

Montessori, Maria, *The Advanced Montessori Method: Scientific Pedagogy as Applied to the Education of Children from Seven to Eleven Years*, vol. 1 – Spontaneous Activity in Education [translated from Italian by Florence Simmonds and Lily Hutchinson] and vol. II – The Montessori Elementary Material [translated from Italian by Arthur Livingston] (London: William Heinemann, 1919 [1918])

Montessori, Maria, *The Discovery of the Child* (Madras: Kalakshetra Publications, 1966 [1948])

Montessori, Maria, *The Montessori Method* (New York: Frederick A. Stokes Company, 1912)

Montgomery, The Rt Rev *Charles Perry Scott: First Bishop in North China* (Westminster: The Society for the Propagation of the Gospel in Foreign Parts, 1928)

Moorman, J.R.H., *A History of the Church in England* (London, 1986)

Mott, John R., *The Decisive Hour of Christian Mission* (New York: Educational Department Board of Foreign Missions of the Presbyterian Church in the USA, 1910)

Muller, James Arthur, *Apostle of China: Samuel Isaac Joseph Schereschewsky 1831–1906* (New York: Morehouse Publishing Co., 1937)

Murray, Iain, *The Puritan Hope: Revival and the Interpretation of Prophecy* (Edinburgh: The Banner of Truth Trust, 1971)

Murray, Stuart, *Church After Christendom* (Milton Keynes: Paternoster Press, 2008)

Murray, Stuart, *Planting Churches: in the 21st century* (Waterloo: Herald Press, 2010)

Muskett, Judith A., 'From Vicarious Religion to Vicarious Social Capital: Information and Passive participation in Voluntary Associations', in Ralph L. Piedmont and Andrew Village (eds), *Research in the Social Scientific Study of Religion*, vol. 23 (Leiden: Brill, 2012), 29–52 (39)

Nazir-Ali, Michael, *From Everywhere to Everywhere: A World View of Christian Mission* (London: Collins Flame, 1991)

Nazir-Ali, Michael, *Frontiers in Muslim-Christian Encounter* (Oxford: Regnum Books, 1987)

Nee, Watchman, *Concerning Our Missions* (1939. Repr. as *The Normal Christian Church Life* (Anaheim: Living Stream Ministry, 1980)

Neill, Stephen, *A History of Christian Missions*, (London: Penguin Books, 1964. Repr., Harmondsworth: Penguin Books, 1986)

Neill, Stephen, *Colonialism & Christian Missions* (London: The Lutterworth Press, 1966)

Neill, Stephen, *The Unfinished Task* (London: The Lutterworth Press, 1957)

Nevius, John L. *The Planting and Development of Missionary Churches* (Shanghai: Presbyterian Press, 1886. Repr., Hancock: Monadnock Press, 2003)

Newbigin, Lesslie, *A Word in Season: Perspectives on Christian World Missions* (Grand Rapids: Eerdmans, 1994)

Newbigin, Lesslie, 'Bringing Our Missionary Methods under the Word of God', *Occasional Bulletin from the Missionary Research Library* 13 (1962): 1-9

Newbigin, Lesslie, *Foolishness to the Greeks: The Gospel and Western Culture*, The Benjamin B. Warfield Lectures given at Princeton Theological Seminary, (London: SPCK, March 1986)

Newbigin, Lesslie, *Honest Religion for Secular Man* (London: SCM Press, 1966)

Newbigin, Lesslie, 'Religious Pluralism and the Uniqueness of Jesus Christ', an article from the *International Bulletin of Missionary Research*, Repr. in *The Best in Theology*, vol. Four, J.I. Packer, gen. ed., (Carol Stream: Christianity Today, 1990), 270

Newbigin, Lesslie, *The Gospel in a Pluralist Society* (London: SPCK, 1989)

Newbigin, Lesslie, 'The New Delhi Report: The Third Assembly of the World Council of Churches', *New Delhi* (New York: Association Press, 1962): 88-89

Newbigin, Lesslie, *The Open Secret: An Introduction to the Theology of Mission* (London: SPCK, 1995)

Newman, John Henry, 'Tract One: Thoughts on the Ministerial Commission', in *Tracts for the Times* (London: J.G. & F. Rivington, 1838)

Nias, John, *Flame from an Oxford Cloister: The Life and Writings of Philip Napier Waggett S.S.J.E. Scientist, Religious, Theologian, Missionary Philosopher, Diplomat, Author, Orator, Poet* (London: The Faith Press, 1961)

Oborji, Francis Anekwe, *Concepts of Mission: The Evolution of Contemporary Missiology* (Maryknoll: Orbis Books, 2006)

O'Connor, Daniel and others, *Three Centuries of Mission: The United Society for the Propagation of the Gospel 1701-2000* (London: Continuum, 2000)

Oden, Thomas, *The Rebirth of Orthodoxy: Signs of New Life in Christianity* (San Francisco: HarperCollins, 2003)

Okoh, Nicholas, Vinay Samuel and Chris Sugden, *Being Faithful: The Shape of Historic Anglicanism Today – A Commentary on the Jerusalem Declaration* (London: The Latimer Trust, 2009)

Oldham, J.H., and Luther A. Weigle, *Religious Education*, 'Report of the Jerusalem Meeting of the International Missionary Council March 24th-April 8th, 1928', Volume II (London: Oxford University Press, 1928)

Oldham, J.H., *The World and the Gospel* (London: United Council for Missionary Education [UCME], 1917 [1916])

O'Loughlin, Thomas, *The Didachē: A window on the earliest Christians* (London: SPCK and Grand Rapids: Baker Academic, 2010)

O'Loughlin, Thomas, 'The Missionary Strategy of the *Didachē*' in *Transformation* 28 (April 2011): 77-92

Paine, Thomas, *Common Sense* (1st edition published [1776]. Repr., New York: Penguin Books, 2012)

Partridge, Christopher and Helen Reid, (eds.), *Finding and Losing Faith: Studies in Conversion* (Milton Keynes, UK: Paternoster Press, 2006)

Paton, David M., *Christian Missions and the Judgment of God* (London: SCM Press, first edition 1953, second edition 1996)

Paton, David M., (ed.), *The Ministry of the Spirit: Selected Writings of Roland Allen* (Grand Rapids: Eerdmans, 1960. Repr., London: World Dominion Press, 1965)

Paton, David, *New Forms of Ministry* (London, Edinburgh House Press, 1965)

Paton, David, *Reform of the Ministry: a Study of the Work of Roland Allen* (London: The Lutterworth Press, 1968)

Payne, J.D., *Roland Allen: Pioneer of Spontaneous Expansion* (Self-published, 2012)

Phillips, Melanie, *Londonistan* (New York: Encounter Books, 2006)

Piedmont, Ralph L. and Andrew Village (eds.), *Research in the Social Scientific Study of Religion*, vol. 23 (Leiden: Brill, 2012)

Pinnock, Clark, 'The Concept of Spirit in the Epistles of Paul', (unpublished PhD dissertation, Manchester, 1963)

Platt, William J., *From Fetish to Faith: The Growth of the Church in West Africa* (London: Cargate, 1935)

Porter, Andrew, *Religion versus empire? British Protestant missionaries and overseas expansion, 1700-1914* (Manchester/New York: Manchester University Press, 2004)

Presler, Titus, *Horizons of Mission* (Cambridge: Cowley Publications, 2001)

Rack, Henry D., *Reasonable Enthusiast: John Wesley and the Rise of Methodism* (London: Epworth Press, 1989)

Ramsay, William Mitchell, *St Paul the Traveller and the Roman Citizen* (London: Hodder and Stoughton, 1895/96. Repr., 1902)

Ratzinger, Joseph Cardinal, *Truth and Tolerance: Christian Belief and World Religions* (San Francisco: Ignatius Press, 2003)

Robinson, Charles Henry, *History of Christian Missions*, International Theological Library [editorial secretary of the Society for the Propagation of the Gospel in Foreign Parts], (New York: Charles Scribner's Sons, 1915)

Robinson, John A.T., *Redating the New Testament* (Philadelphia: Westminster Press, 1976)

Rushdoony, Rousas John, *The One and the Many: Studies in the Philosophy of Order and Ultimacy* (Craig Press, 1971)

Rutt, Steven, 'An Analysis of Roland Allen's Missionary Ecclesiology', *Transformation* 29(3), (Oxford: SAGE Publications, July 2012): 200-213

Rutt, Steven, 'Roland Allen's Apostolic Principles: An Analysis of his "The Ministry of Expansion"' *Transformation* 29(3), (Oxford: SAGE Publications, July 2012): 225-243

Said, Edward W., *Culture and Imperialism* (New York: Vintage, 1993)

Said, Edward W., *Orientalism* (London: Penguin Books, 2003)

Samuel, Vinay and Chris Sugden, *Mission as Transformation: A Theology of the Whole Gospel*, (Eugene: Wipf and Stock Publishers, 1999)

Sanderson, David, *Roland Allen: a Prophet for a "Decade of Evangelism"*, *Quarterly of the Modern Churchpeople's Union*, XXXIV (1993)

Sanneh, Lamin, *Whose Religion Is Christianity? The Gospel beyond the West* (Grand Rapids: Eerdmans, 2003)

Sanneh, Lamin, *Disciples of All Nations: Pillars of World Christianity* (Oxford: Oxford University Press, 2008)

Schillebeeckx, Edward, *Christ the Sacrament* (London: Sheed and Ward, 1980)

Schillebeeckx, Edward, *Ministry: A case for change* (London: SCM Press, 1984)

Schillebeeckx, Edward, *The Church with a Human Face: A New and Expanded Theology of Ministry* (London: SCM Press, 1985)

Schnabel, Eckhard J., *Paul the Missionary: Realities, Strategies and Methods* (Downers Grove: InterVarsity Press, 2008)

Sen, Sunil Kumar, *Working Class Movements in India, 1885-1975* (Delhi: Oxford University Press, 1994)

Shahar, Meir and Robert P. Weller, (Eds.), *Unruly Gods: Divinity and Society in China*, (Honolulu: University of Hawaii Press, 1996)

Sharpe, Eric, *Not to Destroy But to Fulfil: the Contribution of J.N. Farquhar to Protestant Missionary Thought in India before 1914* (Uppsala: Svenska Institutet för Missionsforskning, 1965).

Shenk, Wilbert R., *Changing Frontiers of Mission* (Maryknoll: Orbis Books, 2001)

Shenk, Wilbert R., in 'Missionary Encounter with Culture', *International Bulletin of Missionary Research* 15:104–109

Shenk, Wilbert R., *Henry Venn – Missionary Statesman* (Maryknoll: Orbis Books, 1983)

Shenk, Wilbert R., *The Transfiguration of Mission: Biblical, Theological & Historical Foundations* (Scottdale: Herald Press, 1993)

Shenk, Wilbert R., *Write the Vision: the Church Renewed* (Eugene: Wipf and Stock Publishers, 1995)

Simorangkir, Mangisi, 'Theological Foundation of Mission: An Asian Perspective', Regnum Edinburgh 2010 Series, Volume 4, *Mission Continues: Global Impulses for the 21st Century*, ed. Claudia Wahrisch-Oblau and Fidon Mwombeki (2010)

Smart Ninian, *The World Religions: Old Traditions and Modern Transformations* (Cambridge: Cambridge University Press, 1989)

Smith, Adam, *Wealth of the Nations* (London: Dent [1776], 1910), 2 Vols.

Smith, Daniel, *Bakht Singh of India, a Prophet of God* (Washington: International Students Press, 1959)

Smith, David, *Mission After Christendom* (London: Darton, Longman and Todd, 2007)

Stanley, Brian, *The Bible and the Flag: Protestant Missions and British Imperialism in the Nineteenth and Twentieth Centuries* (Leicester: Apollos [IVP], 1990)

Stanley, Brian, *The World Missionary Conference, Edinburgh 1910*, Studies in the History of Christian Missions (Grand Rapids/Cambridge: Eerdmans, 2009)

Stott, John R.W., *Christian Mission: in the Modern World* (Downers Grove: InterVarsity, 1975)

Stott, John R.W., *One People – Clergy and Laity in God's Church* (London: Falcon Books, 1969)

Sundkler, Bengt and Christopher Steed, *A History of the Church in Africa* (Cambridge: Cambridge University Press, 2000)

Talltorp, Ake, *Sacrament & Growth: a Study in the Sacramental Dimension of Expansion in the Life of the Local Church, as reflected in the Theology of Roland Allen* (Uppsala: Swedish Institute for Missionary Research, 1989)

Talltorp, Ake, 'Sacraments for Growth in Mission: Eucharistic Faith and Practice in the Theology of Roland Allen', *Transformation: An International Journal of Holistic Mission Studies*, 29(3) 214-224, (July 2012): endnote 10 (222)

Tan, Jin Huat, *Planting an Indigenous Church: The Case of the Borneo Evangelical Mission* (Oxford: Regnum, 2011)

Taylor, Dr and Mrs Howard, *Biography of James Hudson Taylor* (London: Overseas Missionary Fellowship, 1965)

Taylor, John V., *The Primal Vision: Christian Presence amid African Religion* (London: SCM Press, 1963)

The Act of Uniformity (1662), 'The Case for Uniformity,' Church of England

The Book of Common Prayer 1662, Cambridge: Cambridge University Press, 2002

The Chicago-Lambeth Quadrilateral, Article III, Part IV, The Reformed Episcopal Church (2002)

The Lambeth Conference of 1888, Resolution 11, Article III, Part IV, The Reformed Episcopal Church (2002)

The Lambeth Conferences (1867-1948): The Reports of the 1920, 1930 and 1948 Conferences, with Selected Resolutions from the Conferences of 1867, 1878, 1888, 1897 and 1908 (London: SPCK, 1948)

'The Nicene Creed' in *The Book of Common Prayer* 1662 (Cambridge: Cambridge University Press, 2002)

Tinker, Melvin (ed.), *The Anglican Evangelical Crisis: A radical agenda for a Bible based church* (Geanies House, Fearn, Ross-shire, Scotland: Christian Focus Publications, 1995)

Thompson, H.P., *Into All Lands: The History of the Society for the Propagation of the Gospel in Foreign Parts 1701-1950* (London: SPCK, 1951)

Tippet, Alan, *People Movements in Southern Polynesia*, 'Studies in the Dynamics of Church-planting and Growth in Tahiti, New Zealand, Tonga, and Samoa' (Chicago: Moody Press, 1971)

Tromp, Sebastian, *Corpus Christi Quod Est Ecclesia*, vol. II, *De Christo Capite Mystici Corporis* (Rome: Gregorian University, 1946. Repr., 1960)

Tucker, Ruth A, *From Jerusalem to Irian Jaya: A Biographical History of Christian Missions* (Grand Rapids, Zondervan, 1983)

Van Engelen, J.M., 'Missiologie op een keerpunt,' *Tijdschrift voor Theologie*, vol. 15, 1975: 291-312 (309)

Van Engen, Charles, *Mission on the Way: Issues in Mission Theology* (Grand Rapids: Baker Books, 1996)

Van Engen, Charles, Dean S. Gilliland and Paul Pierson, (eds.) *The Good News of the Kingdom: Mission Theology for the Third Millennium* (Eugene: Wipf and Stock Publishers, 1999)

van Heerden, Cornelius, *Die spontane uitbreiding van die Kerk by Roland Allen* (Kampen: I.H. Kok, o. J.)

Venn, Henry, *Church Missionary Society*, 'Native Church Organization,' Official Paper, (London, No date recognized)

Viola, Frank, *Finding Organic Church: A Comprehensive Guide to Starting and Sustaining Authentic Christian Communities* (Colorado Springs: David C. Cook, 2009)

Waggett, Philip Napier (SSJE), *Religion and Science*, Handbooks for the Clergy, A.W. Robinson, (Longmans, 1904)

Wagner, C. Peter, *Frontiers in Missionary Strategy* (Chicago: Moody Press, 1971)

Wagner, C. Peter, *Strategies for Church Growth: Tools for Effective mission and Evangelism* (Ventura: Regal Books, 1989)

Wainwright, Geoffrey, *Lesslie Newbigin: A Theological Life* (Oxford: Oxford University Press, 2000). References to Roland Allen on pages: 21, 75-77, 157, 163-64, 172, 175, 181, 189, 417n. 26

Walls, Andrew F., *The Cross-Cultural Process in Christian History* (Edinburgh: T & T Clark, 2002)

Walls, Andrew F., *The Missionary Movement in Christian History: Studies in the Transmission of Faith* (Maryknoll: Orbis Books, 2009 [1996])

Ward, Kevin, and Brian Stanley, (eds.), *The Church Mission Society and World Christianity 1799-1999*, Studies in the History of Christian Missions, (Grand Rapids: Eerdmans, 2000)

Warren, M.A.C., *Caesar the Beloved Enemy: Three Studies in the Relation of Church and State*, Reinecker Lectures at the Virginia Theological Seminary, Alexandria, Virginia, February 1955 (London: SCM Press, 1955)

Warren, Max A.C., *Problems and Promises in Africa Today* (Hodder, 1964)

Warren, Max, *The Christian Mission* (London: SCM Press, 1951)

Warren, Max A.C., *The Missionary Movement from Britain in Modern History*, (London: SCM, 1965)

Warren, Max A.C., *The Triumph of God* (Longmans, 1948)

Warren, Max A.C., *The Truth of Vision* (Canterbury Press, 1948)

Warren, Max, (ed.), *To Apply the Gospel: Selections from the Writings of Henry Venn* (Grand Rapids: Eerdmans, 1971)

Webb, B.G., (ed.), *Exploring the Missionary Church*, Explorations 7, (Homebush West, NSW: Lancer Books, 1993)

Williams, W.R., *Ohio Friends in the Land of Sinim* (Mount Gilead: 1925)

Winter, Ralph D., Stephen C. Hawthorne, (eds.), *Perspectives on the World Christian Movement, A Reader* (Pasadena: William Carey Library, 1981. Revised editions, 1992, 1999)

Wood, Susan K., *Sacramental Orders*, Lex Orandi Series. (Collegeville: The Liturgical Press, 2000)

Woodhead, Linda, *An Introduction to Christianity* (Cambridge: Cambridge University Press, 2011)

Woodhead, Linda, Hiroko Kawanami and Christopher Partridge, (eds.), *Religions in the Modern World: Traditions and Transformations* (London and New York: Routledge, second edition, 2009)

Works, Herbert Melvin Jr., *The Church Growth Movement to 1965*, Doctor of Missiology Thesis for Fuller Theological Seminary, 1974

Wright, N.T., *What St Paul Really Said* (Grand Rapids: Eerdmans and Cincinnati: Forward Movement Publications, 1997)

Yang, H., and Daniel H.N. Yeung (eds.), *Sino-Christian Studies in China* (Newcastle, 2006)

Yates, Timothy, *Christian Mission in the Twentieth Century* (Cambridge: Cambridge University Press, 1996)

Young, Robert, *Postcolonialism: An Historical Introduction* (Oxford and Malden: Blackwell Publishers, 2001)

Young, Robert, *Postcolonialism: A Very Short Introduction* (Oxford: Oxford University Press, 2003)

Periodicals / Journals

Anglican Theological Review, Bardwell L. Smith, 'Liberal Catholicism: An Anglican Perspective' (3/1972), vol. 54, 175-193

Church Missionary Review 'Indigenous Churches: The Way of St Paul' (June 1927) 147-159, a paper read by Roland Allen at the *Church Missionary Society Conference of Missionaries*, High Leigh, Box 2, Number 23, Rhodes House, Oxford

Church Quarterly Review (January 1933)

Church Quarterly Review, 'The Priesthood of the Church', Roland Allen, art. IV (January 1933): 234-44, Rhodes House, Oxford

Church Quarterly Review, Kenneth Scott Latourette, *A History of Christian Missions in China*, book review by Roland Allen (January 1930): 317

European Journal of Theology, XIX (2010), Pavel Cerney 'The Relationship between Theology and Missiology: The Missiological Hermeneutics' (Nottingham: Paternoster Periodicals, 104-109)

International Bulletin of Missionary Research, vol. 34, no. 1, January 2010, 'From the "poor heathen" to "the glory and honour of all nations"': Vocabularies of Race and Custom in Protestant Missions, 1844-1928 by Brian Stanley, pages 3-10, New Haven, Connecticut: Overseas Ministries Study Center (2010)

International Bulletin of Missionary Research 15:104-9, 'Missionary Encounter with Culture' by Wilbert R. Shenk, 104

Journal of Religion in Africa, vol. 41.2 (2011) 180-205, Richard Werbner, 'The Charismatic Individual and the Sacred Self' (Leiden: Brill)

Missiology 10:263-77 'The Soft Age Has Gone' by Johannes Aagaard (1982), cited in Bosch, *Believing in the Future*, 27-28

Missiology, Charles H. Kraft, 'Dynamic Equivalence Churches: An Ethnotheological Approach to Indigeneity' vol. 1, no. 1 (January 1973) 39-57

Pentecost & World (London: Oxford University Press, 1917)

Quarterly Paper of the Mission of the Church of England in North China, vol. III, 17, 27, 48

The East and the West (April 1909)

The Interpreter, 'The Case for Voluntary Clergy: an Anglican Problem' (July 1922): 314ff

The North China Mission Quarterly 'First Impressions' (October 1896): 53–56

Transformation: An International Journal of Holistic Mission Studies, vol. 28, no. 1, OCMS (January 2011) (London: SAGE Publications)

Transformation: An International Journal of Holistic Mission Studies, vol. 29, no. 3, OCMS (January 2011) (London: SAGE Publications)

Internet & DVD Sources

http://www.youtube.com/watch?v=7di4zMGIZY8&feature=g-vI.   Richard Evans, 'Formal and Informal Empire in the 19th Century,' Gresham College lecture

http://www.youtube.com/watch?v=TA.BddvELkk

http://www.jamesault.com 'African Christianity Rising: *Stories from Ghana*' (2008)

Recorded Minutes

Minutes from the *Members of the St. John's College Debating Society*, UGS V.1, St. John's College archives; interview with Michael Riordan, archivist (St. John's College, Oxford)

Minutes from *St. John's College Essay Society*, UGS VI.1, St. John's College archives; interview with Michael Riordan, archivist (St. John's College, Oxford)

PhD Dissertations

Cheruvil, Joseph. *Roland Allen's Missionary Insights: Their Relevance to a North Indian Context*, 296 pages, Belgium: Katholieke Universiteit Leuven, 1993, Publication Number AAT C348052

Payne, Jervis David. *An Evaluation of the Systems Approach to North American Church Multiplication Movements of Robert E. Logan in Light of the Missiology of Roland Allen*, 334 pages, Kentucky: The Southern Baptist Theological Seminary, 2001, Publication Number: AAT 3042375

Thompson, Michael Don. *The Holy Spirit and Human Instrumentality in the Training of New Converts: An Evaluation of the Missiological Thought of Roland Allen*, California: Golden Gate Baptist Theological Seminary, 1989, Publication Number: AAT 8923304

Index of Names

Scripture Index

Old Testament

Genesis
11:9   81

Exodus
12,   6, 176, 183
12:1-4   176

Job   66

Psalms
34:8   157

New Testament

Matthew
18:20   151, 155, 157

Mark
10:32   72

Luke
24:29   80

John
3:16   79-80
12:24   131
16:13   148
17:3   71

Acts   61, 88, 147, 190
1:1-20:28   32-34
1:8   65, 80
2:1-11   81

2:1-4   86
2:2   80
2:14-36   84
2:37-39   86
2:38-40   84
3:12-26   84
5:30-32   84
6:6   86
8:14-17   86, 183
8:37   78
9:17   86
9:19-22   33
10:1-48   81
10:44-48   86
11:15   86
11:17   79
15:1-29   89
15:8   86, 89
15:23, 41   111-112
17:3   72
19:5-6   86
20:13-28   130